PREMONITIONS OF THE *TITANIC* DISASTER

PREMONITIONS OF THE *TITANIC* DISASTER

TERRY KEEFE

Matador
9 Priory Business Park,
Wistow Road, Kibworth Beauchamp,
Leicestershire. LE8 0RX
Tel: 0116 279 2299
Email: books@troubador.co.uk
Web: www.troubador.co.uk/matador
Twitter: @matadorbooks

ISBN 978 1800462 342

British Library Cataloguing in Publication Data.
A catalogue record for this book is available from the British Library.

Printed and bound in Great Britain by 4edge Limited
Typeset in 11pt Minion Pro by Troubador Publishing Ltd, Leicester, UK

Matador is an imprint of Troubador Publishing Ltd

For our grandchildren:
Bram, Liddy, Maddy, and Mirry

Contents

FOREWORD

Passengers who cancelled their tickets for the maiden voyage of *Titanic* in 1912, out of apprehension. A novel published fourteen years earlier, telling of the 'unsinkable' liner *Titan*'s collision with an iceberg and sinking at midnight in April, near the American coast. A famous journalist and social reformer who died on *Titanic*, warned in 1911 that he would be in danger from water in April 1912. A woman watching *Titanic* go by on the Solent, crying out that the ship would sink before reaching America. A female passenger so fearful that she refused to sleep at night on *Titanic*. The inhabitants of the capital of the remote islands of Fiji aware of the sinking of *Titanic* before reports of the collision reached the Pacific. A woman on the Portsmouth shore warned by a 'ghost' that *Titanic* should be ordered to turn back to avert a tragedy in a few days' time. A dying girl who, on 14 April 1912, 'sees' a big ship sinking in the water and mysteriously knows the name of the violinist in the ship's orchestra.

These are just a few of the many alleged premonitions explored by Ian Stevenson, Rustie Brown, Martin Gardner, George Behe and Bertrand Méheust, the writers who have contributed most to the examination of *Titanic* 'premonitions'.

In Chapter 1 of the present work, the *literary* premonitions mentioned by these commentators are treated by individual author, in chronological order. In Chapter 2, premonitions of the death of W.T. Stead (firstly his own premonitions, then those of others) are examined in the order in which they appear in the works of our commentators. In Chapters 3, 4, 5, and 6 general premonition cases are looked at in the chapter on the commentator who first raised them, again in the order in which they appear. Each case is considered just once, with the additional contributions of later authors taken into account. There are 201 cases in all.

I have adopted the following system for identifying cases. Stevenson and Behe both number all of their cases, and their numbering has been followed here in the numbers given in bold: Stevenson's as **(IS,1 …)**, with, for Behe, the addition of letters to indicate 'curious coincidences' **(GB,cc,1 …)**, 'possible psychic phenomena' **(GB,po,1 …)**, and 'probable psychic phenomena' **(GB,pr,1 …)**. The cases introduced by Brown, are numbered in the order in which she raises them **(RB,1 …)**, as are those mentioned by Gardner **(MG,1 …)**, and Goss and Behe **(G&B,1 …)**. Méheust goes through his cases in Part II of his book: I have numbered them in the order in which he takes them up there, **(BM,1 …)**. (Both Behe and Méheust have separate chapters on cases concerning W.T. Stead and these are also numbered in bold in the sequence in which they first appear, **(GB,wts,1 …)** and **(BM,wts,1 …)**).

Appendix 1, 'Full List of Cases', which includes – in the order in which they appear in this book – all of the 201 premonition cases touched upon, also records treatment by authors other than the first; e.g. '**IS,12** – Mrs Tweedale – **(MG,23)**, **(GB,po,21)**, **(BM,73)** *+'.

When the main text or footnotes in this book mention just an author's name, or a book's title (or both), full details of the work concerned may be found in the Bibliography, where information about all the books and articles referred to is provided.

I am grateful for the support and assistance of my wife, Sheila, who proof-read the text and advised on presentation. The translations of Méheust's French text are, in all cases, my own.

Readers so inclined may focus first on the alleged premonitions as such by turning to the sections marked 'Case' or 'Cases' in Chapters 1-6. (P. 3, 6, 22, 49, 63, 109, 138, 163, 205, 226, 239, 270, 287.)

INTRODUCTION

Despite the vast quantity of trivial and purely speculative material – even nonsense – available in print and on the internet on the subject, it is rather remarkable how much we know for sure about White Star's *Titanic* and its fate. Two substantial, large-format volumes provide enormous detail on every aspect of the ship's construction and equipment;[1] the admirable website 'Encyclopedia Titanica' contains biographical information on virtually every passenger and crew member, as well as much else;[2] deck-plans show us the original position of every piece of furniture in every cabin; and at around the time of the 100th anniversary of the sinking, two books, each by a number of *Titanic* experts, summarised comprehensively the state of knowledge at the time.[3]

Yet experts acknowledge that there is still a great deal

1 Bruce Beveridge, Scott Andrews, Steve Hall & Daniel Klistorner; Art Braunschweiger (ed.), *Titanic. The Ship Magnificent. Volume One: Design & Construction*; *Volume Two: Interior Design and Fitting Out* (2009).

2 www.encyclopedia-titanica.org

3 Samuel Halpern *et al*, *Report into the Loss of the SS Titanic. A Centennial Reappraisal* (2011); Tad Fitch, J. Kent Layton, & Bill Wormstedt, *On a Sea of Glass. The Life and Loss of the RMS Titanic* (2012).

that is uncertain, unknown, perplexing about *Titanic* and its fate. The very abundance of eye-witness accounts of what happened between collision with the iceberg and the sinking brings confusion; what are apparently established facts are periodically questioned and contested by new theories; and certain subjects are inherently obscure. The matter of alleged premonitions of the disaster is shrouded in mystery and controversy. It is frequently touched on, usually in somewhat dramatised fashion, but only rarely treated carefully and systematically. The main purpose of this book is to examine and compare the significant work carried out by the five commentators who have contributed most on the topic: Ian Stevenson, Rustie Brown, Martin Gardner, George Behe, and Bertrand Méheust.[4] This is very far from exhausting the subject, but it does entail scrutinising a substantial body of cases, large enough to enable anyone to begin building an informed view on *Titanic* premonitions. It may also offer a kind of framework into which additional cases of premonitions can be fitted.

There are at least three fundamental reasons, however, why this material is of only limited help towards a view of premonitions in general. Firstly, prophetic predictions and divination have a very long history indeed.[5] The similarities and links between historical phenomena and

4 No disrespect whatever is intended towards Michael Goss, who co-edited *Lost at Sea. Ghost Ships and Other Mysteries* (1994) with George Behe. It is simply a matter of convenience to link the one relevant chapter in this publication with Behe's name.

5 Cases of the gods speaking through the voices of women are said to go back to the second millennium BC. Oracles were especially prominent and important in Ancient Greece, and the tradition of divine prophecy exists in most ancient cultures.

the modern (predominantly non-religious) concept of premonitions would need to be examined in a full study of the subject. Furthermore, a detailed and thorough discussion of the *theory* of premonitions as such would also be required before any broad view of the topic could be arrived at. The theoretical issues touched on in this book are more or less limited to those raised – deliberately or not – by our five authors. Perhaps most importantly of all, moreover, none of our commentators gives any kind of extended attention to the alleged scientific or experimental evidence for paranormal phenomena in general, or premonitions in particular, which dates back to the second half of the twentieth century. The evidence that they deal with, and will be dealt with here, is entirely anecdotal (provided that we include the small number of literary cases in this category).[6]

Those with any familiarity with the foundation and development of psychical research or parapsychology will be well aware of the great divide between premonition anecdotes – however numerous – and laboratory research. One scholar, recording that J.B. Rhine (in the 1950s) 'shepherded parapsychology into the laboratory', claims that it was at this juncture that formal parapsychology 'began to lose touch with the very experiences that originally motivated its pursuit', since laboratory activities 'have virtually nothing to do with human experiences

6 Stevenson and others have categorised non-experimental cases as 'spontaneous' ones, but for a number of reasons the term 'anecdotal' is preferable here.

that seem to many to be paranormal'.[7] Despite the occasional suggestion that the natural context in which psychic phenomena appear to occur should be taken into account, laboratory experiments continue to dominate scientific investigations, and the nature of these appears to have changed relatively little over the past sixty years or so.[8] What is more, there is a sharp discrepancy between the very nature of spontaneous precognitive experiences and the ways in which precognition may be tested experimentally.[9] Much experimentation involves a somewhat artificial structuring of experience and bears almost no resemblance at all to the kind of foreseeing of events that constitutes 'premonition' as it is experienced in the course of people's lives.[10]

7 James E. Alcock, 'Give the Null Hypothesis a Chance. Reasons to Remain Doubtful about the Existence of Psi' (2003); pp. 43-44. This article appeared in a special issue of the *Journal of Consciousness Studies*, which was an attempt to present a 'balanced collection of papers'. Alcock argues that verification became a matter of statistics: 'No longer was it a question of whether a person had dreamed of his father's funeral in detail, not knowing that miles away his father had died, but rather, what is the series of cards that will next be turned up.'

8 If anything, the situation is now even more polarised than ever. Recent developments concerning the ganzfeld procedure and subsequent meta-analyses of results have resulted in fairly complex statistical discussions which bear no obvious relation at all to premonition anecdotes.

9 One recent type of scientific measurement of precognition is limited to the anticipation of the kind of image or object that will be presented, and/or to the order in which a series will be presented. And certain experiments seek to check whether the emotional reaction to something shown can occur before the actual showing.

10 Bertrand Méheust claims that spontaneous telepathy is closely related to the extrasensory perceptions displayed by gifted subjects in experimental situations (Méheust, pp. 141-142). But he also argues that the latter only rarely have the intensity and precision of that of 'ordinary' people, giving no evidence or justification of any kind for either claim.

The present study is based on, and confined to, anecdotes of a variety of different kinds. Exploring those different kinds – their nature, their sources, their strengths and weaknesses, their reliability, and so on – will be a significant part of the enterprise in the following pages. What relationship the results of that exploration bear to the results of experiments on psychic phenomena – the outcome of which is itself often unclear, and to one extent or another controversial – will remain an open question. We certainly do not set out to bring conclusions drawn from the scrutiny of anecdotes into line with, or into opposition with, any 'scientific' evidence, or any elaborated theory concerning premonitions. This enables us simply to refer readers interested in developments in parapsychology to the many diverse accounts available in books and on the world-wide web. These accounts, of course, hold a fascination of their own.

Ian Stevenson makes the point that 'some important phenomena, such as the weather, volcanoes, fossils, earthquakes, and meteorites, do not occur in laboratories under controlled conditions, and yet we study them with scientific methods.'[11] But while scientific observation and experiments are governed by agreed procedures, there is no established, generally-accepted protocol or set of rules for investigating premonition anecdotes.[12] Here we are

11 Ian Stevenson, 'Some of My Journeys in Medicine – A Lecture about Science and Reincarnation' (1989).

12 Although thinkers like C.D. Broad have tackled aspects of this general issue. Our own investigation may be seen as having affinities with case study, but although case-study research has a role to play in a number of disciplines, it involves several diverse approaches based on different assumptions.

engaging, with no *specific* methodological commitments, in a basic scrutiny of anecdotal premonition cases and an examination of the accompanying analyses by five writers. All five are self-conscious about their methods to one degree or another, so that, at best, a survey of these writings may point to some general principles or questions relating to methodology.

It is important to recognise that the issue of belief, or non-belief, in premonitions is not entirely a simple matter. Survey results over the years vary significantly, but some suggest that a substantial proportion of the population – not only in the U.K. and the U.S.A., but also in other countries – 'believe in' paranormal phenomena. Many people claim to have had paranormal experiences themselves, and premonitory dreams are sometimes said to constitute more than half of the Extra Sensory Perception (ESP) experiences reported. At the same time, we can be certain that only a very small number of those claiming to believe in the paranormal have any acquaintance at all with the results of parapsychology experiments. In short, even if – and it is a very large 'if' indeed, according to the vast majority of mainstream scientists – the paranormal has some kind of basis in scientific fact, this basis can confidently be said to play very little part at all in the belief in the paranormal apparently displayed by many people. For the most part, the majority undoubtedly make their judgement on the grounds of anecdotes, that is of what they and/or others close to them have seen or heard, or particular experiences they have read about.

Premonitions themselves fall squarely within the broad domain of the paranormal, since they breach the basic principles of science (in particular, the principle that an effect cannot precede its cause). But the paranormal is an extremely wide category, including phenomena such as ghosts, telepathy, clairvoyance, near-death and out-of-body experiences, telekinesis, and so on. Even when we home in on extrasensory perception (where information is said to be acquired directly; that is, without passing through the recognised human senses or through logical inference), this is usually taken to include four main categories: telepathy (information directly obtained from another person), clairvoyance (perceiving people, objects, locations, or events beyond the natural range of the senses), precognition (information about future events), and retrocognition (information about past events). Essentially, these processes are defined negatively, by reference to means that they do *not* use: theories of what means they *do* use are a separate matter, another layer of complexity to add to the question.

It may be tempting to regard premonitions as instances of, or a form of, precognition, also known as prescience, foresight, second sight, future vision, future sight, and so on. But there is actually no reason for this particular hierarchy of terms: 'precognition' and 'premonition' may be used, for the most part, interchangeably. It is true that premonitions (or presentiments) are frequently emotionally charged in one way or another, and that an attempt might be made to see precognition as conscious cognitive awareness, and premonitions more as affective apprehension. Even linking premonitions with a (possibly vague) sense of foreboding, as some explicitly do, is plausible, since although we do occasionally talk of premonitions when we are anticipating something pleasant, in the huge majority of instances this is not the case. In fact, this is the point at which it is appropriate to remember that all of the individual instances examined here relate to *Titanic* in some way. It is possible that there is something special about this case, or, indeed, about precognition of major disasters in general. Anyone wanting to come to general conclusions about premonitions on the basis of *Titanic* examples might do well, initially, to look also at the nature and the pattern of premonitions in connection with events like the Aberfan landslide in 1966, and the catastrophe of 9/11 in New York in 2001, disasters commonly cited in connection with *Titanic* forewarnings.

Some of the manifestations of the paranormal raise questions and problems that have no place at all in an inquiry into premonitions. At the same time, certain general issues concerning the paranormal impinge firmly upon any such inquiry. Perhaps above all, there are matters relating to evidence that cannot be avoided. Do the 'standard' levels of required evidence that prevail apply to anecdotal instances of precognition/ premonition? Or are more rigorous levels than normal appropriate, since major changes in our world view might be needed if premonitions were a demonstrated fact? Anyone examining premonitions must adopt a position on questions of this kind, whether consciously or not, and it is desirable that this position be made explicit. On the particular matter of evidence, it will have to be sufficient here to say that while no formal attempt will be made to impose more rigorous levels than normal (how could any such levels be established, or justified?), the 'normal' levels will be particularly vigilantly and systematically applied in the case of all premonition anecdotes.

A fully comprehensive re-examination of the numerous instances of alleged precognitive experiences connected with the sinking of the *Titanic* (let alone all the other reported examples of related paranormal phenomena of one kind or another) would be a considerable undertaking. Just the double-checking of all the original sources and the scrutiny of additional reports and interviews would probably be best tackled by a team of researchers. At the same time, any attempt to look seriously again at the matter of *Titanic* premonitions undoubtedly involves chasing up *certain* sources; and some investigation of the nature of the evidence and criteria employed must necessarily form an integral part of the process. As already mentioned, our particular inquiry is limited to those premonitions reported in a number of key publications.

The commentators concerned are of varied backgrounds and have different – to some extent complementary – preoccupations. While, in their very different ways, Gardner and Méheust bring out the literary and philosophical links with the *Titanic* disaster, Stevenson's approach may be characterised, in general, as somewhat more 'scientific'. On the other hand, Brown, with her early reference to 'the premonitions, the superstitions, and the so-called "coincidences'",[13] and Behe, who discusses, among other things, 'curious coincidences' and 'mistaken accounts and deliberate hoaxes', both set foreseeing the catastrophe within a rather broader context.

Other premonitions have been reported and are in the public domain,[14] but very often these are unsourced and poorly substantiated. In any case, a line has to be drawn somewhere. Few will deny that the trawl carried out by our five authors, and their presentation of the 201 cases in print, provides an extensive and representative collection of *Titanic* premonitions. It has to be said repeatedly that – leaving aside the reported (and rather vague) premonitions of the death of W.T. Stead – there are remarkably few alleged *Titanic* premonitions actually documented before 14 April, 1912. From immediately after the disaster onwards, on the other hand, it was suggested that premonitions had occurred before the event. Chronologically, the first source of such suggestions is, of course, the newspapers. As early as 16 April, 1912 the *Daily Mirror* recorded that the delaying of *Titanic*'s departure for weather reasons had been regarded as 'ominous' by many.[15] On 17 April the paper recounted a number of other cases: the businessman who wanted his solicitor to agree to be a guardian to his two little boys, since he and his wife were sailing on *Titanic* next day and he felt they would never see their children again;[16]

---

13 Brown, p. 6.

14 See footnote 877 below.

15 **(GB,cc,13).**

16 **(GB,po,16).**

John Coffey, who jumped ship, 'having grave, indefinable misgivings';[17] and the steward who told his wife he wished he had not signed on.[18] By 19 April, the *Daily Mirror* was saying that 'Many strange stories of foreboding that some disaster would overtake the *Titanic* on her maiden voyage continue to come to hand.'[19] As we will see, both Rustie Brown (who was herself a newspaper columnist) and Behe rely heavily on newspapers as sources of the cases they cite.

The first books published about the *Titanic* disaster date from soon after it in 1912, and these contain a few mentions of premonitions. But, because of world wars and economic conditions, there was a great slowing down in the output of books on *Titanic* until Walter Lord revived interest in the ship in the 1950s. His *A Night to Remember* of 1955, however, again contains only a relatively small number of references to premonitions. It was not until Ian Stevenson's two articles in 1960 and 1965 that the matter of premonitions became a permanent feature of the interest in *Titanic*,[20] and possible psychic foresight in the fiction of Morgan Robertson and W.T. Stead a regular theme. Rustie Brown's *The Titanic, the Psychic and the Sea*, published in 1981, was the first book to devote a great deal of space to *Titanic* premonitions in general (paying no particular attention to literary cases or Stead), although she casts her

---

17 **(IS,12b).**

18 **(GB,po,18).**

19 Carol King & Richard Havers, *Titanic. The Unfolding Story* (2011).

20 Ian Stevenson (1), 'A Review and Analysis of Paranormal Experiences Connected with the Sinking of the *Titanic*' (1960); and (2), 'Seven More Paranormal Experiences Associated with the Sinking of the *Titanic*' (1965).

net much wider and takes in a number of quite different striking or odd features of the disaster. Some of her material on premonitions comes from Stevenson. Martin Gardner's *The Wreck of the Titanic Foretold?*, on the other hand, focused strongly, in 1986, on Robertson and Stead, as well as on Stevenson, seeking to show that there is no substance at all in claims of psychic premonitions of the *Titanic* disaster. Both Behe's *Titanic. Psychic Forewarnings of a Tragedy* (1988) and Méheust's *Histoires paranormales du Titanic* [*Paranormal Stories of the Titanic*] (2006) set out to be much more comprehensive, though, even in their cases, there are puzzling omissions. (The relevant chapter in Goss and Behe's *Lost at Sea. Ghost Ships and Other Mysteries* of 1994 had added only 8 cases to those already treated by that date.)

One justification for the present inquiry is that none of these works has had the kind of currency that it might have had. Stevenson's investigation from the 1960s was published in the specialised *Journal of the American Society for Psychic Research*, and his two articles themselves have not been seen by many. Brown's book is not commonly referred to; and Gardner's only slightly more frequently. Méheust's book – not yet translated into English – is used as an original source by still fewer in English-language *Titanic* studies. Behe's book remains the best-known on this subject, but even this is long out of print and has not been read by as many as it might have been.[21] The results of the five commentators' inquiries, moreover, have never been systematically compared.

21 There are quite often references in internet forums to the difficulty of obtaining a copy.

Because the topic of paranormal phenomena is a controversial one, it is important to set out in the open a kind of scale of 'belief'. Stevenson was clearly committed to the reality and genuineness of some paranormal experiences, as was, apparently, Brown. Gardner was a convinced and well-known sceptic. Behe considers some cases to be authentic, but seems more comfortable when talking of 'probability'. Méheust clearly – albeit in some respects cautiously – accepts paranormal phenomena. The approach in this book will be a generally sceptical one, although it is acknowledged that the sheer range of cases concerning *Titanic* can be seen as rather remarkable, and that a small number are somewhat mysterious. There will not be a systematic attempt, as there is in Gardner, to debunk all of the instances mentioned, but it will be assumed that, in principle, each substantial case needs to be carefully scrutinised, and that, despite Behe's unjustified dismissal of sceptics' search for '*any* other explanation' of alleged psychic phenomena,[22] every possibility of doubt should be voiced.

It is vital to emphasise, however, that it is possible to disagree with someone's judgement without impugning their good faith. Needless to say, we set out with no inclination to question the intellectual integrity of the commentators concerned: in evaluating their work, it is appropriate to assume that proper examination of the phenomena has been carried out, unless the evidence suggests otherwise. The hard part of the process is that, sadly, one cannot, on the other hand, simply take for granted the accuracy of all original reports of paranormal phenomena, or even

22 Behe, p. 13.

the honesty of all of those putting forward the claims that researchers examine.[23] The way in which this problem is dealt with in connection with paranormal claims is one of the points that will be taken up.

Websites and internet forums devoted to the *Titanic* provide evidence of a permanent interest in this matter and occasionally raise significant new points. Nevertheless, when a systematic and detailed attempt is made to compare the work of the five principal investigators, one is struck by the different ways in which they approach this difficult topic, as well as by a definite lack of correspondence in their precise results. Both factors bear close examination, and an investigation and analysis of the nature of the evidence and criteria employed by the main researchers is an integral part of our task. Furthermore, a concentration on premonitions rather than the paranormal as such defines the field more tightly and increases the chance of making some progress. This does not mean ruling out of consideration entirely phenomena such as omens and telepathy. After all, omens, which predominantly involve happenings in the physical world rather than presentiments, are seen and acknowledged as such by individuals, who may sometimes be regarded as having premonitions. And the important distinction between premonitions and

---

23 Any more than one can have blind faith in the – often conflicting – 'eye-witness' reports of the *Titanic* sinking itself.

telepathy[24] is exceedingly difficult to draw in certain cases. In these particular respects, therefore, it is sensible in general to follow the selections and emphases of our five authors.

This means not addressing immediately and directly certain potentially controversial issues, but examining them only to the extent that our authors themselves raise such matters. What kind of experiences count as substantive premonitions? How is a 'premonition of the *Titanic* disaster' distinguished from closely related but ultimately distinct experiences (of disaster to *some* liner, of something being wrong about or with the *Titanic*, of *some* disaster on 14-15 April, 1912, and so on)? What criteria have to be strictly adopted – and which, if any, less strictly – to make a case worth consideration? The degree to which our authors bring these issues into the open, as well as the different ways in which they are dealt with, is itself a prime matter of interest. There is, however, one matter of timing, on which a different approach is required. In certain instances, the texts we are scrutinising deal – sometimes at length – with experiences that clearly occurred *after* the *Titanic* disaster, some considerably later. Close examination of one or two of these might help to cast light on the paranormal in general, but most of them may be firmly put aside for our purposes, in order to focus as closely as possible on the question of premonitions as such.

24 Any attempt to conflate these two phenomena should be strongly resisted: premonition necessarily implies a time-gap, while simultaneity seems to be of the essence of telepathy.

Of course, some kind of written record is required for any alleged premonition, but it makes sense to talk of a literary dimension to the inquiry, since our authors deal – to differing degrees – with four works of fiction (and two poems) that have been said to have premonitory qualities. Since the earliest of these dates back to the 1880s, they provide the obvious starting-point for our investigation.

CHAPTER 1

PREMONITIONS IN LITERATURE: POEMS, W.T. STEAD, MORGAN ROBERTSON, 'MAYN CLEW GARNETT'

OUR CASES OF POTENTIAL *TITANIC* PREMONITIONS fall into two categories: literary and non-literary (those concerning the death of W.T. Stead are obviously a sub-category of the latter). But although Gardner's 'strange anthology' is a literary anthology, he makes little of this distinction, writing of premonitions and the paranormal in general (and treating most of Stevenson's cases in some detail). In fact, although all five of our authors refer to literary premonitions, only one – Méheust – takes account of the distinction formally and uses it in a significant way. Indeed, his handling of premonitions in literature is a major feature of his book, and his theories on literary premonitions are quite elaborate.

But how important is the distinction itself? Though a number of those who may have had premonitions

– or someone close to them – later enshrined them in published books, only the four fictions by W.T. Stead (two), Morgan Robertson and 'Mayn Clew Garnett', as well as the poems by Celia Thaxter and Herman Melville can clearly count as *possible* literary premonitions of the *Titanic* disaster. And because it is quite certain that five of these were written before 1912, that already distinguishes them sharply from almost all other cases. Furthermore, alleged literary 'premonitions' are somewhat distinctive in their nature. Often, though not always, non-literary precognition involves a particular, spontaneous experience, whereas direct 'premonitions' in literature are more considered and measured, or at least more carefully integrated into a constructed whole, which generally involves more than one alleged premonition. What is more, whether or not it is claimed that the literary piece as such was written in some kind of paranormal trance, the item will, in practice, have to be examined in a very different way from examples of non-literary precognition. These considerations alone constitute a good reason for bearing the literary/non-literary distinction in mind, even if only one of our commentators sees any particular significance in it.

Despite the tendency to begin consideration of literary premonitions of the *Titanic* disaster by looking at Morgan Robertson – perhaps because this is probably the best example – there seems every reason to respect chronological order and examine his case after Stead's. Thaxter's poem was written earliest of all and should be treated first. For convenience, Melville's poem, which was actually published two years after Stead's first relevant story can be taken next.

Another inclination that needs to be resisted is that of grouping premonitions of Stead's death with his literary pieces: the former need to be treated separately, as a distinct sub-category of non-literary premonitions.[1]

POEMS

In the brief final section of his *The Wreck of the Titanic Foretold?* called '"A Tryst," and Other Poems' Gardner – perhaps implausibly – guesses that hundreds of poems were published around the world before 1912 describing ships going down after hitting icebergs, but admits that he does not know of one 'remotely close to Robertson's novel, or even Garnett's story, in anticipating aspects of the *Titanic* disaster'. Nevertheless, he reprints three poems, although we may ignore Thomas Hardy's 'The Convergence of the Twain', which was written after *Titanic* sank, to be read at a charity concert to raise funds in aid of the tragedy.

CASES

(MG,25) The first poem is **Celia Thaxter's 'A Tryst'**.[2] Without making any comment at all on its quality as a premonition, Gardner reprints it from a complete collection of her poems published in 1896, 'some twenty

1 See our Chapter 2.

2 Celia Thaxter (1835-1894), whose father was a lighthouse keeper, lived on islands for most of her life, and wrote, in addition to stories, many sea poems.

years' after it was written.[3] It is referred to by none of the other commentators.

The poem, of twenty four-line stanzas, follows the southward drift of an iceberg 'From out the desolation of the North', asking:

At whose command? Who bade it sail the deep
With that resistless force?
Who made the dread appointment it must keep?
Who traced its awful course?

In separate stanzas, it also follows the progress of a stately sailing ship carrying 'Brave men, sweet women, little children bright', crossing an ocean that one assumes to be the Atlantic. It is clear from the second and third stanzas onwards that the two must meet, and the contrast between the hopes of the people and the coldness of the iceberg is lyrically brought out. On a night 'with neither moon nor star', on which 'Clouds draped the sky in black', the ship 'rushed upon her ruin', and in 'one awful crash' everyone on the ship perished.

Since ships had already collided with icebergs, and many missing ships had been suspected of doing so, 'A Tryst' might just as easily be taken as historical rather than as precognitive. A ship colliding with an iceberg is the only connection between the content of the poem and the *Titanic* disaster. There are no specific grounds whatever for seeing it as constituting, or being based upon, a premonition of that disaster.

---

3 Gardner (1), pp. 151-154.

(MG,26) The second poem that Gardner quotes is **Herman Melville's 'The Berg (A Dream)'**, published in 1888.[4] Again, there is no reason for seeing the poem as any kind of premonition, much less as a foretelling of the *Titanic* disaster, and none of the other commentators mentions it. It is said to have been inspired by memories of Melville's first transatlantic crossing at the age of 19. Gardner prints the poem in his book, saying only, 'Here is how Herman Melville dealt with the same theme.'[5] The work – thirty-seven lines long – portrays 'a ship of martial build', which steers against 'a solid iceberg' and goes down. But the emphasis is on the fact that the iceberg does not budge, and there is scarcely a mention of people on board the ship.

W.T. STEAD

William Thomas Stead (1849-1912) was a famous, controversial journalist and writer of the Victorian era. Of strong Christian faith, he was publicly involved in a number of social and political campaigns in Darlington, and then from 1880 in London. Editor of the *Pall Mall Gazette*, and later of the *Review of Reviews*, he sought to influence public opinion and government policy through a brand of 'new journalism'. He was a publisher of paperback

4 Herman Melville (1819-1891) drew on the time he spent at sea in his writings, but turned to poetry after his great prose works (including *Moby Dick*) had been written but were largely unrecognised. He had his poems printed mostly in small private editions.

5 Gardner (1), pp. 155-156.

literature and supporter of the peace movement. He travelled to America and Russia, and wrote a number of influential books. From the 1890s on he was increasingly absorbed by spiritualism. He died on *Titanic*.

Stead wrote two fictional items that are commonly taken to constitute or contain a foretelling of the *Titanic* disaster: 'How the Mail Steamer Went Down in Mid Atlantic by a Survivor' (1886), and 'From the Old World to the New' (1892).

Stevenson introduces the stories by suggesting that, although for some years Stead claimed to have obtained communications through automatic writing from 'Julia', these provided him with no forewarning of his death on *Titanic*. Nevertheless, Stead 'did have some interesting hints or premonitions of the circumstances of his death'.[6] Stevenson goes on to mention four: Stead's two fictional items, and two of his own separate premonitions.

CASES

(IS,9a) The first fictional piece is **'How the Mail Steamer Went Down in Mid Atlantic, by a Survivor'**. Stead published it in the *Pall Mall Gazette*, of which he was then editor, in March 1886.[7] Stevenson quotes James Coates's *Has W.T. Stead Returned? A Symposium* (1912)[8] as saying

6 Stevenson (1), p. 1

7 Reprinted in *Review of Reviews*, in June 1912. Stevenson does not mention the titles of Stead's two fictional items anywhere in his two articles.

8 This book is usually listed as a 'Symposium'. One description says it concerns 'Evidence of the authenticity of messages from the deceased W. T. Stead'.

that the item 'showed how the majority of the passengers were doomed beforehand', and he records Stead's famous editorial note to the article: 'This is exactly what *might* take place, and what *will* take place, if liners are sent to sea short of boats.'[9] It is not entirely clear, however, that Stevenson has read Stead's story itself (which he describes as a 'fictional article'), and to present it as a premonition of the circumstances of Stead's own death, without explicitly considering it as anticipating the *Titanic* disaster is, in the context, rather odd.

Brown does little more than register the existence of Stead's story and his comment that this is what might take place.[10] Gardner notes that, in any case, in Stead's story the liner does not sink as a result of hitting an iceberg – he might have gone further and mentioned that there is not a single reference to ice in the whole story. He adds that such fears as Stead expressed were common at the time, as were predictions of great sea disasters.[11] He also includes some general material on Stead, saying – doubtless with a certain irony – that he became a 'gifted automatic writer': 'He would pick up a pen, and his hand would be guided by telepathic communications from the unconscious minds of living persons or from the conscious minds of souls in heaven.'[12]

Behe says very little about the story as such, but, despite acknowledging that the 'basic parallels', as well as

---

9 Stevenson (1), p. 160.

10 Brown, p. 61 **(RB,32)**.

11 Gardner (1), p. 92 **(MG,20)**.

12 Gardner (1), p. 92.

Stead's death on a liner short of lifeboats, are interesting, classifies the case as only a 'curious coincidence'.[13] Méheust, on the other hand, devotes two full chapters to Stead, though much of his material relates to matters other than premonitions of the *Titanic* disaster. He first briefly mentions 'How the Mail Steamer Went Down …' in Part I of his book,[14] then goes on to summarise the story and refer to Stead's editorial note as well as his own death on *Titanic*.[15] He does not include it in his dossier in Part III of his book, but in Part IV he says he believes that although the story is less spectacular and less precisely linked to a sinking than Robertson's, it is still more intriguing.[16] This is because it seems to anticipate not only the sinking of a great liner, but also Stead's own death, although Méheust admits that this is not obvious, appearing only when one analyses the fiction in the way that dreams are analysed.[17]

Méheust says that the first striking thing about the story is that it is told in the first person. He claims it anticipates in 'improbable detail' what Stead will experience on *Titanic*, stressing that the collision between the narrator's (unnamed) steamer and another ship takes place, as does *Titanic*'s disaster, on the fifth night of the voyage, and that it is a 'sudden freak' that first causes the narrator to climb up to look at the lifeboats and discover

---

13 Behe, p. 16, (**GB,cc,1**).

14 Méheust, p. 11 (**BM,wts,1**).

15 Méheust, pp. 47-48.

16 Méheust, p. 255. He thinks this is also the case for 'From the Old World to the New'; see below.

17 Méheust, p. 256.

that they cannot accommodate everyone on board the liner. Stead, too, we are told, was out walking on the deck just before the collision, and, although we obviously do not know what thoughts were in his head at this precise time, Méheust very unconvincingly claims we can infer what they were on the basis of our knowledge of Stead. He has great difficulty in believing that the tale and the final warning it contains, together with at least one (other) prediction of his own death, did not enter Stead's mind.[18] But he admits that there is no evidence for his arbitrary assumption regarding Stead's thoughts. (Why should Stead think these things at that precise time, when he had already been on *Titanic* for five days?).

When Méheust returns to the 'sudden freak', it is to argue that the unmotivated impulse precedes the calculation of numbers and that this sequence is typical of premonitions.[19] Yet whether or not this is so, there is evidently insufficient justification for his subsequent assertion that Stead 'seems' to have anticipated not only his own death but also the phenomena of precognition that preceded and accompanied the sinking. Moreover, a series of claims that Méheust makes concerning exactly what happened to Stead at the time of *Titanic*'s collision and afterwards are seriously unsubstantiated: 'Like his character, he sees the collision, and a thin coat of pulverised ice cover the front of the ship in an instant'; he sees an officer take out his revolver and threaten passengers trying to take charge of the boats; he takes up an iron bar and helps Major Butt to enable women

18 Méheust, pp. 256-257.

19 Méheust, p. 258.

and children to get into the boats; and, having been thrown into the sea, he clings onto a lifeboat, but out of cold and fatigue lets himself slip back. Some of this is fanciful, and the evidence for all of these claims regarding Stead is slender in the extreme, most of it depending upon Stead's posthumous appearances to his disciples.[20]

Méheust is guilty, in a general way, of over-stressing and over-interpreting 'How the Mail Steamer Went Down …', which is a very short story of just over 2,600 words. In itself it does not contain any paranormal element at all. And, above all, it bears strikingly little relation – however it is interpreted – to the *Titanic* disaster. The vessel in the story is much smaller, and slower than *Titanic*, and, above all, its collision with a sailing vessel has not the remotest resemblance to *Titanic*'s brush with an iceberg.[21] It is true, though not especially surprising, that certain aspects of the conduct of both the steamer's crew and certain passengers would to an extent be those displayed on *Titanic* some twenty-six years later: some women and children are put into the lifeboats first, and some boats leave with 'half their proper complement'. But steerage passengers in the

20 Méheust, pp. 257-258. He claims that some of these assertions are justified by 'major testimony' in Steven Biel's *Titanica, the Disaster of the Century in Poetry, Song, and Prose* (1998), but the writer was not a passenger on *Titanic* and offers a highly dramatised account of the sinking, with imagined dialogue. Another source, 'certain testimonies' in the *Daily Mirror* of 30 April, is equally dubious.

21 In certain respects, a case might be made out for seeing the story as foreseeing the French liner SS *La Bourgogne*'s fatal collision with the British sailing ship *Cromartyshire* in dense fog near Nova Scotia in July 1898, although in this incident the steamer sank, whereas the sailing ship did not, and it was reported that the steamer's crew behaved particularly badly (of the 165 survivors, only 70 were passengers, almost none First Class and only one a woman).

fictional piece are violent and virtually out of control, and there are other considerable discrepancies. What is more, the prominent warning about shortage of lifeboats – the story's narrator calculates that they would accommodate 390 of the 916 on board[22] – is far from unusual, having being formulated by a number of others acquainted with the sea. It is comparable in general terms to the non-fictional warnings given concerning the dangerous speed at which steamers were crossing the Atlantic in the early years of the twentieth century.

No one, it seems, has suggested that Stead wrote this story in any kind of trance or abnormal state of mind, and it has to be concluded that far more attention than is justified has been paid to 'How the Mail Steamer Went Down ...' as a supernatural premonition of the *Titanic* disaster. The foresight it contains consists of a common-sense prediction, cast in fictional form, of the potentially catastrophic consequences of inadequate lifeboat legislation.

(IS,9b) The second fictional piece, for which Stevenson gives Estelle Stead's book, *My Father* (1934), as his source, '**From the Old World to the New**', was published in the *Review of Reviews* in 1892. Stevenson says this item imagines the sinking of a liner by collision with an iceberg and the rescue of its sole surviving passenger by the White Star liner *Majestic*. He adds that the captain of the real *Majestic* at the time was Edward Smith.[23]

22 There may be some carelessness in Stead's reference, at the beginning, to 902 passengers.

23 Stevenson (1). p. 160.

Brown, referring to the item first as an 'article', then a 'story' adds nothing, seeing the presence in it of Captain Smith as 'eerie'.[24] Behe is equally brief on the subject, categorising the case as another 'curious coincidence', and not mentioning that only a section of the story is relevant.[25] Gardner takes the story seriously enough to reprint the significant part of it in his book, although he is clear that the alleged premonition element is no more than 'a portion' of Stead's 'sentimental novel'.[26] He makes the valid point that 'It is a measure of Stead's skill as a journalist and researcher that he wrote this novel before making his first trip to America in the fall of 1893', and summarises the story up to and after the extract that he prints (the last part of Chapter VII and the whole of Chapter VIII).[27]

The story is, in fact, one part of the Christmas (1892) issue of the *Review of Reviews*. The issue opens with some 25 pages of advertisements, including a number for planned trips abroad, and ends with 20 pages of more advertisements and advice about travelling in the United States. The tale itself bears the title 'From the Old World to the New. A Christmas Story of the World's Fair, 1893'. Only two of its twenty chapters ('Chapter VII – Coincidence and Clairvoyance', and 'Chapter VIII – The Castaways') contain material that might specifically be thought to prefigure in some way the *Titanic* disaster, and these occupy only some 11 of the 122 pages of the story. Moreover, a third or so of

---

24 Brown, p. 61 (**RB,33**).

25 Behe, p. 17 (**GB,cc,3**).

26 Gardner (1), p. 92 (**MG,21**).

27 Gardner (1), pp. 96-99.

the first of these chapters simply continues the main thread of the story, so that the relevant section is no more than some 8,350 words in all (the last 3,600 of which contain no reference whatever to the paranormal). In the text one of the many illustrations is a photograph of Captain Smith, to which Stead adds an odd footnote: 'I need not say that the whole of this story is purely imaginary. Although I illustrate the account of the voyage with a portrait of the real captain of the *Majestic*, he must not be in any way identified with the captain of this story.'

Once again it is Méheust who pays – by far – greatest attention to this story. Having briefly referred to it early on,[28] later in Part I of his book he points out that Stead reverts here to the subject of a ship sinking, which is never far from his imagination. He says that in the Introduction the author explicitly draws a link between the discovery of America by Columbus and the recent discovery of the continent of psychic phenomena.[29] He also claims – mistaking the dates – that, while the Christmas 1892 issue of *Review of Reviews* had explored the practices of automatic writing, this 'Christmas 1893' issue deals with the discoveries in science and technology on display at the great Chicago Fair that was the event of the year in 1893, though it also returns to psychic phenomena in the story in question. He suggests that, for Stead, the title 'From the Old World to the New' refers to a journey to both the land of America and the 'other world'.[30]

28 Méheust, p. 11 **(BM,wts,2)**.

29 Méheust, pp. 48-49.

30 Méheust, p. 49.

It is difficult to judge the notion that Stead had a certain obsession with sinking ships, but it is true that in the Preface to the story he draws a loose analogy between the discovery of the American continent and that of the 'Invisible World'. Stead, however, does not emphasise 'the discoveries in science and technology' as such at the Chicago Fair, but talks more generally of 'the latest embodiment of the genius, the enterprise and the labour of Man in the material realms'. He also says explicitly that the story incorporates a 'more or less dramatic representation of conclusions arrived at after twelve months' experimental study of psychical phenomena'.[31]

One is bound to wonder, however, whether there is absolutely definite evidence that Stead himself is the author of the story, since he ascribes this 'undertaking which might well daunt the most practised story-teller' to 'one who had the audacity of the novice who always believes that he can do impossibilities in his first story'. Stead adds a final remark that he has not allowed the writer 'when treating of psychometry, clairvoyancy, telepathy, or automatic writing, to go one step beyond the limits, not merely of the possible, but of that which has actually been attained. This I have verified by experiments conducted under conditions precluding fraud or mistake.'

The story as a whole incorporates a number of elements relating to the paranormal. The Prologue itself involves the mysterious appearance of the face of a past love in a mirror. Dreams and hypnotism play an important part in the plot, and at least four characters have experiences of a broadly

31 Preface to 'From the Old World to the New'.

spiritualist nature. At the end of Chapter VI, Compton, the wealthy man whose involvement with automatic writing makes him the main player in Chapters VII and VIII, explains his hopes and plans for the future (heralded by the Chicago World's Fair), in which telepathy will have a major part to play. We are 'just about to enter the Telepathic Era', for Compton knows as a scientific fact 'that it is possible to communicate instantaneously from a common centre, orders, counsel, judgment and suggestion, to trained telepathists all over the world, without the use of any other agency than thought.' But the paranormal elements in the story are set against a more realistic background. There are many genuine details concerning travelling on liners, and Chapter IV contains – albeit in a somewhat didactic form – information about the dangers of Atlantic crossings (fog, icebergs, fire, and collision), which do not include storms: 'There never was a storm brewed in heaven or earth that could wreck the *Majestic*, if she had sea room enough and no fog.' It also gives details of the many ships lost in the first forty years of the steam ferry (said to number 144), and offers the dubious opinion that 'no ship is ever driven at full speed during a fog'. Chapter VII will add that about four ships are lost every year after collision with icebergs.

The relevant section of Chapter VII opens with Mrs Irwin explaining that she has 'occasionally the gift of second sight',[32] and that when she was asleep the previous

32 This gift, said to have been inherited, is brought into the story at a later point, when Mrs Irwin claims she can hear and see sounds and sights inaudible and invisible to other mortals. She also has the faculty of 'thought-reading': 'She was clairvoyant, psychometric and a thought-reader.'

night she 'saw' a ship, the *Ann and Jane* of Montrose, damaged by contact with ice, sink, with only six men and a boy surviving on an iceberg (she later estimates that this took place nearly 200 miles away). Compton divulges that at noon he had received a message, by automatic writing, from a friend, John Thomas, one of the men stranded on the iceberg. He will receive another six such messages (one in the presence of the Captain) before the rescue of Thomas;[33] and the Captain's niece, under hypnosis, will also 'see' John Thomas on the ice. Because Compton has on previous voyages given the Captain messages, obtained through automatic writing, that have 'enabled the captain to avoid imminent dangers into which he was steaming at full speed', he persuades the Captain to stop in sight of the iceberg and send a boat to rescue Thomas.[34] It ought to be said at this point that, although the conditions in which the *Ann and Jane* struck the ice are not given in the story, there are a number of important *contrasts* between the circumstances surrounding the fictional *Majestic* and *Titanic*. Fog is a serious factor for the *Majestic*, which enters an 'ice fog' before the rescue, and the Captain slackens speed. Moreover, the *Majestic* ploughs through drift-ice for some time before reaching the edge of the icebergs. She slows down again and goes a little further south when icebergs are seen, before resuming full speed.

33 There is another, greatly extended, episode of automatic writing later in the story, involving communication from the dead. Stead, as editor, claims that this part of the narrative is not a story, but a 'fact'.

34 It is interesting to note that when the story of the rescue later goes public, the participants choose to tell it without referring to the paranormal elements at all.

Listing the coincidences between the *Titanic* disaster and Stead's 1892 story, Méheust points out that the *Majestic* was White Star's star ship at the time, and that Smith was its captain.[35] He does not include the story in his dossier in Part III, but returns to the subject in Part IV of his book. He finds Stead's assertion that the captain figure in his story is a fiction 'curious' (resembling the psychoanalytical process of 'denial'). He also repeats his claim that Compton is 'obviously' Stead himself ('There is no doubt on this matter'), although it should be said that, despite the fact that both are trying to establish 'a sort of telepathic Internet', the parallels in other respects are, in fact, quite limited. Furthermore, Méheust suggests – he believes he is the first to have noticed this – that the roles that the captain and Compton play before and during the disaster *reverse* what was to happen on *Titanic*, with the captain acting (unlike Smith) prudently, and Compton (unlike Stead) acting on the paranormal information that he has received.[36] But this is a rather arbitrary interpretation that is, in any case, of no obvious significance. Even less plausible and consequential is the parallel that Méheust attempts to draw between Stead and Thomas, the man rescued from the iceberg, 'a tall man, red-haired and bearded, with one eye half-closed that apparently cannot see'. Méheust finds that this description 'curiously' fits Stead himself, although he acknowledges that the reasons for this are rather 'mysterious', and admits that he has not been able to confirm that Stead was tall and red-haired! He says this analogy is just an 'hypothesis', and

35 Méheust, pp. 51-52.

36 Méheust, p. 259.

feebly concludes that Stead is dividing himself in two in his story, to be both the soothsayer and the person calling for assistance.[37]

At this point Méheust seeks to relate the network of people linked by automatic writing in Stead's story to the 'network of people linked in one way or another by the inaugural voyage of *Titanic*' (and, on a smaller scale, to Stead's own spiritualist network), arguing that in September 1911 a telepathic connection was established between Stead and the psychic W. de Kerlor, though Stead was to ignore the latter's warning and embark on *Titanic*. Méheust goes further than this, however, and makes the exaggerated claim that on the night of the *Titanic* disaster 'tens of people will be informed by a vision or presentiment that someone close to them is in danger of death or in the process of drowning'.[38] Hence Stead is said to have anticipated not only his own end at the same time as that of *Titanic*, but also the premonitions that accompanied the drama. Méheust believes that, if there is genuine precognition in this process, this means that, in seeking to describe telepathic links in a work of fiction, he has put them into practice without knowing it, embedding the theme of predestination in his story.[39]

Méheust's point that, in 'From the Old World to the New', Stead embodies the paranormal in the story itself

37 Méheust, p. 260.

38 Méheust, p. 261.

39 Méheust, p. 261. Méheust adds to this case of embedding, or 'mise en abîme', the way in which icebergs as a danger to shipping are actually discussed in a story which involves a ship sinking after collision with an iceberg.

is, of course, incontrovertible (whereas his attempts to establish this in the case of 'How the Mail Steamer Went Down ...' were entirely unsuccessful). Nonetheless, one is reluctant to follow him in the analogies that he draws and the analysis that he conducts on the basis of this fact. Many of the details of his argument are at best half-truths, and once more part of the problem is over-interpretation. It is important to remember that the pertinent sections of the two relevant chapters form only a very small portion of what is a very long short story, or a novella – a novella, moreover, that is indeed a sentimental love story, with extremely substantial segments of historical, and geographical information, and political opinion. This is entirely lost sight of when Méheust asserts that 'The peripeteia and protagonists of the 1912 drama are strangely invoked and redistributed in the 1893 story, which, as a result, is charged with an inexpressible strangeness'.[40] He believes that it is as if the story has the structure and function of a dream, so that one can see in it the processes of displacement and condensation that Freud detected in dreams. The problem with this, however, is that Méheust fails to deliver on his promise to analyse the story in the way that dreams are analysed. Instead of further detailed scrutiny of the two relevant chapters, he passes on to more general features of the whole Stead phenomenon: other people's predictions concerning his fate, how Stead reacted to these, messages from Stead after his death, and so on.

We have, therefore, to conclude that Méheust's consideration of 'From the Old World to the New' leads

40 Méheust, p. 262.

nowhere in itself, and is, in general, over-elaborate, not to say fanciful. It is significant that in this story there is no mention at all of, or reference to, anyone foreseeing the collision of the *Ann and Jane* with an iceberg, and that the paranormal activities concerning the rescue (automatic writing and visions in hypnosis) are all of a telepathic, not precognitive nature. Hence, insofar as Méheust is claiming that the story foretells not just Stead's death and the *Titanic* disaster, but also the network of *precognitive* experiences surrounding it, he makes a leap in his argument that has no logical foundation whatever.

The major differences between the *Titanic* disaster and 'From the Old World to the New' are too numerous to list. The only substantive links or resemblances – none of which is in the least remarkable – are that the (presumed) author of the story was on *Titanic*; and that the fictional captain of the rescue-ship is based on Edward Smith, who was to become captain of *Titanic*. A short, almost self-contained segment of the story centres on a transatlantic liner that collides with an iceberg (but in fog), with catastrophic loss of life (there are only seven survivors from the *Ann and Jane*, six of whom subsequently perish; John Thomas, whose life will be saved, has to be revived by a 'patent galvano-vitalizer').

Méheust claims that there are two hypotheses about the story. The first is that there is no question of it constituting a premonition: we simply note the coincidences and reinterpret them in the light of the later event. The second is that through the fiction paranormal information reached the depths of Stead's unconscious, only to be repressed and then to resurface in the last days of his life. But not only is there little, if any, evidence on which to base the second hypothesis, Méheust pursues it in two fruitless directions: the appearances of Stead to his disciples after his death, and the notion – with which he flirts, but dismisses, perhaps somewhat reluctantly – that Stead and/or his acquaintances may have had some role in bringing to reality the prophecy of Stead's death on *Titanic* (which he calls the 'performative' hypothesis).[41]

Overall there is little, if anything, in the comments of our five authors to substantiate any claim that 'From the Old World …' anticipates Stead's own death, much less that it somehow foretells the *Titanic* disaster. It is true that, unlike 'How the Mail Steamer Went Down …', the story definitely contains paranormal elements. But, in fact, our first four authors scarcely make the case for premonition at all, and the detailed consideration that Méheust gives to the story contains a great number of dubious assertions and is speculative in the extreme. Once again, moreover, none of the commentators suggests that Stead wrote the story in any kind of paranormal trance.

MORGAN ROBERTSON

Morgan Andrew Robertson (1861-1915), son of a ship's captain on the Great Lakes, was at sea as a cabin boy and eventually first mate. He then worked as a diamond setter for ten years, before turning to writing, in 1897, after noting that Kipling had made some errors in a sea story. He

41 Méheust, pp. 264-267.

produced more than two hundred sea stories of his own, but made little money from his writing. He mixed in a small bohemian circle of writers and artists in New York, dying in a hotel room in Atlantic City, probably of heart disease.

CASE

(IS,1) Stevenson records that Morgan Robertson published a novel called ***Futility*** in 1898, describing the construction and an early voyage of a huge steamship named *Titan*.[42] He lists a number of ways in which details of the *Titan* and its sinking resemble those of *Titanic*, saying that we can consider the correspondence either exact or impressive on the following ten points:

> *name of ship; myth of unsinkability; collision with iceberg; sinking in month of April; displacement tonnage; length of ship; speed of ship at impact; number of propellers; number of lifeboats; enormous loss of life.*

He does not dwell on any of these points and his treatment of the whole case is brief. Later, he claims that we should consider less coincidental the matching of unusual details (e.g. the name of the ship), than the matching of commonplace features, like the number of propellers.[43] He tells us nothing at all about Robertson himself and does not explain the discrepancy between the titles *Futility*

42 Stevenson (1), pp. 156-157.

43 Stevenson (1), p. 165.

and *The Wreck of the Titan*; in a footnote he cites the 1898 edition, but he uses the latter as the title of the work.

In looking back over the nineteen cases discussed in his first article, Stevenson is emphatic that 'we certainly cannot exclude inference as a source for Robertson's story'.[44] He points out that at the end of the nineteenth century few limits were discernible to engineering skill and that the novels of Jules Verne and H.G. Wells predicted further extraordinary developments. Arguing that the reach of science from time to time exceeds its grasp – and providing what some might regard as a 'premonition' of his own: that 'the mastery of flight into outer space' will produce disasters like those in the history of the first passenger jet airliners after the Second World War[45] – Stevenson suggests that a writer of the 1890s 'might reasonably infer' that man would overreach himself in the construction of ocean liners. This, in turn, could lead to 'additional inferences about the details of the tragedy to come': 'overconfidence would neglect the importance of lifeboats; recklessness would race the ship through the areas of the Atlantic icebergs; these drift south in the spring, making April a likely month for collision'. And the name *Titan* has connoted power and security for several thousand years. Although he does not elaborate on these points as much as other commentators, one must give Stevenson full credit for making them.[46]

Brown adds nothing to this, except to say (without giving sources) that Robertson claimed he had an 'astral

44 Stevenson (1), p. 164.

45 One might think, in particular, of the breaking apart of Space Shuttle *Challenger* in 1986.

46 As Méheust does: Méheust, p. 247.

partner' as a co-author and was 'in a state of trance' when he wrote.[47] Although she does not list the text, she may be basing her comment on *Morgan Robertson the Man* (1915) edited by 'J.B.K', in which two or three contributors mention Robertson's belief in the occult in general, with one referring to an 'astral helper', a 'psychic partner', and even an 'astral boss'. Yet the evidence of the book is mixed, since other friends emphasise how difficult Robertson found the writing process and how painstaking was his study of a subject before he wrote about it.

Gardner regards Robertson's novel as by far Stevenson's best example of precognition,[48] going on to claim that it is the 'single most impressive example of seeming precognition of the *Titanic* disaster, or any other disaster'.[49] He says that the 145-page book (called *Futility*) was reprinted in 1912 under the title *The Wreck of the Titan; or, Futility*. The reprint also included a longer novella by Robertson and two of his short stories. Gardner notes that Robertson made 'numerous revisions' to his text for the reprint, but they are 'mostly changes of punctuation and phrasing and have almost no bearing on the story's prophetic aspects'. He says that the writer of two privately published books on Robertson, Jack W. Hannah, who was convinced that Robertson had the gift of prophecy and that his novel was divinely inspired, points out that, if anything, the parallels are

47 Brown, pp. 21-22 (**RB,12**).

48 Gardner (1), pp. 18 (**MG,1**).

49 Gardner (1), p. 27. His introduction to the text itself, which his book contains, is on pp. 27-36.

'a trifle stronger' in the 1898 version.[50] It is sometimes suggested that the inflation of *Titan*'s displacement from 45,000 tons to 70,000 tons, and her horsepower from 40,000 to 75,000 – both figures from the later version of Robertson's story being considerably in excess of the figures for *Titanic* (52,000 and 46,000) – indicates that Robertson's intention was to keep his fictional ship *ahead* of current technology.

Before focusing on Robertson, Gardner summarises the *Titanic* story (including aspects of developments since the sinking). His summary corrects a number of 'myths' about the sinking, but it also contains a number of contentious statements and one or two errors.[51] Gardner goes on to tell us that Robertson, who, he acknowledges, had 'a strong personal interest in occult topics', became one of his country's most widely read writers of sea stories, penning more than two hundred tales of varying length, reprinted in fourteen books. He points out that Robertson's short autobiography, 'Gathering No Moss', which is around 9,000 words long, strangely makes no mention of *Titanic* or his own prophetic novel. Nor does it suggest that he writes in any paranormal state.[52]

---

50 Hannah's two books are: *The Futility God: Spiritist Power, Occultism, and Futility* (1975); and *The Titanic: Its Prophecy, Philosophy, and Psychology* (1980).

51 Gardner (1), pp. 27-30.

52 The autobiography, first printed in the *Saturday Evening Post* on 28 March, 1914, is in *Morgan Robertson the Man* (1915), edited by 'J.B.K.', and also in Hannah's 1980 volume. Without giving any reasons, Bill Wormstedt claims that it was actually written by Bozeman Bulger (http://wormstedt.com/TitanicBookSite/RobertsonMorgan.html). Another autobiographical piece in *Morgan Robertson the Man* also appears under Robertson's name: 'My Skirmish with Madness'. Although very different in tone from 'Gathering No Moss', it again casts no light at all on premonitions or the paranormal.

Robertson is said to have had a 'lifelong problem of alcoholism'.[53]

Gardner reminds us that in the 1970s there was a 'public hunger for sensational accounts of the paranormal', and that many of the publications it produced cover Robertson's vision of the *Titanic* disaster. He clearly deplores this, but believes that the parallels between the disaster and Robertson's fiction are so startling that 'it is easy to understand why Robertson's novel is often hailed as paranormal foresight'. He thinks, however, that it is impossible to judge how 'improbable' the parallels were,[54] since there is no way to estimate, even crudely, the relevant probabilities (which echoes a general point that he argues in the Introduction to his book).

Gardner stresses that Stevenson made it clear that we certainly cannot exclude inference as a source of Robertson's story. The strength of Gardner's introduction to Robertson's text is that, in spite of his ranking of the story so highly as a case of 'seeming precognition', he makes a very plausible attempt to put himself in Robertson's shoes as a writer wanting to weave an adventure around the greatest sea disaster he can imagine. He shows how the parallels might have been arrived at largely by inference from knowledge of the sea and ships. Robertson could easily have envisaged a liner larger than any previously made, with watertight compartments that would result in its being hailed as unsinkable. Other details, like length, tonnage, carrying capacity, number of propellers, etc,

53 Gardner (1), pp. 30-31.

54 Hannah arrived at a probability estimate of 1 in 4 billion that the parallels could be chance coincidences, an arbitrary figure that is taken up by Méheust.

would 'jog into place'. Then, what could sink a monstrous liner except a monstrous iceberg? The danger of colliding with an iceberg was, after all, the most-feared event of a ship's crew when it crossed the North Atlantic, the time of greatest peril being in the early spring. Robertson would also have known from his years at sea that damage to a ship is much greater when the collision is with its side rather than head on.[55] Finally, wanting to stress 'the unbounded hubris that caused the ship's owners and officers to be careless', he would naturally give the ship an inadequate supply of lifeboats and have almost all passengers perish. Stressing just how many stories are published about imaginary disasters, Gardner concludes that Robertson's novel happens to be the 'best example we know of a "probable improbability" within the enormously large combinatorial universe of fictional possibilities'.[56]

In *When You Were A Tadpole And I Was A Fish* (2009), when he presents his reprint of the Introduction to his earlier book, Gardner says, 'I argue here that the parallels in Robertson's novel with the *Titanic*'s sinking are no more than coincidences combined with Robertson's knowledge of the White Star company's plans to build a gigantic ocean liner'.[57] It is interesting to note, however, that neither of the introductions to his earlier book and to 'The Wreck of the Titan' within it mentions these plans, let alone Robertson's knowledge of them. It is in Gardner's

55 This is a slightly odd point for Gardner to make, since the *Titan* runs up onto an ice shelf.

56 Gardner (1), pp. 33-36.

57 Gardner (2), p. 75.

Preface to the paperback edition of the earlier book (1998), also reprinted in *When You Were A Tadpole And I Was A Fish*, that he gives us more information about Robertson. In particular, he quotes Robertson's reply to a letter from Ella Wheeler Wilcox, the American poet and spiritualist:

> *As to the motif of my story, I merely tried to write a good story with no idea of being a prophet. But, as in other stories of mine, and in the work of other and better writers, coming discoveries and events have been anticipated. I do not doubt that it is because all creative workers get into a hypnoid, telepathic and percipient condition, in which, while apparently awake, they are half asleep, and tap, not only the better informed minds of others but the subliminal realm of unknown facts.*[58]

Wilcox also raised a question that had intrigued Gardner from the first: how could Robertson fix on 'almost the very name which was afterwards given to the ill-fated sea monster'? In his earlier book, Gardner had discarded the possibility that someone in White Star, having read Robertson's story, simply added 'ic' to the name of his ship, on the grounds that it is difficult to imagine that anyone would want to name a new liner after a fictional ship that sank after hitting an iceberg.[59] He now claims that evidence has recently emerged which makes the coincidence of names far less astonishing, reporting the

58 Gardner (2), p. 95.

59 Gardner (1), p. 35.

discovery of an obscure, 'amateurish' novel by William Young Winthrop, entitled *A 20th Century Cinderella or $20,000 Reward*, published in 1902. It refers to a gigantic ocean liner called *Titanic* that had been built by the White Star Company some time before 1920, the year in which Winthrop's science fiction takes place. Gardner says that this could be 'another coincidence', but suggests that it is entirely possible that White Star, as early as 1898, when Robertson published his novel, had announced plans to construct the world's largest liner and to call it *Titanic*.[60]

In any case, Gardner points out that Eaton and Hass reproduced a news item from *The New York Times*, published as early as September 1892:

> *London, Sept. 16 – The White Star Company has commissioned the great Belfast shipbuilders Harland and Wolff to build an Atlantic steamer that will beat the record in size and speed.*
>
> *She has already been named* Gigantic, *and will be 700 feet long, 65 feet 7½ inches beam and 45,000 horsepower. It is calculated that she will steam 22 knots an hour, with a maximum speed of 27 knots. She will have three screws, two fitted like* Majestic's,

60 It is certain that by 1908, when Matthias McDonnell Bodkin published his short story, 'The Ship's Run', the plans for three *Olympic*-class liners were well established. Bodkin, who may well have read of White Star's plans while researching his story, actually calls his fictional vessel 'the great ship *Titanic*', and 'the largest and fastest passenger boat afloat'. It sails 'at the rate of twenty miles an hour'. But although the story centres on betting on what distance the ship covers in a day, which is what happened on *Titanic*, there is no question of its being in a collision, much less sinking; no question of the story constituting or containing a premonition.

> *and the third in the centre. She is to be ready for sea in March, 1894.*[61]

Although the vessel was never built, Gardner points out that the figures given for the liner's dimensions, horsepower, speed, and number of propellers are very close to those to be used by Robertson for *Titan* six years later. He believes that this makes it clear what happened: Robertson, knowing of plans for the *Gigantic*, 'modelled his ship on this proposed mammoth'. The name *Titanic* being the only unused appropriate name left for a giant liner, he simply dropped *-ic* from the name, since he did not want his doomed *Titan* to be identified with White Star.[62]

It has to be admitted that this last point seems a good deal less clear than Gardner suggests, and that his further argument that White Star did not mind adopting a similar name to Robertson's ship because it was persuaded that *Titanic* was absolutely unsinkable is rather unconvincing. Nevertheless, Gardner has provided enough new evidence to justify his claim that the parallels between the names *Titan* and *Titanic* are 'less astonishing'. He could also have included *Titania* in the picture, since it seems that three

61 John P. Eaton and Charles Hass, *Titanic: Destination Disaster*, (1987), p. 55. Morgan Robertson's story 'The Pirates', included in *Futility, or the Wreck of the Titan* of 1912, incorporates a huge liner, *Gigantia*, 'the latest and largest steamship built'. It is 1,000 feet long and has five funnels: 'the only ship afloat with five funnels since the *Great Eastern*'.

62 I'm not sure that it is has been noted that in his novel, *Atlantis* (1892), Gerhart Johann Robert Hauptman has his hero, Frederick, on his first encounter with the liner *Roland*, think of the ship as 'that Titan of venturesomeness, that floating fairy palace' (p. 15), suggesting that the use of the name had a certain currency, and perhaps making Robertson's use of *Titan* somewhat less surprising.

vessels with that name sank in the North Atlantic before *Futility* was written, one, and possibly two, of them after collision with an iceberg.[63] Gardner concludes his Preface by saying that, in a letter, Richard Branham indicated numerous coincidences involving Robertson's *Titan* and the *Lusitania*, and, 'tongue in cheek', made out as good a case for Robertson precognising the *Lusitania* disaster as for anticipating the *Titanic*'s sinking.[64]

Behe classifies Robertson's novel as only a 'curious coincidence'.[65] After relating what happens to *Titan*, he argues that the 'many similarities' between *Titan* and *Titanic* seem uncanny at first, 'but are actually perfectly understandable'. He adds to Gardner's account the notion that Robertson was forced to project the dimensions of his ship a couple of steps ahead of the vessels of 1898, since he did not want his story to be rapidly outdated by modern advances in shipbuilding and rapid increases in size. But he agrees with Gardner that other details simply follow from the ship's length, so that the similarities are 'not at all remarkable'. Behe also stresses that there is no 'psychic ability' involved in Robertson's awareness of the dangers of the failure to increase the number of lifeboats as the size of ships increased: he merely projected this observation to its 'extreme, but logical end result'. Yet Behe does not give any substantive reason for his contention that Robertson's choice of name for his ship is 'not all that remarkable'. He

63 Research article by Senan Malony: http://wormstedt.com/TitanicBookSite/article_robertson_prophet.html

64 Gardner (2), p. 99.

65 Behe, pp.17-19 **(GB,cc,4)**.

does, however, note two important additional differences between the ships *Titan* and *Titanic*: Robertson assumed that future liners would still use sail, and the crew of *Titan* had actually hoisted great triangular sails on each of the ship's two masts, to help the ship make a speedy crossing, whereas *Titanic* had no sails.[66] And Behe later claims of *Titanic* that the details of her sinking were 'greatly different' from that of the fictional ship.[67]

Méheust devotes a great deal of space to Robertson – two-and-a-half chapters – emphasising that his is just one of a group of fictional stories that appear to foresee the *Titanic* disaster.[68] He gives new dimensions to the case, but his treatment of it is less than satisfactory in a number of respects.

Briefly listing the standard parallels between *Titan* and *Titanic*, Méheust adds to the technical similarities the fact that in both cases there was a 'series of acts of imprudence driven by the demands of commercial competition and by the conviction that the two vessels are unsinkable',[69] although in the case of *Titanic*, it is unclear what alleged acts of imprudence (in addition to excessive speed, which

66 There are other significant differences between *Titan* and *Titanic*: for example, the former has 80 stokeholes, the latter 159.

67 Behe, p. 46.

68 Méheust, p. 11 **(BM,mr,1)**. In recording that *Futility* was reprinted under a different title, Méheust cites *The Wreck of the Titan, a Nineteenth Century Prophecy*, Pocket Books, London, 1998, but he also claims that the reprint dates from 1915, 'shortly after the sinking'. His own page-references are to a French translation: *Le Naufrage du 'Titan'*, Corsaire Editions, Orléans, 2000. He refers throughout to *Futility* rather than *The Wreck of the Titan*.

69 Méheust, p. 29.

has been mentioned separately) are involved. He next goes on to list ten points raised by the parapsychologist, Yves Lignon, implicitly giving his approval to the list.[70] But the appositeness or accuracy of virtually every item can be contested in some respect or other. For example, though it is probably true that *Titanic* was attempting to beat *Olympic*'s crossing time, Lignon's notion that *Titan*'s captain is trying to beat the record won on its maiden voyage is based on a single sentence in the story saying that 'it was unofficially rumoured' among the passengers that this was so; the assertions that *Titanic* almost sank *New York* in Southampton and a French trawler in Queenstown are entirely unfounded; no initial 'Hard-a-port' was given on *Titanic*;[71] no 'Full speed astern' order is given on contact with the ice on *Titan* in Robertson's text, and it is highly dubious whether such an order was given on *Titanic*;[72] it is far from clear that the 'lesser evil' would have been to strike the iceberg full-on; the statement that *Titan* 'makes contact on the starboard side' is not justified by Robertson's text; it is entirely uncertain why the suggestion that either *Titan* or *Titanic* sank on the port side is made; and the claim that 950 people were saved on *Titanic* is a clear, simple, and serious error. Méheust himself adds another coincidence to Lignon's list, saying that both ships were subject to a curse. Rumours in Belfast suggested that *Titanic* was cursed because its builders had offended

70 'Le Titan-ic', *La Gazette fortéenne*, 2005. Méheust, pp. 30-32.

71 As on other liners in 1912, helm orders were reversed (in a hold-over from the times of using tillers to steer ships), so that Murdoch actually initially called out 'hard-a-starboard', meaning 'turn the ship to port'.

72 See Samuel Halpern *et al* (2011), pp. 91-92.

God. And two sailors on the *Royal Age* cursed *Titan* when their ship was cut in two.[73] But while the cursing of *Titan* in Robertson's story is a fact, mere reference to 'rumours in Belfast' amounts to nothing at all.

When Méheust returns to the 'coincidences concerning the technical characteristics of the two ships', he refers once more to Lignon. Almost all of the items on this list are familiar: both ships fly the British flag; length, speed, tonnage, capacity, and number of crew are all similar; both have watertight compartments and are designed to float with a certain number of these flooded; both have three engines and three propellers; both have a telephone exchange; both have two masts; there is a similar number of passengers on board both; both have two orchestras; both sailed at midday; kidnapping of children is associated with both ships. We will look in detail at the significance of most of these parallels later.

Méheust also stresses – quite rightly – that the opening paragraphs of *Futility*, reviewing the revolutionary characteristics of the ship, are remarkably like the descriptions of the *Titanic* fourteen years later. The phrase 'practically unsinkable' was used in both instances, and Méheust now adds that on both ships the watertight doors can be closed together by a single action, and also close automatically in contact with water. In both cases, moreover, because of the central commercial aims of the companies, the ships carried the minimal number of lifeboats, although they were provided with an adequate number of life-jackets.

73 Méheust, p. 32.

At this point in the first of the two chapters concerned, Méheust has a section on the life and works of Morgan Robertson, referring rather puzzlingly to the 'unintentional prophecy' with which his name is now associated. Acknowledging that Robertson never 'broke through' as a writer of maritime stories and led a miserable existence, he correctly and usefully emphasises that *Futility* is first and foremost a strong attack on 'Victorian society, with its cult of technology, power and money', a world heading for catastrophe, condemned to 'futility'.[74] Méheust's claim that the main character in Robertson's story (John Rowland) is an 'autobiographical projection' of Robertson ignores the many obvious differences, including the fact that Rowland is an atheist. In any case, it does nothing directly to strengthen the parallels with *Titanic* or to convince us of the author's powers of precognition. A certain recognition of Robertson is said to have come late on, when he was almost blind, in the form of a publication of his complete works, although Méheust now argues that Robertson was in high esteem in literary circles in New York, where it was acknowledged that he could write only in a 'state of dissociated consciousness similar to a trance', and where he enjoyed (some time before the publication of *Futility*) the reputation of a high-level visionary.[75] Méheust says that he is relying on a work by the parapsychologist and psychoanalyst, Jule

74 Méheust, p. 35. More than half of Robertson's text is situated in offices in London and New York.

75 Méheust, pp. 36-37.

Eisenbud,[76] for this information, and he can only refer to 'numerous stories' relating to Robertson's predictive powers which were circulating in New York.[77] Elsewhere he admits that we simply do not have sufficient evidence to be sure about these powers,[78] and his argument that Robertson's friends probably refrained from commenting on these after the sinking of *Titanic* because it would have been in bad taste is entirely lacking in plausibility.

In his second chapter on Robertson, Méheust stresses that, across the author's works as a whole, the central theme is not the sea, but fate or destiny.[79] He relies more heavily than ever on the analyses of the psychoanalyst Eisenbud, who argues that the fantasy of a possible transgression of the decrees of fate explains why the 'recurrent theme' of precognition is ambivalent in Robertson's works.[80] Eisenbud asks whether prophesying is simply recording fate, or actually altering the course of it, and claims that it is the author's desperate effort to free himself from his fate that sets off his precognitive experiences. While acknowledging that this explanation may seem 'somewhat forced', Méheust believes that this is exactly what happens to characters in *Futility* and another of Robertson's tales, even perhaps to Robertson himself,

76 *Parapsychology and the Unconscious*, (1983). Méheust also refers to Robertson's 'Gathering No Moss. An Autobiography' (1914).

77 Méheust, p. 37.

78 Méheust, p. 240 and p. 249.

79 Méheust, p. 233.

80 Méheust, pp. 233-237. Eisenbud also sees the ambivalence of the precognition theme in Robertson as bound up with the Oedipus Complex and latent homosexuality.

in writing them.[81] He says that, according to one of his friends, Robertson could write only 'in a state of trance', and he places him, accordingly, in the category of writer-medium.[82]

It has to be said, however, that Méheust's claim that *Futility* itself three times brings in the theme of precognition is dubious in the extreme.[83] There is, indeed, the case of little Myra, who rushes on deck 'As though warned by an inner subconsciousness of danger',[84] although this single reference is entirely undeveloped anywhere in the text. But the idea – to which Méheust returns on more than one occasion – that John Rowland ('drunk and drugged') foresees the collision with the iceberg is nowhere justified by the text. In his opening summary of the text, Méheust notes that Rowland, in a drug-induced hallucination, sees 'a dark threatening mass approaching irresistibly'. Then a few sentences further on he repeats that Rowland 'unconsciously senses the dark threat approaching'.[85] But this is a misinterpretation of the English text, where Rowland 'sees' both light and darkness approaching him: 'it seemed to him that this light and darkness were the good and evil of his life'. As he watches to see which will reach him first, the 'shapeless darkness' does so, changing

81 Méheust, p. 236.

82 Méheust, pp. 237-238.

83 Méheust, p. 239.

84 Gardner (1), p. 55.

85 Méheust, p. 27.

'to the form of the first officer'.[86] The third occasion on which Méheust claims that precognition comes into the text is when Rowland 'seems to foresee through his prayer the arrival of the Norwegian ship'.[87] But this is an entirely fanciful reading of Robertson's text, where the question raised is whether Rowland's prayer is answered: '"That bark was there – half a mile back in this wind – before I thought of praying. Is that prayer answered?"'.[88]

To determine whether chance or inference can be the explanation of the parallels between *Futility* and the *Titanic* disaster, Méheust first looks at Robertson's reputation as a visionary and a writer-medium.

On the assumption that, if it could be confirmed on other grounds that Robertson was a visionary, that would strengthen the case for precognition in the story, he admits that we do not have the documents to confirm this.[89] But having earlier attached credence to the idea that Robertson invented the periscope,[90] Méheust now confesses to being 'troubled' by 'another unintentional prophecy' on Robertson's part, which appeared in 1898 in a story belonging to the same collection as *Futility*: a visionary account of the surprise Japanese attack on Pearl Harbour. He is also impressed by an anticipation of radar

86 Gardner (1), pp. 54-55. Although the text is not absolutely clear, Méheust is almost certainly wrong also in his assertion that the whisky given to Rowland by the officers is drugged. It turns out that it was the tea that Rowland drank that was drugged.

87 Méheust, p. 239.

88 Gardner, p. 65.

89 Méheust, p. 240.

90 Méheust, p. 36.

– which might have avoided disasters like the *Titanic* – in the third story in the collection, suggesting that these three premonitions in one collection of stories by a writer-medium who could write only in a state of trance cannot be ignored.[91]

Méheust categorically rules out the possibility that White Star were inspired by *Futility* in naming *Titanic*. More plausibly than Gardner, he argues that there is so much superstition in maritime circles that the idea is foolish.[92] But he comes close to contradicting his earlier claim concerning Robertson's fame in New York when he asserts that at the end of the century Robertson remained 'almost totally unknown'.[93]

Méheust then asks the obvious question whether Robertson based his *Titan* on how ships were developing at the time. He turns to Hannah for the answer,[94] pointing out that of all the transatlantic liners between 1819 and 1910 the only one that corresponds 'in all respects' to the technical measurements and the specifics of *Titan* is the *Titanic*. Robertson had no model, either built or being built, for his fictional ship. But the natural reaction to this, of course, is to ask why Robertson should have had one *single* model. And there is no logical reason whatever, either, to follow Méheust's next step, which is to argue that *Titan* is not a 'projection of existing technology', or to accept his self-contradictory claim that the catastrophe

91 Méheust, p. 240.

92 Méheust, p. 241.

93 Méheust, p. 241.

94 See note 50 above.

in *Futility* is beyond anything that could be conceived at the time.[95]

Pursuing the question of whether the *Titan-Titanic* parallels could be a matter of chance, Méheust draws attention to how Hannah attributes a probability to each item. Hence, since the use of the names of pagan divinities for ships was unusual, Hannah conservatively rates the probability of the *Titan-Titanic* resemblance occurring by chance as one per cent. He puts this together with the chance probability of nine other items, to arrive at the conclusion that the likelihood that the coincidence between the fictional and real disasters is a matter of chance is one in four billion.[96] Méheust agrees that Hannah's figures can be questioned, but refers to Eisenbud's point that, even if Hannah had suggested a probability of 0.25 for each item, that would still give an overall probability of only one in 1,024.[97] He claims that figures in Walter Lord's book reinforce Hannah's point, since almost 90,000 transatlantic crossings by ships under the British flag between 1890 and 1910 produced only thirteen incidents involving ice, with no victims. The *Titanic* disaster remains unique in the annals of seafaring, and if one assigns a probability to 'fatal collision with an iceberg', says Méheust, Hannah's figure is a serious underestimate.[98] Nevertheless, he confesses to

95 Méheust, pp. 241-242. For the second time here (cf. p.33), Méheust writes *Titanic* when he means *Titan*.

96 Méheust, p. 242.

97 There is something outlandish about these figures. Gardner's point about mathematical problems that are not 'well formed' comes back to mind.

98 Méheust, p. 243.

some dissatisfaction with Hannah's analysis, which breaks the question into parts, rather than looking at it globally, 'from the point of view of its significance'.[99] This causes him to act as devil's advocate – on the side of scepticism – and examine the arguments that can be advanced to cast doubt on the prophetic nature of *Futility*.

Méheust now acknowledges the obvious point that Robertson was projecting beyond existing technology to anticipate what would later come to be.[100] He is on equally familiar ground in explaining that the inadequate number of lifeboats related to the Board of Trade's outdated regulations, although he goes further than this, arguing that White Star's reason for not installing significantly more than the minimum number was more symbolic than commercial, since they were marking the break with earlier maritime conditions and practices.[101] He also admits that some of Robertson's other choices (an English vessel, the North Atlantic) were inevitable for the writer. Collision with an iceberg, rather than another massive ship, moreover, was a better option, since it enabled Robertson to bring implacable, cosmic reality into play against man's futile enterprises. And all the other parallel details follow from this initial choice.[102]

Like Gardner, Méheust finds the parallel in the names *Titan* and *Titanic* intriguing. He stresses the point that the mythological name, *Titan*, was entirely appropriate to

99 Méheust, pp. 243-244.

100 Méheust, p. 244.

101 Méheust, p. 245.

102 Méheust, p. 246.

symbolise the arrogant belief in technology at the end of the nineteenth century, and that, in choosing it, Robertson captured the spirit of his time. His implication is that the same arrogance accounts also for the name *Titanic*.[103] Finally, he stresses that the collision with the iceberg, 'the coincidence that governs all of the others', is improbable, but not unforeseeable.[104]

For *Futility* to be considered a true premonition, Robertson would have had to include in the story, Méheust says, the description of a distinctive, non-foreseeable fact that was part of the *Titanic* disaster. He argues that, while there are perplexing similarities, like the fact that both rescue ships were bound for the Mediterranean via Gibraltar (!), there is nothing absolutely decisive.[105] But he continues to be troubled by the case of Robertson for *external* reasons, and firstly because he was known well before 1912 to be a writer-medium and a genuine visionary. His point seems to be that it is highly unlikely a confirmed visionary should apparently foresee the *Titanic* disaster by chance, yet he appears to pull back from this point in saying, once more, that we do not know well enough what visionary acts were attributed to Robertson to be sure.[106] Méheust concludes his second chapter on Robertson by noting that he is also troubled by the strange echoes in *Futility* of Stead's allegedly prophetic stories. In short, it is the whole pattern into which Robertson

103 Méheust, p. 246.

104 Méheust, p. 247.

105 Méheust, p. 248.

106 Méheust, p. 249.

fits that is disturbing. It is the 'network of paranormal communications that seems to have established itself around the sinking of *Titanic*' that is difficult to refute. Méheust will return to this point later in his book.

One might sum up reactions to Robertson's *Futility* by saying that, while a number of commentators regard it as a clear and definite premonition of the *Titanic* disaster, more consider that all of the details that appear to correspond between fiction and subsequent reality could have been arrived at by Robertson – visionary or not – drawing inferences from, and extending, practices and conditions relating to transatlantic crossings and the developments in ship-building near the end of the nineteenth century (even deliberately intending to go beyond them). A more rigorous examination of the parallels may take us a little closer to a balanced conclusion.

If we take Gardner's comprehensive list of the 'major parallels' between the wreck of Robertson's *Titan* and the sinking of *Titanic* as our guide,[107] we find that in virtually all cases these are either offset by major differences or can be explained by the general state of shipbuilding in the period at the end of the nineteenth century.

Titanic *was just over 882 feet long,* Titan *800 feet.*

But *R.M.S. Oceanic* was under construction in 1898, and scheduled to be 704 feet long – to project the length

107 Gardner (1), pp. 31-32. Broadly speaking, this may be considered as a list of the 'technical' parallels: Gardner treats the similarity in the names of the vessels separately. The terms in which each point is expressed are my own, but accurately reflect Gardner's.

of *Titan* as 800 feet is not too much of a leap.[108] And there is a significant (10%) difference between 800 and 882 feet.

Both ships were all steel, with three propellers and two masts.

But steel generally replaced wrought iron in the construction of ships when it became available late in the nineteenth century, and two masts were common. In 1898 there were few liners with three propellers, but this development had been publicly anticipated by White Star as early as 1892. In Robertson's story, unlike *Titanic*'s two triple-expansion engines and one turbine, *Titan* has three triple-expansion engines. We need to remember, too, that the ship, also unlike *Titanic*, had sails: 'sailors set the triangular sails on the two masts, to add their propulsion to the momentum of the record-breaker'.[109]

Both ships were considered unsinkable because of their many watertight compartments: 19 on the Titan, *16 on the* Titanic. *Both ships also had watertight doors: 92 on* Titan, *12 on* Titanic.

But watertight compartments in boats go back more than five hundred years, and the huge discrepancy between the number of watertight doors on *Titan* and *Titanic* is very striking.

Each was called the largest passenger ship ever built.

But the German liner *Kaiser Wilhelm der Grosse*, launched in 1897 was said to be the world's largest

108 Especially as Robertson may well have also seen the article about *Gigantic* in the *New York Times* mentioned above.

109 Gardner (1), p. 39.

moving object ever created by man, and ship after ship subsequently laid claim to this honour.

Each could carry about 3,000 people. Titan *was filled to capacity.* Titanic *carried 2,235.*

In fact, *Futility* refers to *Titan*'s 'three thousand berths',[110] but goes on to mention 'the two thousand passengers who had embarked at New York'.[111] (This also reminds us of the major difference that the ships are sailing in opposite directions.) This makes the parallel in passenger numbers rather closer, but there is no particular reason for ascribing the similar carrying capacity and the fact that both ships had *roughly* the same number of passengers to precognition.

Titanic *had a 66,000-ton displacement.* Titan *was given 45,000 tons in the 1898 edition. In the 1912 revision, it is 70,000 in Chapter 1, 75,000 in Chapter 7. Gross tonnage was 45,000 for* Titan *and 46,328 for* Titanic.

But the original discrepancy in the displacement figures is very considerable. Only the similarity in the gross tonnage figure is of interest, and *Titan*'s 45,000 GRT could easily have been an extrapolation from 1898 numbers.

Titanic*'s horse-power was 46,000. Robertson's* Titan *has 40,000 in his 1898 book. This is changed to 75,000 in the 1912 version.*

But, again, similarity in the original figures is not especially impressive, and, as already mentioned, Robertson's greatly inflated later figure strongly suggests

110 Gardner (1), p. 38.

111 Gardner (1), p. 39; cf. p. 43.

that he may have wished to have his fictional ship ahead of current technology.

Both ships had far too few lifeboats: 20 on Titanic, *24 on* Titan.

But it is well known that the Board of Trade's manner of calculating minimum lifeboat numbers was unchanged between 1894 and 1912, and became seriously outdated by the rapid growth in the size of liners.

Titanic *was going 22.5 knots when it hit the iceberg.* Titan *was going 25 knots.*

But, once more, 'similarity' in the two figures is insignificant. R.M.S *Oceanic*, under construction in 1898, was scheduled to have a maximum speed of 21 knots, and we know that captains – of mail ships, in particular – crossed the Atlantic in this period as quickly as possible, in spite of fog, icebergs and other hazards.

Both ships began their fatal voyage in April. No day of the month is specified in Robertson's novel.

But since spring was the period when liners were most at risk of icebergs, *Titan*'s sailing in April is a reasonable timing for Robertson to imagine.

Both struck an iceberg near midnight. It was a clear moonless night for Titanic. Titan *was in moonlight and heavy fog.*

But darkness is a requirement for Robertson, and midnight is a good, dramatic time to choose. It is difficult to make much sense of 'in moonlight and heavy fog', and there is the further point that the sea was very calm for *Titanic*, whereas, in addition to the fog, *Titan* is experiencing a 'fresh westerly wind'. The discrepancy in weather conditions is very important when one remembers the claim that everything, including the weather, was against *Titanic.*

Both ships grazed an iceberg on the starboard side.

But this is anything but an accurate description of what happened to *Titan*, which does very much more than 'graze' an iceberg, running up onto an ice-shelf: 'she rose out of the sea, higher and higher … she heeled, overbalanced, and crashed down on her side, to starboard.'[112]

Both ships were on the Great Circle connecting New York and England. Titanic *was making her maiden voyage from England to New York.* Titan *was going the other way, and it was her third round-trip.*

But the differences here are at least as memorable as the entirely unremarkable similarity that both ships are on the much-used Great Circle route.

Both ships hit an iceberg at spots a few hundred miles apart.

But the only indication in Robertson's tale of *Titan*'s precise position is Rowland's estimate that it strikes the ice 900 miles from New York. In any case, 'a few hundred miles' is a not-inconsiderable distance.

Both ships were owned by a British firm headquartered in Liverpool, with a branch office on Broadway in Manhattan. The principal stock owners of both ships were American.

But White Star already had its headquarters in Liverpool (and presumably an office in New York) in 1898. And the absorption of White Star into an organisation

112 Gardner (1), p. 56.

like the (American) International Navigation Company – a predecessor of International Mercantile Marine – may well have seemed a likelihood in 1898.

The outstanding difference between the two disasters was that in Robertson's story twice as many people died. About 1,520 Titanic *passengers perished. Of* Titan*'s 3,000, only thirteen survived, including the captain and first mate.*

But is this really the outstanding difference between the two disasters? We have already indicated that in numerous other respects the discrepancies between *Titanic*'s fate and Robertson's tale are significant.

In short, precious little in this list of 'similarities' justifies any talk of the paranormal or premonition. There are, indeed, certain coincidences, but, apart from the closeness of the two ships' names, not one is surprising, granted the nature and state of shipbuilding at the end of the nineteenth century. Furthermore, the clear differences between the real and fictional cases carry at the very least the same weight. It is quite simple to put forward a list of 'corresponding' facts in a way that makes the story look prescient, and, what is more, Robertson, like others well versed in marine matters, was of course 'looking into the future' and *anticipating* an event like the *Titanic* disaster. But this did not require any supernatural power, and there are significant uncertainties in the evidence for saying that Robertson himself claimed to have such power.

Moreover, starting from a different standpoint, one can just as easily fairly summarise *Futility* in a way calculated to raise only the slightest of echoes of *Titanic*, and to bring out the numerous important differences between the real and fictional ships – another of which is that *Titan* is claimed to be able to float with 9 of its compartments flooded – and what happened to them. It cannot be over-stressed that the *Titan*'s sinking is but one element just over a third of the way through a story of love and financial struggle that contains incidents like the slicing in half of a sailing ship, the killing of a polar bear with a penknife, and the rescue of Rowland and a child from an iceberg. As one actually reads the tale, it really is somewhat hard to believe that so much has been made of the idea that it is based on the author's supposed premonitory powers.

'MAYN CLEW GARNETT'

'Mayn Clew Garnett' was the pen name of Thornton Jenkins Hains (1866-1953), who spent time at sea, and published a number of books under his own name between 1894 and 1908, when he was involved in the killing of William Annis by his brother, Peter (the 'Regatta Murder'). Pleading temporary insanity, he was acquitted of manslaughter. He continued to publish stories in pulp magazines, under both his real name and his pen name. He seems to have stopped writing around 1930. 'The White Ghost of Disaster' having been published pseudonymously, many attributed foresight to him without knowing his true identity.

CASE

(MG,24) Gardner is the first of our five authors to introduce the case of Mayn Clew Garnett. Neither Stevenson nor

Brown makes any reference at all to Garnett. Gardner, however, in introducing '**The White Ghost of Disaster**',[113] which he reproduces in his book, notes that Stevenson was unaware of Garnett's story when he wrote his papers, and that he had sent Stevenson a copy. He says that the main interest of the story is that it was written 'only a short time before the *Titanic* sank'. He also asserts that it ran in the American pulp magazine, *The Popular Magazine* in May 1912, though the issue was in press before *Titanic* sank.[114] He draws accurately on the text itself to indicate that the ship in the story, the *Admiral*, is 800 feet long, the same size as Robertson's *Titan*, and that it carries more than a thousand passengers. He also says, slightly ambiguously, that 'Most of them perished because of inadequate lifeboats'. Gardner further points out that the *Admiral* was going at 22.5 knots at the time of the collision – the 'exact speed' of the *Titanic* – but that, unlike *Titanic*, it struck the iceberg head-on, 'plowing 100 feet into the ice', and sank in fifteen minutes. He finds this story 'a more surprising example of coincidence' than Robertson's novella 'because of its close proximity in time to the *Titanic* wreck', but says that for him the story reinforces the fact that many writers, well informed about the dangers of icebergs, were led to tell of big liners sinking in the Atlantic after collisions with them. Gardner acknowledges that he has been unable to learn anything about the author. In his Preface to the paperback edition of his book,[115] he announces

113 *Popular Magazine*, May, 1912.

114 Gardner (1), p. 123 (**MG,24**).

115 Reprinted in Gardner's *When you were a tadpole and I was a fish* (2009), pp. 94-99.

that Charles Chaffe has convinced him that 'Mayn Clew Garnett' was an obvious pseudonym, since a 'clew-garnet' is a 'tackle attached to the clew of a square sail on old sailing ships, used to haul the sail up for furling'.[116] He does not say that he has learned more about the author by this time. Nor does he make the obvious point that 'Mayn Clew' looks like 'main clue'.

Behe classifies Garnett's story as a 'curious coincidence', but it is not entirely clear how close he thinks the parallels with *Titanic* are. He first claims that 'many people' thought the story bore a 'strong resemblance' to the loss of the liner, and says that the similarities to the *Titanic* disaster are 'obvious', citing the speeds of the two ships and the approximate latitude of each collision. But then he argues that 'there are many differences', and that the details of the story are 'only superficially similar to those of the *Titanic* disaster', the real liner's sinking being 'greatly different' from that of the *Admiral* (and that of Robertson's *Titan*).[117] Behe believes that the edition of the *Popular Magazine* was 'coming off the presses at the same time as *Titanic* was preparing for her maiden voyage', and that Garnett had made a 'recent voyage' on *Olympic*, it being rumoured that he had dreamt the details of his narrative while on board and then woven them into fiction ('The truth of this rumour is unknown').

Méheust claims that Garnett sent his story to his editor 'at the very moment when *Titanic* was leaving Southampton', and that the text appeared in May, although it had been

116 Gardner (2), pp. 94-95.

117 Behe, pp. 45-46 **(GB,cc,55)**.

written shortly before this and was in the press during the fatal voyage. He gives no evidence for these claims.[118] He returns to Garnett at the end of his chronological survey of cases in Part II of his book, saying that, without attaining the premonitory precision of Robertson, Garnett's novel presents many similarities with the *Titanic* disaster, but that it is when the story came out that is striking.[119] Méheust also includes Garnett as a case in his dossier in Part III of his book, inadvertently repeating one or two of his own earlier sentences and rating the case as only one-star-plus (three-stars being Méheust's highest grading of cases, one star his lowest).[120] When he returns to it once more near the end of his book, he claims that, as with Robertson and Stead, 'the mainspring of the story is that of predictable catastrophe: human pride, desire to break a record, irresponsible captain, collision with the iceberg, lack of lifeboats, final disaster'.[121] One has to say, however, that the reference to the desire to break a record is entirely unjustified by the text. Méheust argues that there is nothing new here, except for the fact that the story was 'in the press' while *Titanic* was on its way to New York, saying that it matters little whether Garnett had read Stead and Robertson: it is the date of publication that strikes us. Perhaps taking the information from Behe, he also reminds us that Garnett may have claimed to have dreamed his story during a journey on *Olympic*, though he admits that there is too little support for this for us to rely on it.

---

118 Méheust, pp. 11-12.

119 Méheust, p. 135 (**BM,72**).

120 Méheust, pp. 201-202.

121 Méheust, p. 287.

It is perhaps surprising that two of our five commentators had apparently not heard of Garnett's story, and that the other three attach so little weight to it. This is particularly noticeable in the case of Méheust, who makes so much in his book of premonitions in literature. One wonders whether any of the three had actually seen the original May, 1912 issue of *The Popular Magazine*, since 'The White Ghost of Disaster' was also published in a collection of sea stories, *The Chief Mate's Yarns. Twelve Tales of the Sea.*[122] But this is secondary to the question of what exactly the similarities are between Garnett's story and the *Titanic* disaster. And if we can establish that the issue was on sale at the time of the sinking, the matter of precisely when Garnett wrote or submitted his story to the magazine becomes, for our purposes, irrelevant.

Both Gardner and Behe point out that the speed of the real and fictional ships is the same at the moment of collision, but this parallel amounts to nothing, and is to some extent cancelled out by the fact that *Admiral*'s captain slows the ship down for a while (for weather and mist), before petulantly speeding up again. Behe's observation that both ships are in roughly the same latitudinal position also lacks any weight: they are both on the 'Great Circle' route between New York and Liverpool/Cork. Neither is the fact

122 There are many editions of this collection, some versions of 'The White Ghost …' marked 'by Capt. Mayn Clew Garnett', others 'by Thornton Jenkins Hains' (Garnett's real name). The earliest appears to have been published by G.W. Gillingham Company of New York in 1912, though in what month is uncertain. The indications are that the volume was also published under the title *The White Ghost of Disaster. The Chief Mate's Yarn*. It includes a separate introductory section of some three pages that is not reproduced in Gardner's reprint of Garnett's story.

that *Admiral* is 800 feet in length of any significance. Indeed, since Garnett will have known that, like *Olympic*, *Titanic* was around 880 feet long, the length of *Admiral* could be seen as a *dissimilarity*. Moreover, the nature of *Admiral*'s collision with ice, and the short time it takes to sink create great differences with *Titanic*'s fate, as does the prevalence – and importance – of mist and fog in the story. Again, there is no actual reference in 'The White Ghost of Disaster' to the *Admiral*'s number of lifeboats being inadequate. In fact, since at least ten boats get clear of the ship and a couple of others are overturned, it is possible that the lifeboats could have accommodated the 'thousand and more' aboard.

It is true that some of the fictional happenings with regard to lifeboats are strongly reminiscent of the *Titanic* disaster: the struggle for places in the boats, with the 'fireroom crew' coming on deck to add to the pressure; the broadly good behaviour of officers and men, attempting to keep some discipline; the assistance given to women, who are passed onto the boats 'without comment or favour, age or condition'; the swearing and relatively brutal treatment of some passengers by those in charge of the boats, with some of the women upbraiding them for it; the failure of those in the boats to help those in the water. Yet these features of the sinking of a liner are not unique to *Titanic* and could easily have been imagined (even experienced) by a seasoned mariner like Garnett. The 'preface' – not included in all versions – introducing the sailor who relates the story says: 'I am going to give you the facts as they happened this last time, and a few other times besides'. Other aspects of the fate of passengers in lifeboats, like the skirting around of icebergs, even landing on them to seek drinkable water, bear no relation to that of those rescued from *Titanic*.

Nonetheless, this is not quite the end of the matter. The story does also contain curious echoes of *Titanic* which have not been picked up by commentators. It is not specified that *Admiral* is on its maiden voyage, but, in the 'preface', it is referred to as 'the vessel which had the shortest of lives, but which will live in the memory of man for many a year'. Again, the observation of the second officer (whose name is Smith!) – '"Don't you feel it? – the chill, the – well, it's ice, sir – ice, if I know anything"' – reminds us of the great fall in temperature on *Titanic* before the accident (as well as discussions at the two inquiries). And if the lookout's warning, '"Something right ahead, sir"', recalls Fleet's 'Iceberg, right ahead', immediate reactions to the warning are also similar to those on *Titanic*: the captain shouts '"compartments"', and screams, '"Stop her – stop her – hard over your wheel – hard over –."' The state of the sea, furthermore, is certainly similar: 'The sea was as still as a lake'. Even the captain's concern that 'there must be no investigation of his … blame in the matter' is perhaps reminiscent of Ismay's behaviour and the stories of the captain shooting himself and officers committing suicide on *Titanic*. Finally, *Admiral*'s sinking – 'Her stern rose high in the air … Some of the remaining passengers slid off' – resembles that of the White Star liner. The interest of these parallels is that they cannot be explained by the point that Garnett could have had detailed knowledge of *Titanic*, and even its sailing plans. In short, the balance between similarities and dissimilarities can be seen in different ways, but the case for asking whether Garnett might have had some kind of premonition of the *Titanic* catastrophe is certainly no weaker than with the stories by Stead, and perhaps even Robertson's tale.

There is some imprecision regarding dates on the part of our commentators. Gardner, Behe, and Méheust all rightly agree that the story was in the May, 1912 issue of *The Popular Magazine*, but while Gardner says only that the issue was 'in press before *Titanic* sank', Behe claims that it was 'coming off the presses at the same time as *Titanic* was preparing for her maiden voyage', and Méheust that it was in the press 'while *Titanic* was on its way to New York'. None of them suggest on what basis they make their claims. It is not unusual, of course, for magazines to appear (having already been in the press) some time before the dates on their cover, but one has to remember that *The Popular Magazine* at this time was appearing fortnightly, so that, for the first of two May issues to be actually on sale at the time of *Titanic*'s sinking, it had to appear by the formal date of the previous issue! Yet, according to an excellent website which indexes fiction magazines, this is exactly what happened.[123] The cover actually gives the date of 7 April for its appearance, and this kind of time-discrepancy (between formal date and actual date of appearance) was apparently a regular occurrence in this period of the

123 'Galactic Central' (philsp.com) also records that *The Popular Magazine* (1903-1931) came to be one of the most well-regarded pulps of its time. At its peak, it appears to have achieved a circulation of 250,000 to 300,000. For a brief period in 1927-1928, it appeared weekly. Well-known writers like Rider Haggard and H.G. Wells contributed stories to it, as did Morgan Robertson. The magazine's headquarters were in New York.

magazine's existence.[124] This makes Behe's claim the most accurate, and leaves no doubt, therefore, that 'The White Ghost of Disaster' was written before *Titanic*'s sinking. Of course, it also leaves entirely open the separate matters of whether Garnett actually sailed on *Olympic*, and whether he dreamed the narrative of the story.

All in all, the situation appears to be similar to that with Robertson's novella, and, since Robertson was a contributor to *The Popular Magazine*, there is no reason whatever to assume that Garnett could not have read it. In fact, the possible influence of *Futility* upon 'The White Ghost of Disaster' needs to be more carefully explored. Whilst there may be a temptation to see some of the parallels between Garnett's tale and *Titanic*'s fate as close enough to imply precognition on Garnett's part, knowledge of the sea, inference, and other rational processes can, again, pretty plausibly be regarded as adequate sources of almost all aspects of his story.

As we have already mentioned, Méheust is the only one of our five authors to make much of the fact that a number of the alleged premonitions concerning the *Titanic* disaster occurred in works of literature. (Gardner's anthology reprints texts by the writers concerned, but does not emphasise the literary side of the matter; neither Stevenson, Brown, nor Behe takes this up at all.) In the first

124 'Initially *The Popular Magazine* dated its issues, in common with most other magazines, by the date it should be taken «off» sale – thus an issue might be dated «First July Number» and go on sale on June 7th. In late 1914, however, the policy changed to date the issue by the date it was offered for sale…' (philsp.com/data/data414.html#POPULARMAGAZINE).

chapter of Part I of his book ('Literature and Prophecy') Méheust stresses that premonitions in literature are unexpected and disturb our common categories, leaving even parapsychologists uneasy. He strongly praises a book by Pierre Bayard[125] for bringing out this hidden dimension of literature, and gives some prominent examples. But he claims that he himself will be dealing with lesser-known authors and will use (rather than shun) the criteria and method of parapsychologists, which he considers to be at the forefront of human reasoning in this area.[126]

He suggests that Morgan Robertson's *Futility* seems to anticipate the disaster in a series of precise and improbable details, and at first sight goes beyond what chance would allow. But he stresses that Robertson's novel is just one element in a group of works of fiction accurately predicting the sinking, which includes the two texts by Stead (who is said to have embarked on *Titanic* despite warnings from clairvoyants), and Garnett's story.

In a brief final chapter, Méheust maintains that the 'premonitory texts' of Robertson and Stead are even more intriguing when they are looked at in relation to one another, something not done by other commentators.[127] He suggests both authors were 'haunted' by the theme of a sinking, and that both linked the number of deaths after a liner's collision with an iceberg to inadequate lifeboat provision. He also makes a number of other comparisons between the fictional texts of Robertson and Stead, most of which

125 Pierre Bayard, *Demain est écrit* [*Tomorrow is Written Down*], (2005).

126 Méheust, pp. 17-24.

127 Méheust, pp. 283-289.

are doubtful in the extreme.[128] He says that 'in both cases' (there are, of course three stories, with Stead's two) the main character, in a 'modified state of mind', has paranormal awareness of an imminent catastrophe; that, with both, a character manages to avoid a collision, thanks to his psychic powers;[129] that both produce an effect of 'triangulation', in the form of another character who also foresees the disaster; that the psychic experiences in the stories echo those of the authors when they foresaw the *Titanic* disaster; that in both cases the hero is one of the rare survivors, who steps onto an iceberg, with a child; that the heroes owe their survival to paranormal means of communication; that the authors both 'seem to identify partially' with their heroes; and that both authors are passionate about the psychic sciences and are considered clairvoyant in their circles. It will be clear to most that Méheust has rather lost his sense of perspective at this point, and that, in addition to ignoring Garnett for these purposes,[130] and failing to distinguish between Stead's two texts, he presses matters up to, and beyond their limits to make these comparisons, many of which rely on highly stretched and entirely questionable interpretations of the texts.

Méheust admits that Robertson may have known Stead's stories and echoed them, at least unconsciously,

128 Méheust, pp. 283-286.

129 Méheust talks of a 'Finnegan' altering the course of his ship at the last moment in Robertson's tale, but the master of *Titan* is Captain Bryce; Finnegan is not a name that appears in the text.

130 The fact that Méheust includes Garnett in his Part III dossier, but not Robertson or Stead's stories rather confirms that he does not *fully* regard Garnett as a literary case.

but he regards this as unlikely, since any borrowings, he says, are perfectly integrated with Robertson's themes. He claims, nevertheless, that the parallels between Stead and Robertson extend to improbable details and that their fictions are linked by a series of unexpected and sometimes incongruous themes. But this is wholly inadequate. Perhaps largely because there is a tendency to break with chronology and look at Robertson's story before Stead's two, the former's debt to the latter has, in general, not been taken seriously enough by any commentators. It is true that the flights of fantasy in 'From the Old World to the New' are quite different from the rather grim realism of *Futility*, but the very fact that both Stead's 'How the Mail Steamer Went Down …' and Robertson's tale very prominently feature a liner ploughing on and somewhat unscrupulously colliding with and sinking a sailing ship is enough to merit a detailed comparative study of these two stories.

Méheust adds that Garnett's work complicates the network of coincidences somewhat, but his argument that it is more the date of publication than the story itself that is striking is a serious misjudgement. The possible influence of the earlier stories on Garnett's tale deserves more thorough consideration, since there are strong similarities. Central to both Garnett's story and Robertson's is the clash between the liner's captain and a member of the ship's crew; in Garnett and Robertson the collision with an iceberg and the sinking are strikingly similar; in both, as well as in one of Stead's two stories, survivors from the collision land on the iceberg; and so on.

Méheust goes on to say that the comparisons recall the strange affair of 'cross correspondences' at the beginning of the twentieth century, for which a telepathic network emerged as the most likely explanation. He advances the 'risky' idea that a similar network may have been formed in the case of *Titanic*, using Nicholas Royle's hypothesis that a telepathic field linking literary works can be established beneath the surface, without the knowledge of the authors concerned.[131] But he fails to develop this idea in any way.

Without prejudice to the possibility of premonitions in literature in general, it can be said that the alleged cases relating to the *Titanic* disaster are not particularly impressive. It is legitimate to wonder how much consideration would have been given to Stead's two stories as premonitions had he himself not died on *Titanic*, and there is little in the fictions of Robertson and Garnett that cannot be fairly easily accounted for by a combination of inference and imagination. Perhaps above all, none of the writers concerned indisputably claimed that their work was based on premonitions. This last fact makes the literary cases very different from most of the other anecdotal instances. It also places much of the emphasis on *interpretation* of the works, since these do not obviously relate to the *Titanic* disaster at all. Méheust in particular stretches such interpretation beyond reasonable bounds.

131 Nicholas Royle, *Telepathy and Literature, Essays on the Reading Mind* (1991).

CHAPTER 2

PREMONITIONS OF THE DEATH OF W.T. STEAD

A LEAP OF IMAGINATION IS REQUIRED TO BELIEVE that Stead foretells his own death on board *Titanic* in either of his two relevant fictions, but there are a few instances when he apparently had **premonitions of his own death**, although only one relates in any way to drowning.

Brown quotes Leslie Shephard, in the introduction to an edition of Stead's *Borderland* as saying that 'it was astonishing that he did not foresee the manner of his own death, because the signs were clearly there if his attention had been directed to them.'[132] Gardner claims that 'When he booked voyage on the *Titanic*, he had not the slightest premonition of disaster at sea.'[133] And Goss and Behe reaffirm what Behe had claimed in his own book, that,

132 Brown, p. 60. The reference is presumably to W.T. Stead, *Borderland. A Casebook of True Supernatural Stories* (1970).

133 Gardner (1), p. 93.

'Other persons' warnings aside, it is a moot point whether Stead himself experienced some kind of premonition about his coming demise on the *Titanic* … on balance he does not seem to have experienced any "feeling" specific enough to deserve the term "premonition". They also note, in connection with Stead, that 'Most of the clairvoyants seem to have been negligent in the recording of their premonitions about Stead until long after the event – a regrettable lapse that greatly reduces their evidential value.'[134] Méheust believes that Stead constantly thought of the predictions of his death, but does not claim that any of his own premonitions relate specifically to *Titanic*.[135]

CASES

(IS,9c) (This and the following case are the last two of Stevenson's four 'hints or premonitions' of the circumstances of Stead's death.) Without quoting a source, Stevenson refers to a 'vision' of a mob that **Stead** had, which caused him to feel that he would not die 'in a way common to the most of us, but by violence, and one of many in a throng', saying that Stead 'only mentioned this premonition … after a mob had handled him roughly (because of his pacifist views) during the riotous celebration in London of the relief of Mafeking in 1900'.[136] Brown does not mention

134 Goss and Behe, p. 233.

135 After a longish paragraph on Stead's own premonitions, Méheust says he is passing on to another 'register', concerning premonitions *about* Stead (p. 52). Yet half a dozen of his cases later in the chapter involve Stead's own predictions.

136 Stevenson (1), p. 160.

this experience. Gardner does, but adds nothing.[137] Behe records it in the same way as Stevenson (though he adds that Stead would 'periodically' tell his friends about it), wondering whether the premonition may not have been influenced by, or owed its origin to, Stead's rough handling by 'low fellows of the baser sort'.[138]

Méheust also registers this vision, saying, with no obvious evidence to back up the assertion, that it was one of 'several premonitions' that Stead had of his own death, and going on to suggest that he was perfectly aware of them and, indeed, thought of them all the time.[139] He adds that Stead confirmed his premonition of a violent, unusual death in a crowd in a discussion with Dr Ellis, during his last journey to the United States, and that Ellis mentioned this at the meeting that became a memorial to Stead on 21 April, 1912. Méheust thinks Stead 'probably' expected to be assassinated, an idea that never seemed to leave him, and expressed this by saying that he would die 'with his boots on'. He also speculates that this is why Stead constantly consulted soothsayers.

Behe is the only commentator to cite a source for Stead's premonition of death 'in a throng', naming the book by Coates, but some of the details presumably come from Estelle's book about her father.[140] In general, it is hard to see how Stead's vision, with its reference to violence and

137 Gardner (1), pp. 92-93 (**MG,22**).

138 Behe, p. 63 (**GB,wts2**).

139 Méheust, p. 52 (**BM,wts,3**).

140 James Coates, *Has W.T. Stead Returned? A Symposium* (1913). Estelle Stead, *My Father* (1913).

no mention of water, bears any significant relation to the *Titanic* disaster.[141]

(IS,9d) Stevenson records that in 1909 **Stead** gave a lecture in which he pictured himself as shipwrecked and calling for help, citing as his source correspondence in the journal of the American Society for Psychical Research in 1959.[142] He later claims that Stead's 'references to shipwrecks' should be regarded as examples of topical stories and analogies rather than instances of precognition.[143] Brown just registers the lecture, saying that Stead 'told a supposedly fictitious tale about himself being shipwrecked and calling for help'.[144] Gardner takes up this same occasion, saying that Stead 'attacked the British Society for Psychical Research for its efforts to obtain empirical evidence!'. Noting that occult journalists like to cite this as evidence of Stead's unconscious precognition of his death, he claims that Stead imagined himself drowning, but that instead of throwing him a rope his would-be rescuers shouted 'Who are you? What is your name?'. When Stead told them his name and asked them to throw a rope and be quick about it, they insisted: 'How do we know you are Stead? Where were you born? Tell us the name of your grandmother.'[145]

141 Méheust will argue that among Stead's acquaintances the idea of his death gradually evolved into a sea drama.

142 Stevenson (1), p. 160.

143 Stevenson (1), p.165.

144 Brown, p. 61 **(RB,34)**.

145 Gardner (1), p. 91 **(MG,19)**.

Behe adds that Stead's speech was to the Cosmos Club in London, and says that it is 'probably' not the case that Stead's words had a psychic origin. Taking his information from Edith Harper's *Stead, the Man: Personal Reminiscences* (1918), Behe says that Stead had been discussing 'what he felt to be barriers constructed by the Society for Psychical Research against the complete acceptance of the idea of "communication with the Other Side"', and that after painting an image of himself as drowning at sea and calling for help, Stead continued: 'Suppose that instead of throwing me a rope the rescuers should shout back, "Who are you? What is your name?" … Well, that is pretty typical of the "help" given by the SPR to the friends who are trying to hear us from the Other Side.'[146] Behe's more detailed account of the occasion sets it in context and does, indeed, make it appear much more straightforward than Stead foreseeing his own death.

Méheust records the same facts, saying that Stead considered that the British Society for Psychical Research was abandoning those who wanted to communicate with the dead, leaving them to 'drown'. He adds rather vaguely that at the time Stead's speech was taken for what it was, or seemed to be, and of course it would only make sense later.'[147] But he does nothing to add to this by quoting as an apparent 'source' for Stead's comments the use of a drowning metaphor back in 1885, since this bears no significant resemblance to those comments.

146 Behe, p. 64 (**GB,wts,6**).

147 Méheust, p. 54 (**BM,wts,8**).

(RB,20) Without citing sources, Brown records that on the night of Friday 12 April and into the Saturday morning **Stead** had topped all of the ghost stories being recounted by telling of an Egyptian mummy case found in a tomb, claiming that 'whoever retold the tale inscribed in hieroglyphics on the case would meet with a violent death.' She speculates that 'Perhaps, being an evangelist, Stead was unafraid.'[148] Gardner does not mention this story, but, citing the *New York Herald* of 20 April 1912, Behe, too, claims that to prove he was not superstitious Stead called attention to the fact that 'it was Friday when I began this story and the day of its ending, my watch tells me, will fall upon a thirteenth.' But he comments that the story was nothing more than a coincidence which served as a basis for the later – false – rumour that there was a mummy case on board *Titanic*.[149] Méheust, giving a substantial quote from a book by C. Ferruli,[150] also relates that Stead told the story about a mummy.

(RB,29) Brown also thinks that 'Perhaps subconsciously **Stead** did have a premonition about the *Titanic*', although the only evidence she cites is Stead's own statement about other events, in *Borderland*: 'I have had three or four very striking and vivid premonitions in my life which have been fulfilled to the letter.'[151] But he does go on to say that he has had other premonitions 'which await fulfilment', though he cannot speak about them, since he

148 Brown, p. 27.

149 Behe, p. 36 **(GB,cc,36)**.

150 Méheust, p. 66 **(BM,26a)**. C. Ferruli, *"Titanic": l'aventure, le mystère, la trag*édie (2004), p. 30.

151 Brown, pp. 60-61.

might be accused of 'being party to bringing about the fulfilment of my own predictions'.

(RB,35) Brown considers it 'almost inconceivable' that **Stead** did not know 'in some vague, intangible way' what was in store for him, and – without giving any details – says that he 'once remarked, "I knew what the end would be. That after the work was done which my living could do, I should be killed, and my killing would do more good than my life …"'[152]

(GB,wts,5) Behe – this time citing the *Vancouver Daily Province* (19 April, 1912) – notes that in 1907 **Stead** visited Toronto, and again discussed 'the manner of his future death as it had been revealed to him'.[153] He claimed that he would either be beaten to death by a mob in the streets of London, or perish, 'the victim of a great disaster involving hundreds.' Méheust, too, records this occasion, citing Behe as his source.[154]

(GB,wts,12) Referring to the *Daily Express*, Behe says **Stead** told a friend of Mrs E.T. Cook in late 1911 or early 1912 that when his work was done he would die a 'violent death'. He said he could not tell how he knew this, 'but I have had a vision, and I know that it will be true'.[155] Méheust simply repeats Behe's account (although he adds that it was about the nature of his violent death that Stead

152 Brown, p. 63.

153 Behe, p. 64. Behe's 'the manner of his future death as it had been revealed to him' does not make it entirely clear whether this was a premonition of Stead's own, or one experienced by someone else.

154 Méheust, pp. 53-54 **(BM,wts,7)**.

155 Behe, p. 68. Behe's source is the *Daily Express*.

could say no more), giving as his source an article in the *Contemporary Review.*[156]

(GB,wts,17) Behe claims that in a letter posted in Queenstown, **Stead** seemed to indicate that he felt no anxiety about being on *Titanic*, and that he had no premonition of disaster.[157] Méheust does not mention this letter.

(BM,wts,21) Méheust claims that on 3 April, 1912, at his last séance with his spiritualist colleagues, **Stead** chose a text from the gospel of Saint John: 'I have finished the work that you called on me for'. In Edith Harper's memory, though Méheust concedes that this may be a retrospective illusion, there was a 'strange atmosphere of goodbye': Stead was behaving as if he would not see his friends again.[158]

(BM,wts,22) Edith Harper records that on 6 April, 1912 **Stead** wrote to her to say, of his trip to New York: 'I have the feeling that something is going to happen. I don't know where and how. But it will be a good thing.'[159] He asked her to use her powers to ask for indications of the task required of him. Méheust claims that this is Stead once again seeking to know what will happen to him *after* his trip to America.

(BM,wts,23) Stead repeated his feeling that something was going to happen to him shortly in a letter posted in

156 Méheust, p. 59 **(BM,wts,14)**. 'E.T. Cook and the death of W.T. Stead', *The Contemporary Review*, (1912).

157 Behe, p. 70. Edith Harper's book (*Stead, the Man: Personal Reminiscences*, 1918) is Behe's source, though he does not say to whom the letter was written.

158 Méheust, p. 62.

159 Méheust, pp. 62-63.

Queenstown to his friend Dr Clifford, again referring to an unknown task that would be revealed to him by God. Using some of the same terms, Stead reiterated this in a letter to his daughter Estelle, adding that his task might be 'journalistic, spiritual, social, or political'. Ignoring the fact that there is nothing even hinting at his death in these two statements to Clifford and his daughter (or in a letter to Edith Harper, posted at the same time), Méheust rather arbitrarily sees Stead's insistence on his theme as suggesting that he was obsessed by 'the almost apocalyptic feeling of an imminent revelation, of tipping over towards something else'.[160]

But if there is much less substance than is often claimed to the idea that Stead himself had many premonitions of his own death – and no substance at all in the suggestion that he foresaw his death on *Titanic* – stories of **others foreseeing or predicting his death** proliferate, even if almost all bear no clear relation at all to the *Titanic* disaster. It is interesting to note that James Coates, whose symposium *Has W.T. Stead Returned?* answers his own question with a resounding 'Yes', claims that 'A careful examination of all the evidence, makes it clear to me, Mr. Stead had no *definite* warning from any source

160 Méheust, pp. 63-64.

prior to leaving England.'[161] Coates also quotes Stead's daughter, Estelle, as saying 'In April my father passed over. *I do not think he had any conscious premonition*, but, subconsciously he perhaps had.'[162]

(IS,10) Using Coates as his source Stevenson relates that a psychic whom Stead consulted from time to time, Count 'Harmon', said in 1911 that danger to Stead's life 'would be from water, and from nothing else', advising him in a letter (of 21 June, 1911) that 'travel would be dangerous to him in the month of April 1912.[163] He later argues that, because it mentions a specific date for the danger, Harmon's advice belongs to a 'much higher class of prediction (with regard to evidence for precognition)' than vague references to shipwrecks,[164] although he also points out that Harmon did not name *Titanic*, which was then under construction. Brown repeats Stevenson's details,[165] but Gardner, who seems particularly eager to pass on to stories of Stead's alleged communications *after* his death, does not mention this psychic at all.

Behe adds that Count Louis Hamon (sometimes 'Count

161 James Coates, *Has W.T. Stead Returned? A Symposium* (1913), p. 104. He reiterates at p. 169 that Stead 'had many warnings and had listened to many curious statements, but I do not think he had a single *definite* warning as to the "Titanic" disaster.' Coates adds that his remark arises 'out of reflections on Julia's Bureau, and perplexing statements purporting to come from Mr. Stead, subsequently to his transition', and goes on to explore the best-known predictions concerning Stead's future.

162 Coates, p. 186; italics original.

163 Stevenson (1). pp. 160-161.

164 Stevenson (1), p. 165.

165 Brown, p. 61 **(RB,30)**.

Leigh de Hamong') was a palmist also known as '**Cheiro**', whose real name was William John Warner, and that he explicitly assured Stead that he would not meet his death at the hands of a mob, as he had long thought. He also says that Cheiro's letter to Stead cautioned him that 'the most critical months would be July, October, December and April', and warned him that travel would be dangerous to him in April 1912'. Behe comments that Cheiro made this information public in a lecture in May 1912, reading some correspondence with Stead as confirmation. He also records that a researcher has discovered discrepancies between contemporary news articles concerning the accuracy of Cheiro's predictions and his own 'self-flattering' recollections. Behe stresses that our only source for his predictions regarding Stead is Cheiro himself, and wonders whether he altered them after the event.[166]

Méheust offers the same account of Cheiro's predictions for Stead, but he also emphasises how well-known Cheiro was, and mentions his 'spectacular successes', in particular with Oscar Wilde.[167] He later gives a longish quote, which specifically says that if Stead goes to sea in April 1912, he will put his life in danger, 'and the worst may happen'.[168] In Part III of his book Méheust claims that the warning about April 1912 seems 'too good to be true'. He says that

166 Behe, p. 65 (**GB,wts,8**).

167 Méheust, pp. 55-56 (**BM,wts,10**). *Cheiro's Memoirs: the Reminiscences of a Society Palmist* (1912).

168 Méheust, p. 80 (**BM,6**). The quote is said to be taken from Cheiro's letter of June 1911, but Méheust refers to Cheiro's memoirs as his source (*Cheiro's Memoirs: the Reminiscences of a Society Palmist*, 1912), although this work does not include the letter.

Stead had known Cheiro personally for many years,[169] so that Cheiro would have had to be careful, but still altered his letter somewhat after the sinking. He classes the case as only one star, the lowest classification in terms of possible precognition.[170]

(IS,11a) Stevenson claims that in September 1911 the psychic **W. de Kerlor** predicted that Stead would go to America (although Stead had no such plans at the time), saying:

> *I can see … the picture of a huge black ship, of which I see the back portion; where the name of the ship should be written there is a wreath of immortelles … I can only see half of the ship: that symbol may mean by the time this ship will be completed – when one will be able to see it in its whole length – it is perhaps then that you will go on your journey.*[171]

Brown simply repeats Stevenson's account of this and the following incident,[172] while Gardner does not refer to Kerlor at all.

Like Stevenson, Behe uses Coates as his source (as well as a book by Herbert Greenhouse),[173] also mentioning Stead's first appointment with Kerlor, when the psychic foresaw, on the basis of an examination of Stead's hands, that

169 Méheust, p. 273.

170 Méheust, pp. 168-169.

171 Stevenson (1), p. 161.

172 Brown, p. 61 **(RB,31)**.

173 *Premonitions: A Leap into the Future* (1971).

Stead would not bring his future plans into fruition: 'your life will end tragically, it will end in public: you will either be trampled upon or kicked to death, in a most unexpected manner'. At a second appointment on 19 September 1911, Kerlor said he saw something like the blade of a guillotine above Stead's head and urged him to make haste with his plans. He insisted that Stead would be going to America, although his intention was to go to Russia, and Behe argues that it 'seems likely' that Kerlor's view of the 'huge black ship' relates to a trip to America, although Stead specifically asked him to tell him about his proposed Russian trip.[174] It should be said that the additional information Behe offers – about Stead being either 'trampled upon or kicked to death', and the slight doubt about which trip Kerlor's predictions relate to – make the predictions less impressive, although Behe remains struck by Kerlor's vision of the stern half of a huge black ship. In spite of the fact that Kerlor interpreted this to mean that the ship was still under construction (which *Titanic* actually was), Behe compares this vision to the last view that passengers and crew had of *Titanic*, and adds, rather mysteriously: 'Perhaps Mr de Kerlor should have interpreted his vision in a more literal sense.'

Méheust repeats Behe's version of these appointments (with slight variations in Kerlor's quote), but is much more impressed by the second than the first.[175] In Part III of his book, he says that Kerlor did not know that Stead was to sail on *Titanic*, so that unconscious inference is not a significant factor. He thinks it possible that Kerlor had heard of Turvey's

174 Behe, pp. 65-67 (**GB,wts,9**).

175 Méheust, pp. 56-57 (**BM,wts,12**).

first prediction,[176] but that the mystery of Kerlor's premonition remains. He classes Kerlor's case as three stars, retaining it as one of his eight strongest premonitions, although at this point he is grouping together all of Kerlor's predictions.[177]

(IS,11b) Still giving Coates's book as his source, Stevenson also relates that **Kerlor** subsequently had a dream which he related to Stead, in which he was 'in the midst of a catastrophe on the water; there were masses of bodies (more than a thousand) struggling in the water and I was among them. I could hear their cries for help'.[178] When Kerlor told this dream to Stead and repeated his warning that the black ship in the first dream meant 'limitations, difficulties and death', Stead was unimpressed, saying, 'Well, you are a very gloomy prophet.'[179]

Behe, although he also cites Coates, has a slightly different version of the quote from Kerlor, and adds that although Kerlor learned on the morning after his dream that a boat disaster on the Nile had claimed two hundred lives, he did not believe his dream was connected with this event, since he had seen more than a thousand bodies in the water in the dream.[180] Méheust simply repeats the details, crediting Behe.[181]

---

176 **(IS,8)**.

177 Méheust, pp. p. 169.

178 Stevenson (1), p. 161.

179 Stevenson (1) p. 161. Behe says this message was by telephone ('the last time that de Kerlor spoke personally with Mr Stead'), and that Stead added 'Goodbye' and hung up (Behe, p. 67).

180 Behe p. 67 **(GB,wts,10)**.

181 Méheust, pp. 57-58 **(BM,wts,12)**.

(IS,12) Stevenson says that Reverend Charles L. Tweedale, in his book, *Man's Survival After Death* (1921),[182] relates that at 11.30pm on Monday 15 April, 1912, **Tweedales's wife** came running to him, to announce that 'a man with thick eyebrows and a beard under his chin and round his face' had passed through the kitchen where she was. Shortly after, she heard 'wailing, crying sounds, and a kind of moaning', which sounded like 'many people in great trouble'.[183] He claims that by this time they had not heard of the sinking of *Titanic*. When subsequently shown a portrait of Stead, Mrs Tweedale said that the apparition she saw 'bore a strong resemblance to him'.[184] Stevenson thinks this – postcognitive – case is weakened by the relationship between Rev. Tweedale and Stead and the former's knowledge that Stead was sailing on *Titanic*. He also astutely notes that we do not know whether Mrs Tweedale was shown just one photograph to compare with her memory of the apparition, or many, and that learning of Stead's drowning might have stimulated her to see the 'strong resemblance', which she might otherwise not have noticed. In his second article, Stevenson refers to Mrs Tweedale's experience as 'doubtful'.[185]

Brown makes no reference to the Tweedales, but Gardner is scathing about Rev. Tweedale, who he says was

---

182 In the 4 May 1912 issue of *Light* Tweedale had published a brief item entitled 'Mr Stead and the "Titanic" disaster' covering the same incident.

183 Tweedale's article in *Light* (May, 1912) indicates that it was his servants who heard 'loud wailing, moaning, and sobbing' on 8 April.

184 Stevenson (1), pp. 161-162.

185 Stevenson (2), p. 223.

absolutely convinced that the apparition was the ghost of Stead, and who soon claimed that Stead was speaking to him directly in séances. He also says that Tweedale's book was first published in Edinburgh in 1909 and ran through many editions.[186]

Behe points out that Tweedale – 'a strong proponent of spiritualism' – kept a record of the many 'supernatural' manifestations in his vicarage in a daily journal, writing up this diary each morning.[187] This contained a couple of entries which he felt might reveal a connection to Stead and his death on *Titanic*, and Tweedale wrote a 'letter' about this to the spiritualist publication *Light*, published on 4 May, 1912. Despite Behe's assertion that the diary was written up 'each morning', however, Tweedale says in his letter that he is giving 'brief extracts from two consecutive extracts in my diary', and quotes from 9 and 15 April. The first extract, dated 9 April, records servants reporting hearing, 'last night', loud wailing, moaning and sobbing outside their bedroom door. The second, dated 15 April, says that the servants and children told him they had heard 'loud knocks, and also the sound of heavy footsteps'; it also recounts the episode of the apparition that came to his wife. Behe insists that this occurred on the evening of 14 April, although Tweedale's text is far from clear on this.[188] Tweedale concedes, in any case, that he

186 Gardner (1), p. 93 **(MG,23)**.

187 Behe, pp. 104-107 **(GB,po,21)**.

188 Behe also states that 'another study of the Tweedale account' incorrectly dates the events in the second extract as *occurring* on the night of 15-16 April, giving no details of this other study.

is not saying there is a connection between these events and the *Titanic* disaster, but simply placing the events on record.

Behe goes on to argue that in the first of many revised and updated editions of his book (published, he says, in 1920), Tweedale, apparently quoting verbatim from his diary, offers an entry for (Behe says, mistakenly) 14 April that 'differs considerably' from the one quoted in his 1912 letter to *Light*. It is quite true that there are some differences between Tweedale's reports. In particular, he adds details in his later account, so that he is obviously not literally transferring his diary account into his book, although, in fairness, Tweedale did say in his article that he was giving *extracts* from his diary. But oddities exist, too, in Behe's descriptions. In any event, his general view, as stated at this point in his own book, is that 'the strong belief system of the spiritualists makes it very difficult to objectively evaluate the psychic phenomena they reported'. He thinks that the two different diary entries mean that no definite conclusions can be drawn in this case, since it is possible that Tweedale expanded the original diary entry to make it seem more closely connected to the *Titanic* disaster. This is incontrovertible as far as it goes, but it might be added that the further expansion of the account in *Man's Survival After Death* still results in a story bearing only an extremely thin and indirect relationship to *Titanic*.

Behe also suggests that in calculating time-differences Tweedale shifted time in the wrong direction, as the ship's time was three hours *earlier* than the English time zone, not *later*! But the confusions concerning timing are such that this is less weighty than it may seem. Moreover, with the correct time-difference factored in, Mrs Tweedale's apparition (and hearing of wailing) might become a potential premonition rather than something like telepathy. It is peculiar that, in a book devoted to psychic forewarnings of the *Titanic* disaster, Behe should argue that the timing of Mrs Tweedale's experiences should in itself make it 'extremely unlikely' that they can 'reasonably be connected' with the sinking of *Titanic*. In spite of some sound points made, and the rather dubious nature of Tweedale's testimony, Behe is certainly not at his most incisive in his treatment of this case.

Méheust's treatment is no more satisfactory, and much more cursory.[189] Apparently using Stevenson as his only source, since he does not refer to Tweedale's different outlets, he does not mention Mrs Tweedale's apparition at all. Oddly concentrating on Tweedale himself, he feebly speculates that his unconscious fears for Stead's life may have given him hallucinations, and puzzlingly suggests that the indirect references in dreams strongly evoke what we see in telepathic hallucinations where the subject has no expectations. He rates the case as one-star-plus.

All in all, this case – one of the most muddled – is of very little relevance to *Titanic*, and there is more than enough uncertainty and contradiction in it to cause one to treat the Tweedales' experiences with very great suspicion.

(GB,cc,61) Using Edith Harper's book as his source, Behe reports that in December 1911 Stead came into

189 Méheust, pp. 193-194 **(BM,73)**. Presumably inadvertently, Méheust's *only* reference to this case is in in his dossier in Part III, Ch. 6.

possession of a **cross or crucifix** that was supposed to have belonged to Catherine the Great.[190] He was warned that it was 'strongly charged with black magic' and was harmful to persons not 'specially protected'. He very soon fell into an uncharacteristic fit of depression, until an associate took it away to have it 'demagnetised' by someone versed in magical rites. Stead's health and good spirits returned, and he laughingly admitted there '*might* be something in it', adding that such beliefs sounded pretty silly. But in January 1912 Stead told the Russian correspondent of *The Daily Telegraph* of how ill-luck seemed to befall everyone who possessed the crucifix, saying that he was 'curious to see whether any mischief will befall me, and what form it will take.' It is not known whether Stead took the crucifix with him on *Titanic*. Behe classes this case as a curious coincidence. Méheust does not refer to it.

(GB,wts,1) Behe briefly and dismissively refers to a prediction by palmist, **'Teresina'**, that Stead would die at the age of 63 (in 1912), saying that Stead's written response to this was to point out that Madame Blavatsky had told him that he would live until past 75: 'I think one prophecy is about as good as the other.'[191] Méheust refers to the case (but does not include it in his dossier in Part III of his book), and has probably taken it from Behe himself.[192]

(GB,wts,3) Death by water comes into the picture in 1906, according to Behe, when the famous Parisian clairvoyant **Madame de Thèbes** warned Stead that danger

190 Behe, pp. 48-49 **(GB,cc,61)**.

191 Behe, pp. 62-63.

192 Méheust, p. 53 **(BM,wts,4)**.

by water threatened him. But she herself records that Stead laughed at her, saying that he would have warnings from others if any danger menaced him. He later joked with her about her premonition, which she nonetheless repeated. Behe makes the obvious comment that 'Beware of the water' was a 'fairly common warning' given by professional clairvoyants.[193] Méheust simply summarises Behe's report, and acknowledges him as the source,[194] but he does not include this particular warning in his dossier in Part III of his book.

(GB,wts,4) Behe also cites a 1906 report by Stead ('probably connected' with the earlier vision of death in a throng) that an **unnamed clairvoyant** had revealed to him the manner in which he would meet his death: 'I shall be imprisoned twice more before I die. I shall finally be kicked to death in the streets of London. This makes my mind quite easy when I travel, and I never insure myself against risks of any kind.'[195] There is a mention of this by Méheust, who points out that, by his own admission, Stead used the idea of his death in a throng as a 'psychic lightning-conductor', which prevented him from worrying about other perils (although Méheust does not include the case in his dossier in Part III of his book).[196]

(GB,wts,7) Behe records that, at a private séance in May 1911 with the medium **Etta Wriedt**, the spirit of an

193 Behe, p. 63. He quotes the *Providence Evening Bulletin* of 24 April, 1912.

194 Méheust, p. 53 **(BM,wts,5)**.

195 Behe, pp. 63-64. Behe quotes the *Montreal Star* (17 April, 1912) as his source for this report.

196 Méheust, p. 53 **(BM,wts,6)**.

American Indian spoke to Stead, saying, 'Chief Steady! You cross big pond *one time* more, before you shuttee eye!'[197] He comments only that the words (sounding 'more like they were spoken by a Chinese laundryman') did turn out to be true.[198]

Méheust repeats Behe's information (again taken from the book by Edith Harper, whom Méheust mistakenly refers to as Edith Ranger), adding that this is another prediction linking Stead's death with the sea, and that we do not know Stead's reaction to it. (Again, he does not include the case in his dossier in Part III of his book.)[199] Earlier, taking his information from Coates's book, Gardner had highlighted Etta Wriedt.[200] He said that Conan Doyle considered her the best 'direct voice' medium in the world,[201] and that Stead intended to bring Etta back to England.

(GB,wts,11) Citing Coates, Behe says that in October 1911, Miss **May de Witt Hopkins**, considered a gifted psychic by Stead, met him in Paris, on his way to Constantinople. She later wrote that just after seeing him she heard 'clairaudiently' a solemn voice saying, 'The time is soon coming when he will be called home … In the first of the next half year – in six months.' The voice went on, 'His time has come; his career is ended.' She met him

197 Behe, pp. 64-65.

198 Earlier, Behe has said that, following the death of Stead, some of the sittings given by Wriedt exhibited several 'difficult-to-fake' characteristics, especially as they were given in a foreign country (Behe, p. 61).

199 Méheust, p. 55 **(BM,wts,9)**.

200 Gardner (1), p. 93.

201 He says such mediums speak in voices that are close imitations of the actual voices of the dead.

again in Paris, on his return, and claimed that she knew she would never see him again: 'in fact, I *felt* a fate hanging over him though I did not know how it would come.'[202]

Méheust repeats Behe's account, adding that, in a letter to Miss Scatcherd, Hopkins does her best to soften the content of her prediction, by saying, 'Of course, all of that is simply in my imagination'. He says we do not have Stead's reaction to Hopkins's experiences, and that on 18 June 1912 she published her testimony in the journal *Light*.[203] In Part III of his book, Méheust amalgamates Hopkins's experience with a later one, commenting on both together and rating them as only one-star-plus.[204]

(GB,wts,13) Archdeacon Colley was said to have sent a letter to Stead early in 1912 predicting that *Titanic* would sink. Behe cites Greenhouse's book for this case, but says he had been unable to find any more specific reports about it, and that Stead's close associates insist that he never received any *specific* warnings about *Titanic*.[205] Méheust adds nothing to this, and does not include the case in his dossier in Part III of his book.[206]

(GB,wts,14) When Edith Harper, Stead's private secretary, described a message that **Kerlor** gave her for Stead, on 23 February, 1912, in part it repeated his earlier clairvoyant vision of a huge black ship. But it also included a symbolic vision of a stone called an 'agatha', the veins

202 Behe, pp. 67-68.

203 Méheust, p. 58 **(BM,wts,13)**.

204 Méheust, pp. 169-170.

205 Behe, p. 68.

206 Méheust, p 59 **(BM,wts,15)**.

of which were encircling Stead. He took this to denote troubles from which Stead could not free himself. The stone is symbolic of funerals and mourning. Behe suggests that Kerlor's unease regarding Stead had continued without let-up ever since September 1911, and that he was moved to warn Stead one last time.[207] Méheust simply repeats Behe's account.[208]

(GB,wts,15) On 9 April, 1912 Stead wrote to his friend **Mr R. Penny**, in response to a letter from the latter, to say that he sincerely hoped that none of the misfortunes that Penny seemed to think might happen to him or his wife would take place, and that he would write on his return (from America). Penny subsequently said only that his letter referred to certain mishaps which, it seemed to him, probably would occur in the near future.[209] Méheust simply records Behe's account, and credits him for it.[210] He does not include this case in his dossier in Part III of his book.

(GB,wts,16) It was reported (in the *Johnstown Tribune*, on 18 April 1912) that **Stead** informed his friends that his 'spirit friends' were telling him not to sail on *Titanic*, but he became determined to sail on her. Behe considers that this was probably 'only a rumour reported as fact', repeating that none of Stead's associates knew of any specific warning about *Titanic* before the sailing.[211] Méheust does not mention this particular report.

---

207 Behe, pp. 68-69. Behe gives Coates as his source.

208 Méheust, p. 59 **(BM,wts,16)**.

209 Behe, p. 69. Behe quotes *The Cornishman* (Penzance) of 25 April, 1912 as his source.

210 Méheust, p. 61 **(BM,wts,20)**.

211 Behe, p. 70.

(GB,wts,18) Stead wrote **May de Witt Hopkins** a letter some days before sailing on *Titanic*, but without mentioning which ship he would be on. Coates says that Hopkins wrote that she was haunted by an 'unaccountable perfume of roses' the day after the *Titanic* disaster, and claimed: 'There is someone I know who is dead and trying to make me aware of it.' She says she knew Stead was dead as soon as she learned from the papers that he was on *Titanic*, and she had a 'mental vision' of Stead sometime later: 'I saw him very pale, dressed in black, hatless and dripping wet ....' Behe points out that Hopkins added that she was 'rather sceptical' about her own psychic powers, and did not know whether her vision of Stead was 'merely imagination or something more'. He comments that Hopkins's experience of the perfume of roses seems related to the 'stopped clock' type of experience, and that it is impossible to know whether the odour existed objectively.[212]

At first Méheust repeats Behe's account (though not his comments),[213] but in Part III of his book – running together the voice message she received in October 1911 and her smelling of roses (without mentioning Hopkins's later 'vision' of Stead) – he evaluates Hopkins's experiences critically and rates them as only one-star-plus. He claims it is quite possible that in spiritualist circles she had heard of Kerlor's vision of September 1911, and that there are a number of possible explanations of the scent of roses episode. She may, in fact, have heard the news of *Titanic*

212 Behe, pp. 70-71.

213 Méheust, pp. 69, 128-129 **(BM,wts,27, BM,63)**.

and only *then* have given a meaning to the smell of roses by relating the smell to the news. Méheust also argues that, although Stead had not mentioned *Titanic* in his letter, he had told Hopkins of his journey, and this – fuelled by her earlier premonition – could have set a process of subliminal inference in train. But he notes that a *real* smell of roses may have been the basis of a genuine paranormal experience: we simply do not have enough information to decide between the different hypotheses.[214]

(GB,wts,19)[215] 'A day or two' after the sinking of *Titanic* Felicia **Scatcherd** was at lunch with friends in Greece. She had heard that all first-class passengers were safe, but a strange feeling came over her and she sensed the 'spirit presence' of Stead, who was anxious that a friend was about to say or do something he would afterwards regret. That evening the friend in question told Scatcherd that 'something or someone' had held him back from acting in a way he would have infinitely regretted. With Coates once more as his source, Behe reports that Scatcherd later claimed that she had a 'vague idea' that if Stead had died on 15 April she would have known it. He finds it 'curious' that, since Scatcherd was accustomed to communicating with Stead's 'influence', she should first feel that her odd experience proved that he was alive and safe. He thinks it questionable whether Stead and Scatcherd could, in fact, communicate via automatic writing, and argues that there

214 Méheust, pp. 169-170

215 This and the two following cases are alleged premonitions in the sense that the subject is said to have had the experience *before* receiving confirmation of Stead's death. Compare **(GB,cc,52)**.

is evidence that such communications originate in the subconscious. Scatcherd may have unconsciously heard enough of the table conversation to infer the situation of the friend, and interpreted her unconscious mind's attempt to make her aware of this as Stead's attempt to communicate with her, although Behe points out that we do not know if Scatcherd understood Greek well.[216] Méheust makes no mention of Scatcherd's experience on this occasion.

(GB,wts,20) Behe records Edith Harper noting that, on the afternoon of 17 April (while the family were still awaiting definite news of Stead's fate), **her mother, Adela**, clairvoyantly 'saw' Stead and feared he had lost his life on *Titanic* 'as he looked so white and dazed, his face anxious, his eyes dim ....'[217] He does not say that the family, presumably hoping against hope, 'refused to attach any serious meaning to her vision'.[218] Méheust does not refer to this case.

(GB,wts,21) Citing Coates as his source, Behe notes that, on the night of 17 April, 1912, **Lady Archibald Campbell**, before press agencies had confirmed who was lost or saved, suddenly 'heard' the words: 'W.T. Stead – drowned!', and had a vision of *Titanic* – seeming to actually be on board – rising up and sinking. She then heard clairaudiently words which she said came from the 'influence' of Stead. He philosophised and asked the

216 Behe, pp. 71-73.

217 Behe, p. 73.

218 Edith Harper, *Stead: The Man. Personal Reminiscences* (1918), p. 246.

living to pray for the dead.[219] Behe does not record that Coates also says that 'the message partakes of the style of the writer, and *not* of Mr Stead', although Coates does not believe this detracts from its genuineness.[220] Méheust adds nothing to this case.[221]

(G&B,6) Citing a book by **Shaw Desmond** himself as their source,[222] Goss and Behe say that the young journalist was walking along the Strand with Stead, shortly before *Titanic* sailed, with Stead talking mainly about the liner and his trip to America, when he was suddenly gripped by an odd feeling: 'There came to me for the first time in my life, but not the last, the conviction of impending death. In this case, that the man at my side would die within a very short time. It was overpowering and I felt rather helpless, nor did I for a moment associate it with the liner of which he had been speaking.'[223] He did not mention the feeling to Stead, but when he arrived home he jotted down a brief notation regarding his premonition and dated it 'for future reference'. (The authors later point out that 'we aren't informed that he showed it to anyone who might confirm that important allegation.')[224] When he learned of the *Titanic* disaster and the rumours that Stead had survived, Desmond said to his wife, 'He is not saved. He is drowned'. Goss and Behe appear to be impressed by this

---

219 Behe, p. 73.

220 Coates, pp. 26-27.

221 Méheust, pp. 69-70 (**BM,wts,28**).

222 Shaw Desmond, *My Adventures in the Occult* (1946).

223 Goss and Behe, pp.232-233.

224 Goss and Behe, p. 249.

case, although they do not repeat that Desmond did not 'for a moment' associate his certainty that Stead would die with *Titanic*. They later say that we know Desmond was 'an eloquent propagandist of Spiritualism', and that his story, told years after in an autobiographical book, could have been an attempt to aggrandise the writer and spiritualism, although they find a strong conviction amounting to a certainty in it.[225]

Méheust gives the same account of this incident, with most of the same details.[226] But in Part III of his book, he claims of the case that 'with regard to the criteria demanded by parapsychologists, it is insufficiently supported'. Instead of developing this point, however, he stresses that Desmond's sense of imminent death was not linked with *Titanic*, and states that the case would have been weaker if it had been. Based on the (implausible) idea that Desmond had not *heard* of *Titanic* at all, he argues, somewhat bizarrely, that the notion of an instant unconscious inference is improbable, since it would have required 'all the work of collective elaboration in action around the idea of divine punishment'! He classes the case as two stars.[227]

(G&B,10) On the night of 14 April 1912, **Mrs H.M. Chase**, of Groton, Massachusetts, was alone in her study when a face suddenly appeared to her, 'disembodied and floating at arm's length in front of her'. She distinguished the features of a bearded man giving the impression of

225 Goss and Behe, pp. 248-249.

226 Méheust, pp. 60-61 **(BM,wts,17)**.

227 Méheust, p. 175.

great power of mind and physical endurance. Chase felt it was the face of someone who had died with great suffering and noticed that the hair and beard were 'stringy', as if wet and windblown. When newspapers reported *Titanic*'s collision with an iceberg, but did not know the vessel had foundered, Chase was 'somehow certain' that different news would soon arrive regarding the liner's fate. After receiving, on the morning of 16 April, the news that fifteen hundred people had perished on *Titanic*, she told her daughter what she had seen: 'I wish I could know any individual among the *Titanic* passengers who was elderly and had a face like the one I saw.' When she saw a photograph of Stead in the *Boston American*, later on the same day, she immediately recognised the face as the one she had seen in her study, although the face in the photograph seemed younger.[228]

Goss and Behe are impressed that she instinctively made the connection between the face of her vision and the fate of the ship, apparently certain that the bearded features belonged to one of the passengers. But, on the basis of the evidence they present, it is not entirely clear that this is the case: 'I wish I could know ….' Again, it is hard to see how they can be so precise as to say that Chase saw the face 'just ten minutes after the *Titanic* had struck the iceberg', though, because of the time-difference, Chase's vision clearly predates the sinking. But their speculation that 'Something – some communicating power – wished to make Chase conscious of the disaster; it visualized the event in a symbolic fashion, using Stead as a kind of metaphor

228 Goss and Behe, pp. 237-238.

that stood for the disaster' seems unjustified, especially as they cannot say why Chase and not somebody else was contacted, since she had no relationship with Stead. But the last point does not prevent them from asserting that confirmed spiritualists will identify the mysterious communicating power with Stead himself.

Goss and Behe later say that in publishing Chase's account the American Society for Psychical Research did not put its 'cachet of approval' on the incident, but threw the matter open to wider scrutiny. Yet by its very nature there was little in the narrative to be investigated further. Chase was a 'credible-enough-seeming' witness, and corroboration of her account rested on the details that (a) she mentioned her vision of Stead's face *before* identifying it in the newspaper photograph; and (b) the face in the photo truly matched the one in her vision. The authors say that, while 'realistically, sympathetically' we have no reason to reject the statement that these details are correct, we cannot be sure that she saw Stead's face at all, or that it matched the photo. Yet if we argue for 'retroactive cognisance', for the view that she saw a bearded face but was led to put a name to it by seeing Stead's features in the paper, Goss and Behe claim, we simply complicate the issue: 'Why should Chase see a bearded apparition at all?' As long as the factor of the witness seeing something of the sort is unchallenged, they say, the account remains suggestive. And, accepting that her experience came at about the time of *Titanic*'s accident, it might be better than that.[229] Méheust does not mention this case.

229 Goss and Behe, pp. 246-247.

(BM,wts,18) Giving Harper's book as his source, Méheust claims that some weeks before *Titanic*'s sailing an **unnamed medium** told Stead: 'You are going to lose and win ... You are going to see in the darkness the disembodied people you have loved.' After the sinking, those close to Stead saw this as a prediction of his death, but at the time Stead thought it was indicating a development of his clairvoyant powers.[230] Méheust does not return to this case in Part III of his book.

(BM,wts,19) At the end of a séance in March 1912, **Miss Scatcherd**, one of Stead's spiritualist associates, has a message for Stead: 'Put your work, your mission, before everything. The day is well advanced. The time that remains to you to accomplish your task is very short.'[231] Again, Méheust does not take up the case in Part III of his book.

(BM,wts,24) Méheust records that, on 10 April, 1912, at a 'Julia's Bureau' séance in London, **Mrs Wesley Adams** delivered a message that included the following: '*I will guide them with my advice, and then I will receive them into the Glory of the Lord*. That is addressed to the gentleman on a voyage, Mr Stead.'[232] (Méheust inadvertently repeats the case, using a number of the same sentences, in Part II of his book.)[233] In Part III, Méheust gives the date as 11 April, saying that the medium's pronouncement is 'ambiguous', but that its most obvious meaning is a

230 Méheust, p. 61.

231 Méheust, p. 61.

232 Méheust, p. 64.

233 Méheust, p. 102 (**BM,39**).

prediction of death. It seems to relate this prediction to Stead's journey, but again in an ambiguous and indirect way, since it might also be taken to mean simply that when Stead dies he will be received into the Glory of the Lord. Méheust says that this is a classic instance of the difficulty prophetic language poses for interpretation, and rates the case as only one-star-plus.[234]

(BM,wts,26) Citing Estelle Stead's Preface to *Blue Island* (1922),[235] Méheust says that on 14 April, 1912 Stead's daughter was taking tea with a young actor named **Pardoe Woodman**. Out of the blue, he began talking of an imminent maritime disaster, which would involve an elderly man with whom she had links. He mentioned the name of neither the ship nor the man concerned, and, astonishingly, at the time Estelle did not associate the prediction with her father. Woodman subsequently became a medium and made contact with the dead Stead. Again, Méheust exactly repeats six sentences in a second account of this incident.[236]

In Part III of his book Méheust claims that Woodman apparently was not aware that Estelle's father was on *Titanic*, speculating that he would have kept his prediction to himself, had he known. But he emphasises that the premonition is precise and could not have been arrived at by inference. He thinks that the fact that Woodman was not yet conscious of his gifts as a medium is another reason for

234 Méheust, pp. 183-184.

235 *Blue Island, Experiences of a New Arrival beyond the Veil, communicated by W.T. Stead*, Recorded by Pardoe Woodman and Estelle Stead (1922).

236 Méheust, pp. 64-65, 111 (**BM,wts,26, BM,49**).

thinking that this is a case of genuine precognition with its timing sufficiently well attested. But he does not include it among his eight strongest premonition cases, rating it as two-stars-plus.[237]

All five commentators – Stevenson, Brown, Gardner, Behe, and Méheust – refer to the claims that Stead appeared to friends, colleagues, and others after his death.[238] Stevenson devotes little space to the issue, however, simply noting the different – and incompatible – accounts that he is alleged to have given of his last moments (and citing Lord as establishing that Stead could not have persuaded the orchestra to play *Nearer My God to Thee* as *Titanic* sank).[239] Brown records a couple of post-death appearances.[240] Gardner devotes minimal space to the matter, making little comment, although he is scathing about Rev. Tweedale ('an Anglican vicar of unbounded stupidity').[241] And Behe, despite the fact that the title of his book includes 'forewarnings' of a tragedy, deals with many cases in greater detail than his earlier ones. His results are mixed, and he clearly has mixed feelings, stressing that a number of experiences would have been extremely difficult to produce fraudulently.[242] Méheust talks of the 'incredible

237 Méheust, pp. 188-189.

238 In some instances it is a matter not of Stead appearing, but of his sending a message via automatic writing.

239 Stevenson (1), p. 156.

240 Brown, pp. 62-63.

241 Gardner (1), pp. 93-94 (**MG,23**). On Tweedale, see above (**IS,12**).

242 Behe, pp. 73-87.

chronicle' of Stead's posthumous appearances, and takes the issue seriously.[243] The relatively strict terms of reference of the present study – concentrating on premonitions of the *Titanic* disaster – preclude examination of this type of paranormal activity, which essentially post-dates the tragedy. But it is, perhaps, worth recording that in at least one such apparition Stead is said to have communicated that he was sorry to have ignored Kerlor's predictions![244]

In Part III of his book Behe devotes some five pages to general consideration of Stead's connections with the paranormal, first discussing Stead's belief 'in the reality of communication with the spirits of deceased persons', and his use of automatic writing.[245] At slightly greater length, he examines the 'second method of contacting the Other Side', that is through the offices of a medium. He explains with some care how seances involving a medium could be conducted in two different ways (with the lights dimmed or put out, and in a 'cabinet' or separate enclosure with doors or curtains to the side, into which the medium would retire alone), and details the techniques by which fraudulent mediums could 'produce striking "manifestations" through perfectly ordinary means'.[246] These pages – which have as much relevance to the topic of Part II ('Mistaken accounts and deliberate hoaxes') as to Stead – are of great interest as background to any study of

243 Méheust, pp. 69-73.

244 The obvious point from which to begin an examination of Stead's posthumous appearances is: James Coates, *Has W.T. Stead Returned? A Symposium* (1913).

245 Behe, pp. 58-59.

246 Behe, pp. 59-60.

the 'fashion' for the paranormal at the turn of the twentieth century, and should, once more, be borne in mind as one looks at how Behe (and others) deal with certain premonition cases. And exactly the same can be said of Behe's paragraphs on fortune-tellers, clairvoyants, and palmists, which emphasise the 'ever-present possibility of trickery', while stating that some seances would produce things 'which would *seem* to be beyond the ability of a medium to achieve by fraudulent means'.[247]

At this point Behe recommends caution in dealing with written accounts by spiritualists, saying that they are sometimes coloured by their strong belief system. He also urges us to remember that 'a written account of a seance is only as good as the observer who wrote the account', since some details thought insignificant by the teller might go a long way towards explaining how fraudulent means might have been employed. Nevertheless, he contends that not all observers are uncritical, gullible people, and that even sceptics have sometimes been forced to accept the evidence of their own senses.[248] He says we do not know how much Stead and his followers were aware of the techniques of trickery, but that one would have expected Stead to receive some 'psychic forewarning' of the tragedy in which he was to lose his life. He finds the evidence, however, 'ambiguous': some predictions of his fate turned out to be untrue, others were general warnings used by professional clairvoyants, and others again were probably simple coincidences. Yet certain accounts are 'provocative', and suggest that 'contact

247 Behe, pp. 60-61.

248 Behe, pp. 61-62.

with the Other Side *may* have taken place both before and after the sinking of *Titanic*.'[249] Although he does not say which they are, Behe leaves final judgement on the claimed psychic nature of these cases to the reader, and, indeed, as he goes through the Stead experiences one by one, he appears somewhat reluctant to express his own view.[250] One might, at least, have expected that Behe would give some indication of where each case stands in relation to his own categories of curious coincidences, and possible or probable psychic phenomena.

Méheust believes that the sinking of *Titanic* provided a fitting end for Stead, bringing together the multiple facets of his personality and ensuring that he became a legend.[251] Relying heavily on Estelle Stead's book about her father,[252] he gives a fairly detailed account of Stead's life, highlighting that he was, in the general sense, a visionary and prophetic writer from early on, as well as a major innovator in journalism and politics. Méheust accepts Stead's claim that he often had 'extraordinary premonitions', and notes that he began practising automatic writing in 1892. He argues that, like Morgan Robertson, Stead enjoyed a reputation for his skill at the practice. He also claims that whenever Stead went abroad he consulted clairvoyants about his future, possibly out of scientific curiosity, but probably equally to confirm his own premonitions about his destiny.[253]

249 Behe, p. 62.

250 He had earlier claimed that 'Some may be genuine: others are not' (Behe, p. 12).

251 Méheust, p. 38.

252 Estelle Stead, *Stead, my Father* (1913).

253 Méheust, pp. 251-266.

When he returns to the topic in Part IV of his book, Méheust says he will review the 'saga of the spiritualist leader', Stead, in the light of his own earlier analyses. He is struck by the tragic grandeur of Stead's own death and believes it seems to constitute one of the finest cases of a prophecy fulfilled in modern history. He reiterates that it was, in fact, preceded by several converging prophecies. The closeness and collaboration that prevailed in the small world of spiritualists in which Stead was so prominent was an ideal environment for the development of precognition. Stead himself was the 'resonance box' through which the collective effort of this small world was channelled. He points out that Stead was as distant as possible from the work carried out in parapsychology laboratories and even criticised the Society for Psychical Research. Stead experimented with his own life. He was himself 'titanic' and the fate of the ship matched his own excesses. Méheust says that to investigate these ideas he will temporarily abandon the criteria he adopted in examining paranormal phenomena linked with *Titanic*. There will be a loss of certainty as a result, but also a gain in 'suggestive ideas'.[254]

Perhaps the reason why Méheust includes so few of others' predictions of Stead's death in his dossier in Part III of his book is that, having outlined them one by one in his run-through of *Titanic* premonitions in Part II, his perspective on the whole matter in Part IV is a different one.[255] He talks of a 'collective construction' of the premonition and argues that, as Stead went from one

254 Méheust, p. 255.

255 Méheust, pp. 268-279.

clairvoyant to another the vague idea of his death gradually evolved into a sea drama, although this was already present in some of the earliest predictions. He is clear that, granted the level of contact between Stead's acquaintances, later clairvoyants were influenced by the predictions of the earlier ones, and that the final premonition of Kerlor emerged as a result of a collective effort to foresee Stead's fate. Stead himself contributed to this process in the speech in which he envisaged himself shipwrecked and in other maritime comparisons. Méheust claims that it seems that the theme that Stead was in imminent danger was constantly discussed in his circle, with kinds of death other than that by water gradually fading and that of a sinking coming to dominate.

Méheust finds it difficult to understand why Stead was prepared to embark on *Titanic* in spite of all the warnings, but his own suggestion is at least equally incomprehensible. He claims that either Stead was the most extreme of sceptics concerning premonitions, or he boarded the ship to carry out the predictions of those who foresaw his death. He admits that the second hypothesis cannot be verified, but finds it 'fascinating'. For most people, however, it is likely to remain a remote and indeterminate speculation, which is rendered no more likely or plausible by Méheust's subsequent, largely unsubstantiated musings on Stead's final hours on *Titanic*. He acknowledges that we shall never know the 'details' of his last thoughts, but claims, with no evidence whatever, that it seems certain that, just before the end, Stead fell back on the premonitions of his death. Moreover, by now Méheust seems to be boldly *asserting* that Stead deliberately sacrificed himself on *Titanic*, and lyrically describing his last moments.[256]

Méheust concludes his second look at Stead's case by recapitulating the four possible hypotheses, saying that the reader must choose between them.[257] He himself rejects (1) the possibility that nothing paranormal is involved, and says that (3) the idea that Stead subconsciously understood that he would die on *Titanic* is interesting but unprovable. He now suggests that he mentioned (4) – the possibility of Stead actually 'choosing' to fulfil the predictions of his death – just for the record, to show the abysmal depths opened up when one refuses to accept precognition. His own stated view is finally that the rational, balanced hypothesis (2) suggests that Stead glimpsed the drama in which he would lose his life as the result of precognitive perceptions – his own or those of others – but was never able to, or perhaps never wanted to, accept this consciously, embarking on *Titanic* in total ignorance of his own fate.

The problem with Méheust's choice of (2), however, is not just that it is extremely difficult to distinguish from (3) in the terms in which both are couched, but also that in the light of his vigorous rejection of (4), we now need to look back at his previous pages in a different way. It seems that we do not have to take them seriously after all. Was

256 Méheust, pp. 275-280. There are very few references to Stead in the careful reconstruction of events between the collision and the sinking in *On a Sea of Glass* (2012), but a quoted comment by May Futrelle (p.213) suggests that sometime after 1.30am 'Especially William T Stead, the British editor, was sure we couldn't sink.'

257 Méheust, pp. 280-282.

his somewhat fanciful speculation there what he had in mind in saying that he was about to abandon his earlier criteria, to lose certainty but gain in suggestive ideas?[258] In any case, if the 'fascinating', 'unprovable' notion of Stead somehow deliberately fulfilling the predictions of his fate is not to be entirely dismissed out of hand, it is one that requires a very great deal more refinement and explanation than Méheust offers. There is very little else in this second chapter on Stead that actually adds to what has already been said in his book.

It is not surprising that Stevenson, Behe, Méheust, and Gardner (if we include his reprinting of Stead's texts) should have devoted so much space to Stead. His is probably the single most important name attached to the matter of *Titanic* premonitions. What is more, his fictional pieces and alleged forewarnings of his death clearly contain material of relevance to spiritualism in general (and its history). But their real relation to the *Titanic* disaster is questionable. Had Stead died violently 'in a throng' on land, many of the supposedly supernatural anticipations of his death would have carried the same force, or suffered the same lack of it. Furthermore, just as, granted the general emphasis on its 'unsinkability', there is a curious inevitability about the existence of alleged examples of precognition of *Titanic*'s sinking, so the premature death of an eminent spiritualist was bound to generate claims that it had been foreseen. And the fact that there is no significant evidence of the manner of his death on the ship

258 Méheust, p. 255.

simply increases the scope for speculation and fantasy.

Because they all concern the fate of Stead, the individual premonitions in this set are more closely linked than those in any other category that we examine. Méheust is right to draw attention to the close group of friends and acquaintances amongst whom talk of danger to Stead constantly circulated. Yet the premonitions are very far from reinforcing one another, and it is particularly noticeable that none of them predicted Stead's death on *Titanic* in a direct, straightforward manner. Indeed, in virtually all instances it is a stretch to make them relate in any way to *Titanic*. They are, moreover, strongly marked by vagueness, obscurity, confusions, even contradictions. Perhaps paradoxically, since so many spiritualists are involved, all of these factors make it especially difficult to find firm evidence of premonitions in this particular category of cases.

CHAPTER 3

IAN STEVENSON

Ian Pretyman Stevenson (1918-2007) worked at the University of Virginia for fifty years. As Professor of Psychiatry, he founded in 1967 the Division of Perceptual Studies (which investigated the paranormal), and became known for his research into reincarnation, on which he wrote some three hundred papers and fourteen books (one of 2,268 pages). He travelled extensively and is said to have collected at least 2,500 cases of children, many of whom claimed to have memories of a previous life. Some commentators have severely criticised his handling of these cases, which Stevenson was working on when he published his two articles on *Titanic* premonitions in 1960 and 1965. There are methodological parallels in the two inquiries.

Acknowledging the help of Professor C.J. Ducasse and Walter Lord (who drew his attention to one of his cases), Stevenson begins his first article by referring to 'collective' experiences, which he says form a 'substantial group of spontaneous extrasensory phenomena'.[259] He mentions the frequently-cited piece by W.E. Cox, which is said to show that 'on days when a number of important railway accidents occurred, most of the trains involved in the accidents carried fewer passengers than these same trains ordinarily did under comparable traffic conditions'.[260] Somewhat puzzlingly, Stevenson 'presumes' that collective precognitive experiences usually occur unconsciously; that is, without the percipient becoming aware of the experience, and, in the case of putting off a journey, perhaps plausibly offering some other motive for deferring the trip. He admits that 'such unconscious influences of extrasensory perceptions, if they occur, prevent the further study of these experiences', but claims that the occurrence of 'unconscious precognition' suggests that collective paranormal experiences occur more often than we realise, and deserve the most careful study when recognised.[261] Stevenson concludes his short general introduction by pointing out that 'a considerable number of apparently extrasensory experiences' occurred in connection with the sinking of *Titanic* (some apparently precognitive, others contemporaneous with the tragedy), and notes that all the materials he quotes have already been published elsewhere, although no one has previously gathered all of them together 'with a view to their study as

259 Stevenson (1), p. 153.

260 W.E. Cox, 'Precognition: An Analysis, II' (1956).

261 Stevenson (1), p. 153.

collective experiences'.[262] He claims that his discussion will make it clear that he thinks that some experiences show paranormal cognition, while others do not.[263]

This is anything but a sharp and convincing opening to his article. Even the relatively small number of cases that Stevenson will examine exhibit, as he later admits, enough diversity to make use of the phrase 'collective experiences' somewhat inappropriate. His acknowledgement that some are precognitive and others not may also rather weaken his investigation, or at least reduce its scope. And, in addition to some general difficulties concerning the very notion of 'unconscious premonitions', there is woolliness in his reference to the 'unconscious influences' of extrasensory perceptions, in that it is not clear exactly how these relate to 'unconscious precognition'. We also badly need more detail on the processes by which unconscious collective experiences come to be 'recognised' (as what? by whom?). Finally, his implied claim that his first article will somehow involve study of the cases 'as collective experiences' will prove unjustified, unless one interprets the phrase in an entirely unhelpful loose sense.

Stevenson's summarised account of the *Titanic* and its sinking contains a few minor inaccuracies and speculations (where is the evidence that Andrews had 'some difficulty' in persuading Captain Smith that the ship was going down?), but is mostly sound. More interesting is his contention that the general conviction of unsinkability has relevance to the question of paranormal experiences.

262 Stevenson (1), pp. 153-154.

263 Stevenson (1), p. 154, footnote 4.

The complete confidence that accompanied *Titanic*'s maiden voyage is said to contrast significantly with the expectations of danger that characterised the last voyage of *Lusitania*, about which a few apparently paranormal phenomena have also been recorded, the point being that *Titanic*'s perceived unsinkability makes 'unlikely, although not impossible' inference of the sinking from the published facts of the ship. Since inference is the most commonly used alternative explanation for allegedly precognitive experiences, this point seems potentially an important factor, but in practice inference is usually invoked in connection with facts about the ship themselves rather than as a direct source of visions of its sinking.

Stevenson does not cite newspapers as his source for any of his cases in either article,[264] and this probably accounts for the fact that his two articles consider only 26 cases in all. Understandably, he uses journals of psychic research as his sources.[265] He also acknowledges the support of the Parapsychology Foundation and the help of Walter Lord, whose influential *A Night to Remember* appeared in 1955, just some five years before Stevenson's first article. He refers to one or two of the classic books on *Titanic* produced soon after the disaster (like Gracie's and Beesley's),[266] although by 1960 relatively little had been

264 He does thank the *Daily Mirror* for a copy of a photograph in connection with (IS,17).

265 For instance, the *Journal of the Society for Psychical Research*, the *Proceedings of the Society for Psychical Research*, and the *Journal of the American Society for Psychic Research*.

266 Archibald Gracie, *The Truth About the Titanic* (1913). Lawrence Beesley, *The Loss of the Titanic. Its Story and its Lessons* (1912).

published on the subject, and mostly he depends upon rather more specialised books on, or related to, paranormal topics. In short, not much more could reasonably have been expected of him with regard to sources, or even the range of cases he considers. Some twenty years later, Rustie Brown, casting her net much wider, would add around thirty cases (some particularly flimsy). And although eight years later still George Behe, relying heavily on newspaper evidence, increased the number very considerably, he did so partly by considering many instances that he himself believed had no paranormal origin at all. Stevenson was an academic, writing in an academic context, at a fairly early stage of serious work on *Titanic*, and is pretty scrupulous in quoting his sources.

He notes that in some instances inadequate recordings of exact times make impossible a precise separation of these cases into precognitive, contemporaneous, or postcognitive, and that he has not attempted to make the distinction with regard to experiences occurring on the night of 14-15 April. He also registers that he has excluded from his article three accounts of possible extrasensory perceptions, since they lacked adequate witnessing 'before the events became normally known', and that two of them contained improbable details which throw doubt on other parts of the accounts. Stevenson further points out that he has excluded 'all of the abundant material communicated through mediums following the sinking of the *Titanic* that purported to come from deceased passengers and crewmen of the ship'.[267] He believes that

267 Stevenson (1), p. 156, footnotes 9 and 10.

the inconsistencies in much of this material cautions against accepting all mediumistic communications at face value, and is – rightly – specifically critical of the flawed and contradictory accounts of the way in which W.T. Stead met his death. All of this serves to increase our confidence in the judgement of Stevenson, but is, of course, no kind of guarantee that he will exercise that judgement soundly and reliably in the cases he considers.

In one way or another, moreover, Stevenson devotes a great deal of space, in his first article, to Stead, and surprisingly little to other particular cases. It is also noticeable that, in that article, the balance of scrutiny of individual experiences on the one hand and general comment on premonitions on the other is strongly in favour of the latter – roughly, 11 pages against 7. Stevenson not only refers back to particular cases in the course of his general discussion, but also, rather irritatingly, sometimes adds further information about them there. In itself, this does not undermine his investigation, but it does nothing to counter any doubts one may have about its scope and the depth of detail concerning particular examples of premonition.

Only eight of Stevenson's cases over his two articles are covered by all four subsequent authors. Both Gardner and Behe refer to Stevenson's 'nineteen cases', but, as 'Experience 9', Stevenson refers to four incidents involving W.T. Stead. He also adds three cases as 'Miscellaneous Experiences and Events' to those numbered 1-12, and mentions two quite separate premonitions by Kerlor under 'Experience 11' so that, strictly, Stevenson deals with twenty-six cases in his two articles. His first **(IS,1)** relates to Robertson, and **(IS,9a-9d)**, **(IS,10)**, **(IS,11a-11b)**, **(IS,12)** to Stead: these have already been discussed.

CASES

(IS,2) Mr **J. Connon Middleton**, an English businessman, booked a passage on *Titanic* in March 1912, then cancelled it in the first few days of April, after receiving a telegram from the United States advising him to postpone his trip for business reasons. He wrote a letter to the Society for Psychical Research – published in the Society's *Proceedings* (Stevenson's source) in June 1912,[268] – saying that he had had a dream on two successive nights between the booking and the cancellation,[269] in which he saw the *Titanic* 'floating on the sea, keel upwards and her passengers and crew swimming around her'. The dreams made him 'uncomfortable', and he was subsequently 'most depressed and even despondent'. Stevenson later claims that Middleton's 'experienced emotion' was 'probably secondary to the visual perception', and says, rather oddly, that it could not have been a communication from suffering passengers, since at the time of their experiences the sinking of *Titanic* was 'difficult to imagine, much less assert openly'.[270]

Middleton claimed to have told members of his family and friends about this dream prior to the sailing and sinking

268 Connon Middleton, *Proceedings of the Society for Psychical Research*, (1912), p.264.

269 His first dream is later said to have occurred on 30 March (Stevenson (1), p. 166).

270 Stevenson (1), p. 168.

of the ship, and a number of his friends subsequently testified that he had done so, two of them adding that he had said that in his dream he himself 'seemed to be floating in the air just above the wreck'.[271] Nevertheless, Stevenson later admits that accounts differ on when exactly Middleton told anyone about his dreams, and that Middleton's wife testified that he had said 'how foolish it would seem if he postponed his business on account of a dream'.[272]

Stevenson acknowledges that, disturbed as Middleton was by his dream, he did not cancel his reservation until receiving the telegram. His acceptance that Middleton's vision of the ship as keel upwards was 'clearly incorrect' makes it difficult to understand his claim that the ship is 'correctly' identified,[273] and it is not perfectly clear that Middleton did, in fact, identify the *Titanic* as 'going to sink'.[274] Stevenson is sure that for Middleton psychic experiences were rare in the extreme, arguing that the fact that he was about to travel on *Titanic* seems to have 'heightened an otherwise negligible and dormant faculty for extrasensory perception to a functional level', and contrasting his case with those of people with 'more abundant' gifts for extrasensory perception, which '"happened"' to come into play in connection with *Titanic*, without special personal involvement on their part.[275]

---

271 Stevenson (1), p. 157.

272 Stevenson (1), p. 169. A French website claims that it was not until 18 April, after the sinking, that Middleton told his family and friends about his dream.

273 Stevenson (1), p. 167.

274 Stevenson (1), p. 165.

275 Stevenson (1), p. 169.

Brown simply follows Stevenson,[276] although she also claims that the incident is mentioned in a book by Stephen Rudley,[277] as well as one by Robertson and Stevenson.[278] Gardner adds nothing substantive to the case, other than pointing out that 'dreams of this sort must have been extremely common'.[279] And while Behe makes no reference to the case at all, Méheust follows Stevenson's account.[280] In Part III of his book, he suggests that, because Middleton knew he was travelling on *Titanic*, his 'premonition' can be regarded as 'particularly suspect of unconscious inference', although, as in other cases, he fails to provide an explanation of the exact meaning of this concept. He argues that, to avoid this objection, Middleton would have had to offer 'some special view' of the sinking, whereas his description does not exceed what might be imagined. The case, Méheust concludes, is 'undecidable', and in his system of classification he awards it only one star, with three stars marking the strongest instances of premonition.[281]

Despite the suggestion that evidence like Middleton's return ticket, and the actual business telegram, strengthens his claims, there seems to be very little that is remarkable in the case as a whole, much less evidence of precognition.

276 Brown, p. 13 **(RB,3)**.

277 Stephen Rudley, *Psychic Detective* (1979).

278 *The Wreck of the Titan: Or, Futility; Paranormal Experiences Connected with the Sinking of the Titanic*, (1974).

279 Gardner (1), p. 18 **(MG,2)**. Gardner's ascription to Stevenson of the view that mistakes or discrepancies are 'characteristic of most precognitive dreams. The event gets distorted in the dream' is based on Stevenson's *second* article.

280 Méheust, pp. 87-88 **(BM,19)**.

281 Méheust, pp. 174-175.

Even granting that Middleton's description of his dream is accurate and that it is correct to time it as before the sinking, the content of the dream as such is no kind of prediction that the *Titanic* will strike an iceberg, break apart and sink. Gardner's point that dreams with content like that of Middleton would have been common is valid; they look very much like an expression of the worry that anyone might have before a cross-Atlantic trip on a new ship.

(IS,3) During the night of 14-15 April 1912, Stevenson says, a **woman in New York** woke her husband to relate a vivid dream that her mother was in 'a crowded lifeboat rocking in the ocean swell'; 'this wasn't just a bad dream – it was … frightening, and all so real'.[282] She subsequently learned of the sinking of the *Titanic* and discovered with horror the name of her mother 'in the passenger list'. Her mother had wanted to surprise her by crossing the Atlantic on the ship. Although Stevenson does not give a precise time for the dream, he says it was 'at the very time' when the mother was in a lifeboat, thereby hinting at telepathy rather than precognition. As with Middleton, he supposes that the woman had 'an otherwise negligible and dormant faculty for extrasensory perception''.[283]

Brown simply uses Stevenson's details,[284] while Gardner suggests that the case 'seems impressive until we learn

282 Stevenson (1), p. 157.

283 Stevenson (1), p. 169.

284 Brown, pp. 141-142 **(RB,46)**. She is discussing dreams at this stage, and comments that it is 'mind boggling to think of the number of predictions that could have been sent in concerning the *Titanic* disaster' had a registry been in operation at the time.

that the account comes from a book called *The Mystery of Dreams*, in which the author, W.O. Stevens, does not even tell us the names of the mother and daughter!'[285] Behe does not mention this case, and unfortunately Méheust's treatment does not inspire confidence. He quotes only Stevenson as a source (without even mentioning Stevens' book), yet says that the daughter's dream took place at around 1.30 a.m., 'at the moment when *Titanic* is sinking', in spite of saying later that the time margin is 'too imprecise'.[286] (He gives no indication at this stage of awareness of the time-difference between New York time and 'Apparent Time Ship' on *Titanic*, which was probably two hours and two minutes.)[287]

This is bound up with uncertainty over whether the dream is an example of telepathy or precognition. Méheust first asserts that it is a 'telepathic communication', then later categorises it as a 'premonitory dream'.[288] There is also near-confusion about the level of precision in the dream. Méheust talks in Part III of his book of the imprecision in the time margins of the dream, saying – puzzlingly – this is a reason for regarding it as telepathic rather than precognitive, and arguing that the dream would have been more precise (for instance, 'naming' the *Titanic*) if the account of the dream had been drawn up or modified *after*

285 Gardner (1), p. 18 **(MG,3)**. Stevens's book, *The Mystery of Dreams* (1949), is, indeed, Stevenson's only quoted source.

286 Méheust, pp. 129-130, 197 **(BM,65)**.

287 See *Report into the Loss of the SS* Titanic*: A Centennial Reappraisal*, ed. Samuel Halpern *et al* (2011), pp. 76-79.

288 Méheust, pp. 197, 216.

the daughter learned of the sinking.[289] But, in discussing premonitory dreams in his section on psychic processes, he stresses that the daughter was struck by 'the intensity and the precision of the scene'.[290]

Méheust rightly recognises the (potential) importance of the point that the daughter did not know that her mother was at sea, arguing that it is 'highly improbable' that many people would dream by chance of a sinking 'at the very moment' when someone close to them was involved in a sinking, and that the fact rules out any unconscious fear about the mother.[291] But he allows uncertainties to remain regarding exactly when and how the woman learned that her mother was on *Titanic*. Stevenson says 'the following day', Méheust 'a few days later'; and there are questions concerning whether she saw her mother's name on a list (of passengers, of survivors?), and of when such lists were available.

In awarding the case three stars, Méheust sums up by saying, 'Here we are faced with a very strong case, an almost ideal case: the *unknown* presence of someone close rules out chance and weakens inference, while the relative imprecision of the account weakens the hypothesis of subsequent modification.'[292] He includes the case in the privileged group of eight (out of around seventy) which 'satisfy, if not all of our demands (the ideal case does not exist), at least the greatest number of them'.[293] Yet

289 Méheust, p. 197.

290 Méheust, p. 216.

291 Méheust, p. 197.

292 Méheust, pp. 197-198.

293 Méheust, p. 207.

the nature and date of the ultimate source for this whole case (Stevens' book of 1949) will be regarded by many as a major reason for hesitating to take it as significant evidence for precognition.

(IS,4) Mrs **Blanche Marshall**, with her husband and family, watched *Titanic* passing by her home on the Solent on its maiden voyage on 10 April, 1912. In a state of agitation, she cried out: 'That ship is going to sink before she reaches America', then, refusing to be reassured, said angrily: 'Don't stand there staring at me! Do something! You fools, I can see hundreds of people struggling in the icy water! Are you all so blind that you are going to let them drown?'.[294] Stevenson's source for this incident is the autobiography of Mrs Marshall's daughter, Joan Grant (who witnessed it), published, with the – unpromising – title, *Far Memory*, in 1956.[295]

Gardner adds nothing to this specific incident,[296] but Brown, also citing *Far Memory*, brings in the matter of Marshall and the *Lusitania* sinking some three years later, saying that she 'may' have avoided disaster for her entire family by refusing to travel on the ship on the date for which her husband had originally booked passage.[297] Brown does not actually specify, however, that this was the journey on which *Lusitania* sank, and there is also some slight implausibility in her claim that Mrs Marshall was

294 Stevenson (1), p. 158.

295 J. Grant, *Far Memory* (1956). Even as a child, Joan Grant claimed to have lived several lives before her present one.

296 Gardner (1), p. 18 **(MG,4)**.

297 Brown, pp. 14-15 **(RB,5)**.

happy to sail on *Lusitania* on an earlier voyage ('she knew the *Lusitania* wasn't going to sink until later').

Behe includes this case in his list of 'probable psychic phenomena'.[298] He uses a few insignificant details, presumably taken from *Far Memory*, which is his only quoted source, but also draws attention to the comment by another daughter that Mrs Marshall 'has always been afraid of shipwreck', because her best friend was on the *Waratah*, which vanished without trace (in 1909). Yet Behe does not regard this as weakening the case, as 'Her premonition occurred very suddenly, and was specifically focused on *Titanic*'s maiden voyage.' (It is not entirely clear why Behe stresses that this was a *sudden* occurrence.) He devotes as much space to Mrs Marshall's alleged prediction – three weeks before the event – that the *Lusitania* would be torpedoed and sink on its voyage beginning on 1 May, 1915 (which he claims is the voyage for which the family had booked passage), concluding:

> *The chances were very remote that Mrs Marshall could correctly predict the loss of the 'unsinkable'* Titanic *on her maiden voyage. How remote, then, was the chance that she could also specify the exact voyage which would see the torpedoing of* Lusitania*? The probability of these two correct predictions occurring strictly by chance is almost non-existent. That Mrs Marshall was occasionally gifted with precognitive ability is a much more likely explanation.*

298 Behe, pp. 139-41 (**GB,pr,21**).

However, it is noticeable that Mrs Marshall's reaction to the two separate cases is recorded as being very different. While she regards others as being 'blind' to the fate of *Titanic*'s passengers and urges them to 'do something' to prevent the drownings, she feels sorry for *Lusitania*'s passengers, but, illogically, claims 'there is nothing we can do about it in wartime'. There is also something slightly odd about the daughter's speculation that her mother was almost relieved when she learned of the fate of *Titanic* ('not nearly so lonely as waiting until it happened').[299]

Even granting that the *Lusitania* case *looks* impressive, we must acknowledge that, some forty years after the events, the distant memories of the daughter, Joan Grant – she was just short of five years old at the time of the *Titanic* incident! – can hardly be said to register the exact words that her mother used in either case, and this must cast some doubt over the general level of accuracy of the two accounts. Behe does not mention, although Rustie Brown does, that Grant also claims that when her mother, a natural clairvoyant, 'foresaw' that the roof of an indoor tennis court being constructed at her home was doomed to collapse and ordered the workmen out, the roof did indeed fall in, five minutes later![300]

Méheust follows the treatment of this case by Stevenson and Behe quite closely.[301] In Part III of his book he says that the hypothesis of unconscious inference is 'very strong', with 'a whole subliminal process' being involved.

299 Stevenson (1), p. 158.

300 Rustie Brown, p. 14

301 Méheust, pp. 101-102 **(BM,38)**.

But he emphasises both the simple connection with the ship through direct view and the violence and suddenness of the emotional shock. And, dwelling on the *Lusitania* incident, he concludes that 'there is reason to wonder' whether Mrs Marshall did not have the gift of foreseeing certain future events. He rates the case as two stars. Yet there is no compelling reason to accept the implication of both Behe and Méheust that, if she correctly foresaw the *Lusitania*'s fate, this makes it inherently more likely that she had earlier foreseen that of *Titanic*.

(IS,5) Mrs Charles Francis Potter gave the following account of her dream on the night of 14-15 April, 1912, which was vivid enough to cause her to wake up her husband:

> *I saw what seemed to be a high structure, something like an elevated railroad. There were people hanging on the outside of it as if they were holding on by their hands to the top rail of a guard fence. Many of them were in nightclothes, and they were gradually losing their hold and slipping down the inclined sides of this structure. I felt that they were dropping to certain death. They were all terrified, and I felt the terror so strongly that it wakened me.*

Stevenson records that when artists reconstructed the scene of the sinking of the *Titanic* from the accounts of survivors, Mrs Potter said: 'That is just what I saw.'[302]

Since the only source that he quotes is a book by Mrs

302 Stevenson (1), pp. 158-159.

Potter herself, published in 1939,[303] the same reservations about the accuracy of her recollections may be entertained as in the previous case. Furthermore, the parallels between her dream and the *Titanic* disaster are not especially close. Later Stevenson notes that 'something like an elevated railroad' reports 'an association, not the first percept', arguing that her report of her perception would almost certainly have differed had she lived in a 'rural or primitive country', and that, although present knowledge does not allow us to say whether her perception itself would have differed, he believes it would.[304] Gardner points out that water does not figure at all in the dream, and implies that mention of 'something like an elevated railroad' does not improve the case.[305]

Neither Brown nor Behe mentions Mrs Potter at all, but Méheust, again quoting only her own book as a source, relates the same story.[306] In Part III of his book he takes it seriously, not as a precognition, but as an instance of remote viewing. For reasons that he does not make clear, he says that we cannot be absolutely sure in this case that the dream was not modified or 'rewritten' after the disaster. But, as in other examples, he argues 'paradoxically' – though many would say unjustifiably – that its relative imprecision provides its strength. He suggests that the fact that the ship's name does not occur in the dream makes it 'probable' that it was fixed in the memory *before* being adjusted to the event. The same reasons, Méheust says,

303 C.F. Potter, *Beyond the Senses* (1939).

304 Stevenson (1), footnote 27 on p. 168.

305 Gardner (1), pp. 18-19 **(MG,5)**.

306 Méheust, p. 127 **(BM,61)**.

make unconscious inference unlikely.

Emphasising that Mrs Potter had no direct or indirect link with *Titanic*, he claims that she may be part of the statistically predictable group of Europeans who dreamed of a shipwreck on the night concerned, although this is seriously undermined by the point that there is no question of a shipwreck in the dream-report itself. Moreover, Méheust's parallel between the dream and the fact that some third-class passengers tried to climb up the cranes and that most 'had to let go' is far-fetched.[307] When later discussing psychic processes, Méheust unconvincingly suggests that the point that the people in the dream are in night-clothes hints that the great metallic structure is a ship, and that this illustrates the indirect nature of such dreams and the 'economy of means' employed.[308] He awards the case two stars.

(IS,6) In Winnipeg, the **Reverend Charles Morgan**, in a 'trancelike state', saw the number of an unfamiliar hymn presented to him on the evening of 14 April, 1912 and felt compelled to have it sung at his service. Stevenson, quoting correspondence in a book by R. de W. Miller,[309] claims that at the time Morgan's congregation was singing 'Hear, Father, while we pray to Thee, for those in peril on the sea' ('about two hours' before *Titanic* struck the iceberg), second-class passengers on *Titanic* were also singing it.[310] Again, there is no indication of whether a time-difference between Winnipeg and *Titanic* is taken into account –

307 Méheust, p. 193.

308 Méheust, p. 214.

309 R. de W. Miller, *You Do Take It with You* (1955).

310 Stevenson (1), p. 159.

and, if so, what it is.

Brown claims that a second-class passenger on *Titanic* was simultaneously requesting the same hymn at the evening prayer meeting,[311] while Gardner simply relates Stevenson's account.[312] Behe makes no reference to Reverend Morgan at all, but Méheust takes up the case, saying that Colonel Gracie describes this episode in his memoirs, although, in fact, Gracie refers to an entirely different 'coincidence' concerning the hymn![313] Méheust suggests that Morgan forgot the number after his dream, then remembered it just before the evening service.[314] In Part III of his book he argues that no text bears witness to the timing of the dream, and that there is nothing to exclude the possibility of a coincidence. Nevertheless, he is struck by the fact that it is a *number* that imposes itself on Morgan, although he rates the case as only one star.[315] When later analysing psychic processes, Méheust says that this may be an example of a form of clairvoyance frequently encountered in the literature.[316]

(IS,7) The wealthy **Charles Hays** predicted, a few hours before *Titanic* struck the iceberg, that the time would soon come for 'the greatest and most appalling of all disasters at sea'. After the collision, he said, 'You cannot sink this boat', and, later still, 'This ship is good

311 Brown, p. 28 **(RB,21)**.

312 Gardner (1), p. 19 **(MG, 6)**.

313 Méheust, p. 119. See: Archibald Gracie, *Titanic. A Survivor's Story* (2008), p. 5.

314 Méheust, p. 112 **(BM,50)**.

315 Méheust, p. 189.

316 Méheust, p. 215.

for eight hours yet'.[317] Stevenson refers to Lord[318] as his source for this case, and is careful to remark that Hays is 'quoted' as making the last two comments, though he does not indicate that Lord claims Hays added to his eight-hours prediction the point that 'I have just been getting this from one of the best old seamen, Mr Crosby of Milwaukee'.[319]

Brown does not take up the case at all, and it is easy to see why Gardner is so dismissive of it ('Why Stevenson bothered to list this beats me.'),[320] when only the first comment by Hays is potentially any kind of relevant premonition. Behe makes little of the case, classifying it as a 'curious coincidence' (and saying that Hays predicted *Titanic* was good for *ten* hours),[321] but the fact that he refers to Gracie's book confirms that this is the ultimate source for the Hays predictions.

Méheust quotes Behe as his source for the same details.[322] He points out in Part III of his book that one can question the accuracy of declarations picked up just before and during such dramatic situations (saying that it is Hays's wife who records the remarks), and that, in any case, the exact circumstances and the tone of the remarks are unknown. It is notable that he does not believe Hays's

---

317 Stevenson (1), p. 159.

318 W. Lord, *A Night to Remember*, (1955).

319 Lord, p. 76.

320 Gardner (1), p. 19 **(MG,7)**.

321 Behe, p. 40 **(GB,cc,45)**. The American Inquiry quotes Hays as saying 'eight or ten hours'.

322 Méheust, p. 114 **(BM,51)**.

earliest remark should be considered as a premonition at all. He rates the case as only one star.[323]

(IS,8) Stevenson claims that on the day *Titanic* sailed (10 April 1912), the clairvoyant, Mr **Vincent Turvey** predicted that 'a great liner will be lost'. He recorded this in a letter to Madame Isabelle de Steiger dated 13 April, together with a statement that the liner would be lost in two days. Steiger received the letter on Monday 15 April. Stevenson cites as his source for this case correspondence by Steiger published in the spiritualist journal *Light* on 29 June 1912, but adds that the letter by Steiger was transcribed for him.[324] He later suggests that, because it does not name a ship, Turvey's warning seems less predictive than those of Middleton and Marshall.[325] Stevenson's attitude to the significance of actually naming *Titanic* contrasts quite sharply with that of Méheust.

Stevenson devotes less space to this case than to any of his other major ones, and it seems certain that he examined the transcription (by one Miss Ruby Yeatman) rather than the edition of *Light*. He is simply wrong to say that Turvey's letter to Steiger is dated 13 April. This is the Saturday on which Steiger paid a visit to the 'seer'. Turvey himself refers *back* to this visit, and his letter explains that he has already read 'in the papers' of the loss of *Titanic*, which indicates that it was written on 16 April at the earliest. But the item in *Light* is inconclusive on the matter of whether he mentioned the name of the ship to Steiger during her visit:

323 Méheust, p. 190.

324 Stevenson (1), pp. 159-60.

325 Stevenson (1), p. 165.

'"I gave you a very broad hint of today's truly awful disaster to the *Titanic*"'.

Brown uses Stevenson's details,[326] and Gardner does no more than briefly record Stevenson's report,[327] but Behe elaborates on it, classifying it as a 'possible' psychic phenomenon.[328] He claims Turvey was described as a gentleman and a 'most gifted clairvoyant', and foresaw, on 10 April, an approaching disaster which would befall an ocean liner, telling an unnamed acquaintance of his conviction on the following day. Behe does not mention Stevenson in connection with this case, and cites as his source only the book *Has W.T. Stead Returned?* by J. Coates, which relies entirely on Steiger's item in *Light*.[329] It is hard to see why the accuracy of either Steiger or Coates should be regarded as unquestionable, yet Behe believes there is 'no doubt' that Turvey told Steiger about his premonition of a liner disaster in two days on 13 April. He does, however, acknowledge that there seems to be 'a slight uncertainty' about exactly when Steiger received Turvey's letter. Word of the loss of *Titanic* and 1,500 victims did not arrive until very late in the day on 15 April and was not generally known until the morning newspapers of 16 April. This causes Behe to argue that Steiger could not have received the letter until 16 April 'at the earliest', though his claim that Turvey must have written it – referring to both 'today's truly awful disaster to the *Titanic*' and the great loss

---

326 Brown, pp. 18-19 **(RB,7)**.

327 Gardner (1), p.19.

328 Behe, pp.103-104 **(GB,po,20)**.

329 *Has W.T. Stead Returned?* (1913).

of life – late on the afternoon of 15 April is nothing more than rather puzzling speculation. In any case, Behe insists that Turvey accurately predicted the precise day on which a great liner would be lost and regards the prediction as 'impressive' even though it did not specify *Titanic*. Indeed, he thinks its accuracy is 'uncanny' but, following his general principle of doubting professional psychics, classes it as only *possibly* psychic, since we do not know if Turvey was a professional psychic or merely an enthusiastic amateur.

There are significant discrepancies and muddles in Méheust's treatment of this case. At first he says that, if one believes Turvey, he had a premonition on the Friday before the sinking that a great liner would sink in two days, conveying this to a friend the next day. But, confusingly, Méheust calls *the day after that* Saturday.[330] In any case, he later dates Turvey's original premonition to Wednesday 10 April.[331] Méheust further claims that Turvey repeated his prediction to Steiger on 13 April, and, despite the fact that newspapers did not report the sinking on the morning of Monday 15 April, he goes on to say that Steiger receives the letter from Turvey on that Monday morning, 'when she has just learned of the sinking of *Titanic* from the newspaper'. He claims that she attested in writing that the letter was sent 'the day before', that is on Sunday 14 April. But this statement must certainly be false at some level, since Turvey mentions the *Titanic* disaster. Méheust is also

330 Méheust, p. 64 **(BM,wts,25)**. It is slightly odd that Méheust first raises the Turvey case in his first chapter on Stead (Part I, Ch.3), since Turvey's letter makes no reference to Stead.

331 Méheust, p. 108 **(BM,46)**.

confused over the date on which Steiger's letter to *Light* was published, at one point giving 17 June (the date on Steiger's letter itself),[332] at another 18 April,[333] neither of which is correct.

In Part III of his book Méheust adds further information to the case. He does not quote any sources as such, but points out that Turvey was part of the circle of acquaintances of Stead, who wrote a Preface, in 1909, to Turvey's 'book on clairvoyance'.[334] The Preface is said to tell us a number of things about Turvey, but Méheust claims only that it leaves the 'impression' that Turvey was an established clairvoyant who had demonstrated his gift on many occasions. Méheust, entirely wrongly, has no doubt that Turvey's letter to Steiger pre-dates the disaster, and sees the lack of a reference to *Titanic* as a point in favour of the prediction. But he suspects that unconscious inference may have been at play, apparently because of Turvey's link with Stead (!), and ranks the case with only two stars.[335] At least, in bringing to light the Stead-Turvey connection Méheust raises the interesting question of whether Turvey knew that Stead was on *Titanic*. He suggests that the letter to Steiger tends to suggest not, arguing that Turvey would otherwise not have failed to bring the fact into his prediction.

---

332 Méheust, p. 64.

333 Méheust, p. 108.

334 Méheust gives no details, but the book is Vincent N. Turvey, *The Beginnings of Seership : Astral Projection, Clairvoyance and Prophecy* (1909). A 1954 reprint is said to include an abridgement of the original Preface by Stead, as well as a letter of recommendation from Conan Doyle. Neither Behe, nor the website 'W.T. Stead Resource Site' makes mention of this Preface by Stead.

335 Méheust, pp. 184-185.

Hanging over this whole case is the state of Turvey's mind at the time. His letter to Steiger says: 'I … told you that "I" caused what "I" foresaw – or *felt* as if I did', and Steiger acknowledges that 'his psychic condition, owing also to the weakness of his physical organism, added very much to his suffering in mind and body'. And yet we have only Turvey's word for the fact that he had a premonition on Wednesday 10 April, and no indication at all of the person to whom he conveyed this, or of whether at that stage he predicted 15 April for the sinking of the liner. There are far too many uncertainties for this experience to be one strengthening the case for precognition.

(IS,12a) Miss **Edith Evans** recalled, as the ship sank, says Stevenson, that 'a fortune-teller had once told her to "beware of the water"'.[336] Stevenson cites Lord's *A Night to Remember* as his source for this, but that book contains just a single sentence recording the comment.[337] Brown, who quotes 'Beware of the water … always beware of the water', simply 'wonders' whether Evans remembered the fortune-teller's comment when she gave up her place in a lifeboat.[338] Gardner says only that all three of Stevenson's extra, 'miscellaneous' cases are even weaker that his first twelve.[339] Behe classifies this one as a 'curious coincidence'.[340] As Lord presumably did, he uses Gracie as

336 Stevenson (1), p. 162.

337 Lord, *A Night to Remember* (1955), p. 112. Lord gives no source for his statement.

338 Brown, p. 47 **(RB,26)**.

339 Gardner (1), p. 19 **(MG,9)**.

340 Behe, p. 42 **(GB,cc,49)**.

his source,[341] and adds that Evans said that 'now she knew she would be drowned', although she displayed no sign of fear. He argues that in a way the fortune-teller's warning may be regarded as a 'self-fulfilling prophecy', as Evans 'deliberately gave up her last opportunity to be saved so that Mrs Brown, the mother of several children, would have a chance to live'.[342]

Méheust – who wrongly claims that the prediction was that Miss Evans would die – also suggests that it is because Evans feels the weight of the prediction that she accepts the sentence and does not get into the boat.[343] But their point is rather undermined by Behe's earlier observation that she was previously in another lifeboat and did not want to die. In Part III of his book Méheust claims that this case is 'undecidable' and cannot be considered as a true premonition. He touches on the real weakness of the case when he notes that fortune-tellers at the time commonly warned of the dangers of the sea. He, too, suggests we may be dealing with a self-fulfilling prophecy and rates the case as only one star.[344]

(IS,12b) Again citing Lord, Stevenson points out that a crewman deserted *Titanic* when she stopped at Queenstown. He acknowledges, however, that 'he did not leave a record of his motives' and says 'we can only surmise

---

341 Archibald Gracie, *Titanic. A Survivor's Story. Its Story and its Lessons* (1913), pp. 24-25.

342 Behe, p. 42. See Gracie, pp. 15-16.

343 Méheust, pp. 121, 124, 199 **(BM,59)**. Mrs Brown was rescued from collapsible D, the last lifeboat to be launched, with possibly as few as 20 people in it: Lightoller told the British Inquiry that there were no women seeking places when the boat left *Titanic*.

344 Méheust, p. 199.

that these might have included a foreknowledge, perhaps unconscious, of the forthcoming disaster', admitting that he might well have acted from any one or more of numerous other motives.[345]

Gardner adds nothing to Stevenson's account.[346] But Brown names the 'fireman' as **John Coffey**, refers specifically to his 'premonition of disaster', and says he 'deserted', signing on the *Mauretania* the following Sunday.[347] Behe says that he was a stoker, and, using a Southampton newspaper and the *Titanic Commutator* as his sources,[348] claims that it was only 'later' that the rumour arose that Coffey had had a premonition of danger and deserted the ship for that reason. He says specifically that 'No premonition was involved', and that Coffey told fireman John Podesta that he was going to see his mother,[349] classifying the case as just a 'curious coincidence'. Méheust does not refer to this case at all.

It has to be said that, since there is no positive reason whatever to suppose that Coffey acted on the basis of a premonition of any kind, this is a prime example of how something can be made out of nothing in the matter of paranormal activity.

(IS,12c) Stevenson very briefly records that **Major Archibald Butt** (a military aide to US President Taft, and his close friend and advisor), who died on the *Titanic*,

345 Stevenson (1), p. 162.

346 Gardner (1), p. 19 **(MG,10)**.

347 Brown, p.22 **(RB,13)**.

348 The *Hampshire Independent*, 20 April, 1912; the *Titanic Commutator*, December, 1964.

349 Behe, p. 35 **(GB,cc,34)**.

wrote to his sister-in-law, Mrs Clara Butt, on 23 February, 1912, saying of his proposed trip to Europe:

> *Don't forget that all my papers are in the storage warehouse, and if the old ship goes down you will find my affairs in shipshape condition. As I always write to you in this way whenever I go anywhere, you will not be bothered by presentiments now.*

Stevenson points out that Butt wrote this before he knew that he would return from Europe on *Titanic*. He uses a collection of Butt's letters as his source.[350] Brown simply repeats Stevenson's account, although she claims only that 'one could speculate' on whether Butt 'might not have had a slight premonition of disaster'.[351] Gardner, too uses Stevenson's report.[352]

Behe (who names Butt's sister-in-law as Mrs *Lewis* Butt) registers that Butt was having 'personal forebodings of approaching danger' and insisted that he had 'never had such a peculiar and constant feeling of impending trouble'.[353] The feeling was strong enough to cause him to cancel his bookings, and when the President talked him out of this Butt had his will drawn up. Taft himself later commented that Butt 'told some of the Secret Service people who witnessed the will for him that he

350 Stevenson (1), p. 162. The collection is *Taft and Roosevelt: The Intimate Letters of Archie Butt* (1930).

351 Brown, p. 60 (**RB,28**).

352 Gardner (1), pp. 19-20 (**MG, 11**).

353 Behe, pp. 120-122 (**GB,pr,3**).

had an unaccountable feeling that he would encounter some terrible danger before he returned'. Another friend of Butt's confirms that for several weeks Butt had been unable to shake off the 'strongest feeling he had ever had in his life that he was to be at the centre of some awful calamity.' But Behe somewhat undermines his classification of this case as a 'probable' psychic phenomenon when he also claims that during Butt's stay in Italy 'he apparently felt that the danger would soon be past', telling the Italian Minister to Mexico that he would get back to Washington in time and that 'when I step aboard *Titanic*, I shall feel absolutely safe. You know she is unsinkable.' Behe, too, quotes the collection of Butt's letters as his source, but also cites five newspapers. He comments that Butt's presentiments of danger were not focused specifically upon *Titanic*, but were connected with his trip in general.

When Goss and Behe take up the Butt case again in *Lost at Sea*, they cite Behe's earlier book and one additional newspaper source.[354] Perhaps because of what they found in that additional source, they now claim that by the time he arrived in London 'Butt's presentiments seem to have returned and intensified.' Butt was 'strangely depressed' for several days before *Titanic* sailed, and his friends were concerned. He told them on 9 April, 'I must go along to see Westminster Abbey, because if I miss the abbey now

354 Goss and Behe, pp. 233-235 **(G&B,7)**. The newspaper is the *Southern Daily Echo* (Southampton), 22 April, 1912. Later still Behe was to publish four volumes on Butt: three volumes called *Archie* (2010), and *A Death on the Titanic* (2011).

I shall never see it again.'[355] The authors are not especially impressed by this remark, but find it 'difficult to fathom' why Butt's depression would suddenly become so acute as to elicit comment from his friends.

Méheust uses Behe as his source. He does not mention the later book by Goss and Behe, but he also relates the Westminster Abbey incident.[356] He believes the Butt case is a perfect example of the 'long-lasting' premonitions that constitute the most intriguing characteristic of his corpus. But there are some slight confusions in his treatment. He mistakenly calls Major Butt's sister-in-law his 'niece' (twice). And he talks of Butt giving up his place on the 'old German ship' (which is the SS *Berlin*, on which Butt sailed *to* Europe) for one on *Titanic*, saying this is an excellent instance of someone taking a precaution against a premonition and thereby contributing to the realisation of the premonition itself. Without exactly ascribing Butt's depression to his stressful circumstances – Butt was the friend of *both* of the participants in a battle for the presidential nomination: Taft and Theodore Roosevelt – Méheust conjectures that they may somehow be behind Butt's premonition of death (although, in fact, this is not at all a precise description of Butt's depression – at a later point Méheust suggests that Butt 'fears nothing in particular').[357] He also suggests that a scan of Butt's correspondence indicates that he was far from foreseeing

355 Behe gives no source for this quote, but one might assume that this is the *Southern Daily Echo*.

356 Méheust, pp. 86, 95 (**BM,16**).

357 Méheust, p. 222.

catastrophe before each crossing of the Atlantic, which is what he claimed to Mrs Butt. He rates the Butt case as two-stars-plus.[358]

Behe understates the case in saying that Butt's fears were not focused on *Titanic*. Their nature is particularly vague (Behe assumes at one point that Butt expected to return to Washington, but only having passed through some great personal danger). And although Méheust considers them long-lasting, there are indications that, to some extent, they came and went. Then there is the confusion over whether or not Butt foresaw catastrophe before each crossing. Stevenson, too, points out that, on the three previous occasions when he was travelling, Butt's letters to his sister-in-law contained 'no predictions of disaster such as he subsequently claimed … he "always" made'.[359] But it is not clear whether he is referring to all journeys or specifically to Atlantic crossings, and, in any case, the question remains of why Butt should make this claim if it is not true.

The eminence of Butt (as well as his allegedly heroic conduct during the sinking) may well have contributed to the relative prominence of this case. Long-lasting or not, moreover, it is very hard to see that Butt's fears relate specifically in any significant way to *Titanic*.

In the 'DISCUSSION' of his cases in his first article Stevenson admits that they differ 'in the accuracy of recording and witnessing', and that some people forget

358 Méheust, pp. 173-174.

359 Stevenson (1), p. 163.

that they have repeatedly predicted disaster, so that it is only coincidence when events actually turn out as 'foreseen'.[360] He reminds us that for an experience to count as precognition, we must exclude rational inference 'as far as possible'. Citing a book by Saltmarsh as particularly good on the difference between precognition and inference,[361] he recognises wide variations in the capacity for inference, and lists the following features as important in distinguishing between the two: (a) number of items that match between prediction and actual event; (b) accuracy of timing; (c) nature of the items that match.

His point that the greater the number of matching items, the greater the 'probability' of precognition has some general validity, but he indicates that as many as ten items may match without our excluding inference completely, and the point remains vague. The assertion that a general warning to beware of water is commonly given by fortune-tellers and is plausible in the context of the number of marine disasters between 1870 and 1914 is not strictly relevant to discussion of (b), but leads into repetition of the reminder that we tend to forget unfulfilled prophecies, and the claim that Stead's 'references to shipwrecks' should be regarded as topical stories and analogies rather than instances of precognition.[362] In discussing (c), Stevenson suggests the nature of matching items becomes 'of great importance' in further analysis of the data, and compares and contrasts some of his cases.

---

360 Stevenson (1), p. 163.

361 Stevenson (1), p. 163. The book is H.F. Saltmarsh, *Foreknowledge* (1938).

362 Stevenson (1), p. 165.

In citing Tyrell as arguing that collective experiences are very important in strengthening the evidence for apparitions, but that collective hallucinations can occur,[363] Stevenson urges that we should not ignore the latter possibility. He now suggests that the *Titanic* cases differ from the 'usual' examples of collectively perceived apparitions, in that the percipients were separated in space and that some of their perceptions differed in the times of their occurrence. But he argues that the 'collectivity' of these cases cannot be regarded as an instance of 'infectious hallucinations', since none of the percipients knew, or had heard of, the others. (He also claims, naively, that all of the experiences were told to at least one witness before the events occurred, or became 'normally' known to the percipients.)[364] Yet it is scarcely worth questioning Stevenson's reasoning here, because he goes on to point out that for the most part each perception differs from the others 'as to details in the experience', so that no one experience gains any additional strength as a paranormal phenomenon from the occurrence of the others.[365] Not only does this admission render the reference to Tyrrell irrelevant, it also seriously undermines Stevenson's emphasis on collective experiences at the beginning of his article.

Stevenson goes on to discuss extrasensory perception as such, in which he clearly believes, saying that it 'depends on the presence of an obscure faculty possessed more abundantly by some people than by others' and varies

363 G.N.M. Tyrrell, *Apparitions* (1953).

364 Stevenson (1), p. 166.

365 Stevenson (1), p. 166.

within any one person at different times.[366] Indeed, he has a particular theory:

> *Granting the faculty for extrasensory perception and its operation, the incoming stimuli may activate or push into consciousness images already present in the subconscious layers of the percipient's mind. The images which become conscious then vary according to the available contents in the different stimulated minds of the percipients.*[367]

Unfortunately, this theory leaves a number of crucial obscurities, which reference back to a number of his cases does nothing to elucidate. To what exactly does 'incoming stimuli' refer? Are they themselves conscious or unconscious? If they 'may' push images from the subconscious into the conscious mind, are there experiences where this is not the case? If so, to what do these amount? And Stevenson's claim that 'The relationship between the contents (available images) in the mind of a percipient and extrasensory communications deserves much further study'[368] is not in the least surprising! A footnote complicates matters still further, in saying that 'Images almost immediately attract associations which may then influence further statements and possibly perceptions'. What precisely he is referring to when he says that 'we have some evidence that available mental

366 Stevenson (1), p. 167.

367 Stevenson (1), p. 167.

368 Stevenson (1), pp. 167-168.

images can modify the actual perceptions' is not made clear, although he speculates that future studies may show to what extent perceptions are 'modified or deflected by existing images of the mind'. Curiously, the net effect of Stevenson's reflections is to give us less confidence in the stability and reality of extrasensory perception.

He also says that our present knowledge does not indicate whether the strong emotions experienced by many of his percipients result from the vividness of the perception or are 'an integral part of the communications', although the consequences of the latter are left unexplored.[369] He wonders why, granted that strong emotional ties must have connected nearly all of those on board with friends and relatives on shore, there were not still more perceptions. He can only suppose that many of those experiencing strong emotion on the sinking ship did not have a susceptible percipient among families and friends, and suggests that the thoughts of such persons do not always or even often focus on loved ones at home, but on other matters – measures to save life, or even absurd trivia. He concludes, unsurprisingly, that, although personal attachments and strong emotions seem to facilitate extrasensory perception, they do not alone suffice to produce them; nor are they necessary to such perceptions.[370]

Stevenson ends his first article by reminding us that three of his percipients (Middleton, Stead and Hays) seem to have had warning experiences which they did

369 Stevenson (1), p. 168.

370 Stevenson (1), p. 169.

not apply to themselves sufficiently to take appropriate action, suggesting that accurate predictions probably occur too rarely to form a reasonable basis for action. But he believes that we should take an interest in the motives of those who do act upon premonitions, and argues that a climate more favourable to psychical experiences might encourage more people to do so. He does not think that any of his cases is strong evidence of acting upon unconscious precognition, which is suggested by Cox's report, and refers to a superstitious fear of maiden voyages as a possible reason for cancellation of *Titanic* tickets, although he leaves open the possibility that some people reacted sensibly to an unconscious precognition while attributing their behaviour to an irrational belief.[371]

In general, Stevenson's separate discussion of his cases is no more impressive than the opening of the piece. Despite his belief in extrasensory perception, he is tentative in his claims, and there is some confusion and near-contradiction in his reasoning. He devotes a fair amount of space to W.T. Stead and relatively little to each of his other cases. Yet, he raises some interesting points, making some progress towards bringing out, though not clarifying, some of the key issues.

Published nearly five years after the first, Stevenson's second article treats seven more cases.

CASES

371 Stevenson (1), pp. 170-171.

(IS,13) Stevenson records[372] that in a letter sent to the American Society for Psychical Research shortly after the loss of the *Titanic*, and included in an article by W.F. Prince,[373] **Mr M.** claims that he dreamed, between 10.30pm on 14 April and 2.20am on 15 April, 1912, that his dead father came into the room and told a family group 'that there had been a terrible accident at sea, that an ocean liner had run into an iceberg, and that a great many people had been drowned.' The next morning Mr M. read the news of the loss of the *Titanic*, and told his wife of his dream. He notes the curious 'accuracy' of his dream, although the reports that reached Boston on 15 April were that no lives had been lost. Prince records vaguely that Mr M.'s 'report' was made 'within about three weeks',[374] and weakly adds that, although corroborations were not given, 'a trusted member of the Society knows Mr M. well and considers him reliable.'[375]

Stevenson is suspicious that Mr M. modified his account of the dream later, setting its last possible time (2.20am) as that when *Titanic* sank, but again he does not take into account the time-difference between Boston and the ship's time. And because of the discrepancy that Stevenson notes between Mr M.'s claim that he read of the loss of *Titanic* the next morning and his acknowledgement that such news was not available at the time, it is a little surprising that he should believe that there is 'no reason

372 Stevenson (2), pp. 211-212.

373 'Some Coincidental Dreams (Continued)' (1919).

374 This may relate Mr M's dating his letter 6 May.

375 Stevenson (2), p. 211-212.

to doubt' that Mr M. was accurate in recalling the *date* of his dream.

Gardner says that Mr M.'s letter was received 'several weeks' after the sinking.[376] Neither Brown nor Behe mentions the case. Méheust follows Stevenson's treatment of it quite closely.[377] He notes in Part III of his book, where he rates the case as only one-star-plus, that the account was probably modified somewhat after the event, suggesting that if the memory of the dream had been modified even more the name of the *Titanic* would have figured in it. He does not exclude the possibility that Mr M., who had no connection with *Titanic*, was simply one of the people who, by chance, dreamed of a shipwreck on the night in question[378] – something also, perhaps, suggested by the title of Prince's article: 'Some Coincidental Dreams'. Later in his book Méheust uses Mr M.'s case to illustrate the point that dreams use things from everyday life to underline the exceptional (even lethal) nature of the event.[379]

(IS,14) Stevenson says that in a report on spontaneous telepathic experiences in 1923, Mrs Henry Sidgwick, a spiritualist, quotes a letter sent by Miss Alice L. Head, who asked that pseudonyms be substituted for all real names.[380] The letter, dated 4 July, 1912, tells of a friend,

376 Gardner (1), p. 20 **(MG,12)**.

377 Méheust, pp. 127-128 **(BM,62)**.

378 Méheust, p. 194. He mistakenly lists this case twice in Part III, chapter 6, with the different headings 'E.M.' (p. 194) and 'M.M.' (p. 200).

379 Méheust, p. 214.

380 Stevenson (2), pp. 213-214. The article is: Mrs Henry Sidgwick, 'An Examination and Analysis of Cases of Telepathy between Living Persons' (1923).

'Miss Margaret Simpson', who lost her brother in the wreck of the *Titanic*. She knew that he had taken a post on the ship, but her married sister, '**Mrs Henderson**', did not. Mrs Henderson, writing a letter to another sister on 19 April, 1912, claimed to have seen the wife and child of the lost brother 'crying and clinging to one another' on 16 April: 'I seemed to be in a kind of dream and yet I was wide awake and had not even been thinking of them.' In a further letter, dated 13 June, she added: 'I was alone in the house, and they seemed to appear to me in a sort of mist; I could not see their faces.' She said she had told two friends of her experience that evening. To corroborate this account by Miss Head, Margaret Simpson also signed the letter.

As Stevenson acknowledges, unless this is to be taken as a case of telepathy, it is potentially postcognitive rather than precognitive.[381] And Gardner's trenchant evaluation – 'Since we don't know the names of anyone involved, and Mrs Sidgwick is reporting a letter from a woman who in turn is reporting what a friend told her about a dream of the friend's sister, the anecdote seems hardly worth mentioning'[382] – has more than a little justification. Somewhat bizarrely, Stevenson himself, who claims that Mrs Henderson had just heard of the wreck of *Titanic*, but emphasises that she did not know her brother was on board, ignores the tortuous line of communication and lists what 'an investigator of this case today' would want know about the 'officer's' last moments and about

381 Stevenson (2), p.224, footnote 6.

382 Gardner (1), p. 20 (**MG,13**).

the 'relationship between the percipient and her brother, sisters, and niece'!

Brown and Behe again do not deal with this experience. But Méheust takes it up (although, using Stevenson as his source, he mistakenly names Behe in a footnote). Like Stevenson, he simply ignores the very indirect nature of the evidence, and even arbitrarily *adds* the detail that Mrs Henderson 'sensed her brother's death'.[383] In Part III of his book, despite the fact that he acknowledges there is no corroborative support for what Mrs Henderson says, he regards her story as 'very strong' and argues – building on his own unjustified addition – that it is extremely unlikely that she would have dreamed of her sister-in-law and niece in distress 'at the very moment' when her brother had just died, especially since she did not know he was on *Titanic*.

Once more, Méheust stresses that the 'dream' was 'indirect and allusive': the idea of a maritime catastrophe would have appeared more clearly if the dream had been made up or modified after the event. He claims that here again we are faced with a dream that has the typical structure of telepathic dreams, and concludes that there is 'every reason to think' that the dream records a real telepathic communication, rating the case as three stars and including it among his strongest eight cases.[384] When discussing psychic processes, he talks of the 'indirect routes' taken by dreams and agrees with Stevenson that, to understand why Mrs Henderson dreamed of her brother's child and her sister-in-law rather than of her brother,

383 Méheust, pp. 132-133 (**BM,69**).

384 Méheust, pp. 194-195.

we would need to know more about Mrs Henderson's relations with her brother and sister-in-law.[385]

(IS,15) Stevenson claims that on the morning of 15 April, 1912, **Mr Black**, the company manager of a travelling troupe of actors, had to be forcibly awakened from a deep sleep, and said: 'Folks, something terrible has happened! I saw a large ship sinking and hundreds of people being drowned.' (He claimed to have seen the (1906) San Francisco earthquake and fire in the same way 'at the time it happened'.) On the same morning, the company agent received word over the telegraph of the *Titanic* disaster. Black's reaction was to say: 'I told you so! I saw it!'. He never discussed the matter any further.[386] Stevenson learned of this incident in a letter from a Mr Sharpe, in 1962. When he corresponded with Sharpe to point out that, by the morning of 15 April, it was not known that hundreds had drowned, Sharpe replied only that he believed they heard the news 'early in the morning'. Rather arbitrarily, Stevenson speculates that the company agent may have embellished the story by adding the details of the loss of the ship and people, and, even more arbitrarily, wonders whether the agent himself had some extrasensory perception of the disaster.

Gardner accuses Stevenson of stretching the anecdote 'to the limit' in his attempt to account for a discrepancy in the story.[387] Neither Brown nor Behe refers to the case.

385 Méheust, pp. 214-215.

386 Stevenson (2), pp. 214-215.

387 Gardner (1), pp. 20-21 **(MG,14)**.

Citing Stevenson, Méheust uses his details,[388] and in Part III of his book again stresses that the name of the *Titanic* is not mentioned, arguing that this undermines the hypotheses of subliminal inference and a modification of the dream after the event. Stressing that Black had no connection with *Titanic*, he once more falls back on the possibility that Black is just one of those who happened to dream of a shipwreck during the night of 14 April. Without questioning the reliability of his testimony, he attaches importance to Black's premonition of the San Francisco earthquake, but awards the *Titanic* case only one-star-plus.[389]

(IS,16) In the depths of Brazil on the night of the *Titanic* sinking, Stevenson says, Mrs **Ida Lorenz** awakened her husband and asked him to note down the exact time, since she had seen a great ship which had hit an iceberg: 'It had three funnels. There was great commotion on the ship, but the band was playing music. She said the name was *Titanic*.' It was several weeks before newspapers carrying news of the sinking of *Titanic* reached their little village.[390] Having been told this story by Mrs Lorenz's son, who had heard it from his father, Stevenson had 'no reason to doubt' that Mrs Lorenz's son had 'fairly accurately' reproduced his father's narration of the episode. But, for once, he did not think that this merely second-hand evidence alone warranted full confidence.

388 Méheust, pp. 110-111 (**BM,48**).

389 Méheust, p. 189. In Part III of his book Méheust mistakenly refers (twice) to Sharpe as having the dream.

390 Stevenson (2), pp. 215-217.

Then, several days later, Mrs Lorenz's daughter told him that (at the age of four) she had heard of her mother's premonitory dream the morning after the night of its occurrence, adding that her mother had said the proof of the dream lay in the fatigue she had felt from working hard to save the passengers on the ship. The daughter also recalled seeing the note her father had made of the time and day of the dream, and comparing it with newspaper reports. She cited 'some other examples' of her mother's extrasensory perception. Stevenson muses that the fourth funnel may have been 'dropped' by one of the narrators, or by the percipient herself. He says that the other details of the dream establish the match of the reported dream and the sinking of the *Titanic* 'quite firmly'.

Gardner is understandably sceptical that Stevenson should regard the account of someone who was four at the time as corroboration.[391] Brown and Behe do not refer to this case. Méheust, without citing any sources at all, *adds* that Mrs Lorenz had her dream at around 11pm on 14 April.[392] In general, he appears rather muddled in his treatment of time and place. He argues that, while, normally, naming *Titanic* in a dream would give it suspicious precision, the delay in the arrival of news of the sinking counterbalances this. But it is far from clear why this should be so, and Méheust now claims that 'At the time of her dream, she was therefore three weeks behind the news and probably did not know that *Titanic* was making its maiden voyage'. Moreover, his claim that as a result of Lorenz's location

391 Gardner (1), p.21 **(MG,15)**.

392 Méheust, p. 131 **(BM,68)**.

at the time 'the precision of her dream, which, if she had lived in London, would have been a handicap, becomes a trump card' is less than convincing, as is his belief that the inaccuracy of 'three funnels' shows that the account of the dream was 'probably' not modified after news of the sinking. He rates the incident as three stars.[393]

It is remarkable, especially in light of the fact that Méheust includes this case in his list of eight favoured cases (although it meets only some of the criteria he has set), that he pays no attention whatever to the dubious reliability of narration made, at two removes, up to 50 years after the event!

(IS,17) Stevenson says that during the night of 12 April, 1912, at the age of fourteen, a girl, later **Mrs Charles Hughes**, was awakened by a dream in which she was on the main road in Hanford (in the English Potteries) and saw 'a very large ship a short distance away as if in Trentham Park'. There were figures walking about on it 'and then suddenly it lowered at one end and I heard a terrific scream'. She went back to sleep and saw 'the very same scene' once again. Being very upset, she told her mother the following morning. Subsequently, her attention was drawn to a picture in that morning's *Daily Mirror*, showing the crew serving on the *Titanic*. She recognised her uncle in it, and her mother broke the news to her grandmother that her son had been drowned, 'a scene I'll never forget'.[394]

Stevenson learned of this story in a letter written to him by Mrs Hughes in 1963. When he visited her, she

393 Méheust, p. 195.

394 Stevenson (2), pp. 217-219.

added that her uncle's wife had known he was on the *Titanic* but the rest of the family had not. She emphasised the 'vividness and emotional intensity' of her two dreams, and stressed that they were the same. She used to go to Trentham Park during her holidays, but also to another park in Hanley, which 'seemed to be as prominently in her conscious mind as Trentham Park'. Stevenson was unable to get independent corroboration of any of this, since both Hughes's mother and her grandmother had died.

Stevenson learned from Walter Lord that the magazine *Sphere*, on 4 May, 1912 – after the family would have had news of the death – carried a photograph of a group of *Titanic* engineers which included Mrs Hughes's uncle (Leonard Hodgkinson, Fourth Engineer). He also discovered that the *Daily Mirror* did not publish the photo (of which they nonetheless sent him a copy), but thought it 'probable' that some other newspaper did, and that Mrs Hughes erroneously attributed it to the *Daily Mirror*. It appears that he did not check other newspapers. He also acknowledged that she made a mistake in claiming to have seen the photo on 15 April, when the loss of *Titanic* was not known. Mrs Hughes told him that it 'might have been Tuesday'. Stevenson also found out that there was a very large lake adjoining Trentham Park which would be included in the field of vision, so that a boat in the lake might well seem to be 'as if in Trentham Park'. His point seems to be that sailing a toy boat on the lake is what triggered Mrs Hughes's images, but it is difficult to understand why he should make so much of this last point. Indeed, uncharacteristically, Stevenson's whole account contains substantial repetition and redundant detail.

Gardner makes no substantive comment on Stevenson's story,[395] and neither Brown nor Behe mentions it. Yet, once again, citing Stevenson as his source. Méheust includes this in his 'hard core' of eight favoured cases of paranormal activity. However, he mistakenly says Mrs Hughes told her *grandmother* the next morning, and puts the grandmother at the centre of the incident of seeing the photo.[396] He either has another – unnamed – source or is adding a few details of his own making, since the account of this incident is quite different from Stevenson's. In any case, Méheust has Mr Hodgkinson transferred onto *Titanic* both 'some weeks earlier' and 'at the last moment'.[397] In Part III of his book he claims that this story is 'very strong', and again argues that the fact that *Titanic* is not named in the dream (in which there is an 'absence of references to the drama') suggests that 'the dream was related as it was fixed in her memory just after the events'. In fact, he says that this is his 'ideal' kind of case. He thinks that the strange 'structure' of the dream supports its 'reality', apparently believing that the vision of a huge ship in a public garden sinking into the ground is something that we could never invent! He claims that the dream is definitely premonitory and rates the case three stars.

In a section reviewing the processes involved in the examples in his dossier ('Analysis of the Processes'), Méheust turns to the complexity of dream-work and the indirectness with which dreams 'say' things. He sees Mrs

395 Gardner (1), p. 21 (**MG,16**).

396 Méheust, pp. 109, 128 (**BM,47**).

397 Méheust, p. 128 and p. 188.

Hughes's dream as an extraordinary example, with the ship's dipping and beginning to bury itself into the ground representing daily reality breaking up, 'as if civilisation itself were sinking … Buñuel could not have done better'. He uses Stevenson's discovery concerning the nearby lake as an illustration of Freud's view that dreams use *anything* as means of expression: the paranormal 'information' slips through by using the girl's recent memories of sailing toy boats on the lake.[398] One has the impression that Méheust is carried away, at this point, by his general theorising about dreams. It is almost as if Mrs Hughes's account fifty years after the event – the reliability of which he at no stage questions, or raises – could be used as material to exemplify certain points about paranormal dreams whether or not it accurately records what she actually dreamed.

(IS,18) According to Stevenson, **Miss Norah Mathews**, at about eleven years of age, knowing that her mother, Mary Roberts, is about to sail on the *Titanic* feels sad when she hears her mother singing '… I don't care what becomes of me …', and has a 'strange sense of doom'. She tells her mother that she does not want her to sail on the ship. Her father is impressed, since she was nine years old when she first had 'most powerful and correct impressions'. Miss Mathews sent a 'written account' of her experience and a covering letter to Stevenson in 1964, and in a follow-up letter claimed that she thought 'something was going to happen both to my mother and also to the fine new boat', but could not say exactly how long before

398 Méheust, p.213.

Titanic sailed she had these thoughts.[399] Stevenson admits that he could not obtain corroboration of the 'warning' Miss Mathews had given, but says she sent him accounts of other impressions or visual images she had had when some misfortune was about to happen or was happening to a member of her family, including another sinking (of the *Rohilla*) from which her mother escaped.

As Gardner points out, Stevenson reports no effort to verify the later escape ('about 1916'),[400] and the whole case seems particularly vague, and uncertain, being based, once again, on the evidence of a single person some fifty years after the event. Brown and Behe do not treat the case, but Méheust considers it 'intriguing', since subliminal inference can virtually be ruled out in an eleven-year-old.[401] He finds it difficult to explain the 'brutal' reaction of the girl, who might have been expected to be fascinated and excited at the prospect of her mother on the biggest ship in the world. He also stresses the later sinking, speculating that the hospital-ship – which he mistakenly names *Rhodilla* – was probably torpedoed by a German submarine.[402] In general, Méheust over-dramatises the case somewhat, though at least he seems to see the potential importance of the actual words the mother had been singing: 'I don't care what becomes of me'. He rates the case as two stars.

Simple research – apparently not carried out by

399 Stevenson (2), pp. 219-220.

400 Gardner (1), p. 21 (**MG,17**).

401 Méheust, pp. 90, 171 (**BM,21**).

402 Méheust, p. 171. He also erroneously refers to 'Ian Wilson', rather than Ian Stevenson at one point.

Stevenson, Gardner or Méheust – shows that, in a famous incident, the *Rohilla* hit rocks just off Whitby in 1914, and that the nurse, Mary Roberts, was indeed one of the 145 people saved.[403] But Miss Mathews's inaccurate dating of the sinking does nothing to strengthen this case for precognition.

(IS,19) At the age of thirty-three, **Colin Macdonald**, says Stevenson, three times declined the offer of the prestigious post of Second Engineer on *Titanic*, having a 'hunch' – no image of the sinking, just a strong impression that 'something was going to happen to the ship' – that he should not sail on her. Macdonald's daughter told Stevenson of this in an interview in 1964, also loaning him a newspaper account which, duly corrected, accorded with what her father remembered and often narrated to his family and others. She also said her father had had other experiences of 'non-rational foreknowledge of events affecting himself or their family'.[404]

Neither Stevenson himself nor Gardner[405] makes any comment on this case. Brown and Behe omit it altogether. Méheust does not make much of it either,[406] though he stresses that Macdonald's feeling must have been powerful, since one does not turn down such a significant offer of promotion without good reason. He classes the case as

403 See, for instance: www.eskside.co.uk/ss_rohilla/rohilla_tragedy.htm

404 Stevenson (2), pp. 220-221. In footnote 4 on p. 224, Stevenson admits that we do not know when this experience occurred, and unjustifiably suggests that it was 'almost certainly … some months before the ship sailed.'

405 Gardner (1), p. 22 **(MG,18)**.

406 Méheust, p. 83 **(BM,10)**.

one-star-plus.[407] Needless to say, this is all very flimsy, especially as the report is once more made fifty years afterwards.

Stevenson's second article is different in most respects from the first. There is no reference at all to W.T. Stead in this second piece. It introduces only half as many cases, and devotes much more space to them (including a 'Comment' section on all but one), with less than a third of the piece occupied by 'Discussion' at the end, and little of this referring back specifically to experiences already examined. Except in the first two instances (both of which were published but unknown to him before his first article), he had personal contact with either the percipient or someone related to the percipient. This adds a certain immediacy to his reports, but has the disadvantage that almost all of his evidence dates from fifty years or more after the disaster.

In short, Stevenson appears to have sharpened and refined his methodology and his presentation, to a significant degree (his bibliographical information is included as 'References' at the end of his second article, not in footnotes, as in the first). Even his introduction is more focused, not referring to 'collective' experiences at all, and stressing the questions of timing and 'independent corroboration from other persons' for the cases. All seven cases came to his attention after the publication of his first article. He claims – absurdly, if one takes newspapers into account – that the two articles together cover 'the entire

407 Méheust, pp. 170-171.

collection of known cases related to the *Titanic* disaster.[408] He again acknowledges the help of Walter Lord, and, on this occasion, the support of the Parapsychology Foundation.[409]

After examining his seven new cases, Stevenson claims, in a section again headed 'DISCUSSION', that, together with those included in his first article, they make the *Titanic* disaster 'the one most associated with reported extrasensory perception', although he admits that there may be other disasters where such reports have not come to the public attention.[410] He thinks this may be due to 'the combination of the numbers of persons involved in the disaster and its suddenness'. Contrasting the *Titanic* case with large-scale deaths in battles, he stresses its unexpectedness, suggesting that the sudden, unexpected anticipation of death 'generated a greater than usual amount of emotion and "agency" in the passengers', and repeats his point that strength of emotion is an important feature in 'successful agency in extrasensory perception', arguing that we have evidence from other studies of spontaneous cases and laboratory experiments that this is so.[411]

He suggests that personal relationships, too, seem to facilitate extrasensory perception, but argues that there are 'comparatively few' personal relationships between

408 Stevenson (2), p. 211.

409 Stevenson (2), p. 211, footnote 1.

410 Stevenson (2), p. 221.

411 Stevenson (2), p. 222.

people on *Titanic* and those experiencing premonitions.[412] However, his three paragraphs discussing these points are *extremely* confusing and entirely unconvincing. For one thing, he introduces two sets of crucial terms ('acquaintances and strangers', and 'agents and percipients') which he fails to explain at all adequately as his argument proceeds. The juxtaposition of 'acquaintances' and 'strangers' – which one would normally take as contrasting terms – as a single category ('strangers (or acquaintances only) to the people on the ship') is particularly disorienting: Stevenson actually takes to referring to cases where the percipient is *either* an acquaintance of, *or* a stranger to, the person on the ship as '"stranger" cases'.

Moreover, it turns out, bizarrely, that by 'agents' he means people on the ship who are the subject of the 'percipient's' premonition. This seems to be a particularly unfortunate term in itself, and has connotations of telepathy rather than premonition. Contrasting it with 'percipient', furthermore, becomes impossible, as Stevenson acknowledges, where a person on board is himself/herself alleged to have experienced a premonition. He wants to say that, whereas, in spontaneous cases in general, extrasensory perceptions of events happening to those we know occur 'rather rarely', the ratio of 'stranger' cases to 'personal relationship' cases is 'markedly different' with the *Titanic* disaster, being still higher. But, quite apart from the fact that the very sense of the claim itself is seriously undermined by terminological confusions,

412 Stevenson (2), pp. 222-223. He suggests there are personal relationships in only 4 of his 'nineteen' cases.

the statistical basis for it is so slender as to be entirely insignificant.

Stevenson goes on to say that many of his percipients claimed to have had other extrasensory experiences, although he insists that the information is 'rather scanty'.[413] He speculates that:

> *When motivation of agents runs high (as in the sinking of the Titanic) but personally interested potential percipients lack sufficient capacity for extrasensory perception, the 'message' may reach other percipients who lack personal interest in the event, but have thinner barriers to the penetration of the communication into consciousness.*[414]

His reason for making this suggestion (for which he gives no reference, much less any evidence) is that he thinks it may account for the alleged higher incidence of 'stranger' percipients in the case of *Titanic*. But, needless to say, this is simply to pile an apparently arbitrary speculation on top of a dubious premise. He is on safer ground in developing the point that capacity for extrasensory perception varies considerably in one percipient from time to time, and stressing that *Titanic* cases 'emphasise the importance of the dream state in heightening capacity', since a high proportion occurred during sleep. Yet whether he is justified in having 'no doubt' that for many people sleep 'provides better conditions for extrasensory perception

413 Stevenson (2), p. 223.

414 Stevenson (2), p. 223.

than does the waking state' is considerably more contentious.[415]

Stevenson implicitly reverts to the idea of 'collective' experiences near the end of his second article, saying that his cases provide an example of what C.D. Broad calls 'disseminated co-referential hallucinations'.[416] The term refers to 'hallucinations differing in content, but all referring to the same event or associated events', but it is hard to see that this advances Stevenson's argument in any way. He repeats his earlier point that his *Titanic* cases differ very much from each other, now stating that this contrasts with the 'usual' similarity of perceptions by persons viewing the same events occurring in their presence. For reasons that are unclear, he feels obliged at this point to stress that in psychical perceptions true details become 'distorted or blended with various other details associated in the mind of the percipient'.

Stevenson concludes his second article by saying that 'a preponderance … of contemporaneous perceptions occurred and also a relative increase in the number of precognitive perceptions as the time of the disaster approached', but he also makes the point that, although his series of cases is too small for any independent conclusions on this point, it does accord with the analyses of the time intervals in other series of spontaneous cases.[417]

Methodologically he is somewhat more sophisticated in his second article than in the first, and dwells at

415 Stevenson (2), pp. 223-224.

416 C.D. Broad, *Lectures on Psychical Research* (1962), p. 201.

417 Stevenson (2), pp. 224-225.

more length on each of the experiences he takes up. His concluding discussion also deals with aspects of extrasensory perception not raised in the first. Although there are again serious confusions in his argument, given the state of interest in, and knowledge about, paranormal phenomena in 1960, in the two articles as a whole his is quite a bold attempt to tackle matters that had received relatively little public attention but may have begun to generate interest.

CHAPTER 4

RUSTIE BROWN AND MARTIN GARDNER

RUSTIE BROWN

Rustie Brown was an American award-winning newspaper and magazine journalist, whose interest in *Titanic* was triggered by reading Walter Lord's *A Night to Remember*. In addition to *The Titanic, the Psychic, and the Sea* (1981), she published *The Mariner's Trivia Book* in 1986, which is said to be a 'compendium of unusual and useful information'.

In a Foreword to Brown's book, Alan Vaughan claims that 'few tragedies have been foretold by so many with so much accuracy', mentioning 'documented premonitions' and 'synchronicities (meaningful coincidences)'.[418] He gives no indication at all of what a 'meaningful coincidence' might be, but – like 'synchronicity' – it is a term probably coined

418 Brown, p. vii.

by Carl Jung, to refer to events occurring without causal relationship, yet apparently meaningfully related.

After making some general comments on *Titanic*, Brown, in her 'Preface to the Titanic Experience', begins by acknowledging that, following her reading of Lord's *A Night to Remember*, she became acquainted with Edwina MacKenzie (commonly referred to as Edwina Troutt). She listened to her accounts of premonitions connected with the *Titanic* disaster, and was 'absolutely enthralled with *Titanic* lore, the sea, and superstitions connected with it'. Over a ten-year period, Brown talked with every survivor she could find, as well as relatives and friends of survivors.[419] She admits, however, that a 'focal point' of her whole book is MacKenzie, whom she discovered to be living 'practically in my own back yard here in California' when her interest in *Titanic* was first aroused, so that one is bound to wonder to what extent MacKenzie's accounts are the source of Brown's many unattributed premonition anecdotes. Neither this issue nor that of the accuracy of any such accounts can be readily resolved, but it is worth bearing in mind that MacKenzie was 97 years old when Brown published her book.

Brown cites Herbert Greenhouse as saying that there were forebodings of disaster 'weeks in advance of the *Titanic*'s fatal voyage',[420] before recording that she visited Stevenson in 1977, to 'chat', then referring briefly to works by Alan Vaughan ('*nothing* happens by chance')[421] and

419 Brown, pp. 2-3.

420 Herbert Greenhouse, *Premonitions: A Leap into the Future* (1971).

421 Alan Vaughan, *Patterns of Prophecy* (1973).

David Seabury ('we bring about what we believe').[422] But she gives strongest emphasis to the research of William Cox,[423] who claimed that people did actually avoid accident-bound trains, having 'at a subconscious level, precognitive flashes that somehow altered their normal daily routine'. She stresses that *Titanic* carried only 58% of her passenger capacity. Brown also says that Maurice Maeterlinck speculated on the same theme in 1908 ('A ship that sinks usually has fewer passengers on board than usual; two trains that collide ... are generally emptier than on days on which these disasters do not happen').[424]

It is very easy to be severely critical of Brown's Preface, since her general discussion of premonitions is extremely unsatisfactory. Written some twenty years after the publication of Stevenson's first article, it is seriously lacking in methodological awareness and sophistication. Passing references to the London *Evening Standard*'s invitation to the public to send in their predictions to a 'premonition bureau' in 1967, and to the Aberfan disaster, add nothing to the case of *Titanic*, and if the points made by the authors she cites are to carry any weight, they require much more detailed examination. What is more, simply to *hint* that there is some significance in the fact that many people had 'negative (as well as positive) thoughts concerning the *Titanic*'s reaching New York' is woefully inadequate. The

422 David Seabury, *Pull Yourself Together* (1967).

423 W.E. Cox, 'Precognition: An Analysis, II' (1956). Gardner claims that Cox is best known for his 'tireless efforts to prove that Uri Geller's psychic powers are genuine' (Gardner (1), p. 17).

424 Brown, p. 6.

reference to twenty-two crew members who missed the boat, too, is particularly weak in the light of her admission that 'We will probably never know exactly what caused each to be late or not show up at all.' She gives no reference for Cox's work either here or in the Bibliography at the end of her book, making it clear in the text that her knowledge of Cox comes from a book by Charles Panati.[425] And although there is mention of an essay called 'Fate' by Maeterlinck, nowhere in her book does Brown give details.[426]

It is not a justification of these faults to say that it is 'up to the readers to decide' whether *Titanic* was 'hoo-doo'd', a victim of fickle fate, or an avoidable disaster.[427] But, at least, the Preface tells us something of Brown's intentions. She claims that many more survivors have come forth since Lord's book to tell their own stories, and that 'It's time to catch up',[428] although the exact relationship between this and the paranormal is left unexplained. Furthermore, her comment that 'No one has written a comprehensive book pertaining to the dozens of psychic happenings surrounding the *Titanic* experience – the premonitions, the superstitions, and the so-called "coincidences"', although giving a good indication of the content of her book, implies that this is what she is setting out to do. In fact, she mentions three aims: to bring the reader 'a bit closer to the remaining survivors', to perpetuate the

425 Brown, p. 5. Charles Panati, *Supersenses – Our Potential for Parasensory Experience* (1974).

426 This is presumably a reference to Maeterlinck's book, *La Sagesse et la destinée* (1899).

427 Brown, p. 6.

428 Brown, p. 6.

memory of those who survive 'in another realm', and to bring out 'a few small truths'. There is a modesty about this that may seem to disarm detailed criticisms,[429] but the vagueness of the Preface as a whole acts as a warning when we move on to look at her treatment of anecdotal cases, the first of which comes immediately after Brown has described MacKenzie's family background.

It is something of a puzzle that Brown does not mention 11 of Stevenson's cases at all, including all 7 from his second article. But she takes 15 of those from his first article and often does no more than repeat the details that he gives. More generally, there are, however, 30 instances where Brown's treatment of cases is the first in book form. Behe, like Méheust, takes up many of these, and both include a higher proportion than might be expected among the experiences they regard as being the most likely to be psychic. Some of them have also become among the most famous of *Titanic* 'premonitions'.

On the other hand, there is no point in even registering all of the cases where Brown says simply that someone cancelled their *Titanic* passage, without even faintly suggesting that any premonitions were involved.[430]

---

429 Although there are a number of 'facts' in the book that are simply mistaken. Brown talks, for instance, of a '300-foot incision in the great ship's right side' (p. 34).

430 It is now known that more than 50 passengers – including some with famous names, like J.P. Morgan – cancelled bookings on the ship. In addition, a number of crew members who had signed on for the voyage did not appear for muster on 10 April and were classed as 'failed to join'. Those who passed muster, then left the ship and failed to return by sailing time were classed as 'deserted'. There were around 24 crew members in the two categories combined. See www.encyclopedia-titanica.org/canceled-titanic-passages.html

Moreover, we need to remember that Brown's terms of reference in her book are very wide and encompass a great deal more than premonitions, or even the paranormal. She is essentially seeking to bring the *Titanic* story to life, including all kinds of details to which no particular mystery is attached, as well as fascinating facts of human interest.[431] Quite often it is not clear what, if anything, an isolated fact is meant to imply. In such cases – early examples are the report that Thomas Andrews confided to a stewardess that he had become 'very sad since he left home',[432] and reference to Quartermaster Rowe's entry in the ship's log: 'There was not a single sea bird following us leaving Fastnet Rock', to which Brown adds: 'most unusual'.[433] Any assumption that something premonitory or even paranormal is being hinted at in such instances is less than fully justified, although some of the cases below might be seen to fall in that category.

CASES

(RB,1) According to Brown, when the **father of Mrs Louise Finlay**, a friend of Edwina MacKenzie, heard that Edwina was due to sail on *Titanic*, he told her that he would rather she were sailing on a ship that had actually completed its maiden voyage. MacKenzie told him not to be silly, that *Titanic* was the biggest ship that had ever been

431 See, for example, references to the lack of binoculars in the crow's nest, as well as the coal-bunker fire: Brown, p. 20.

432 Brown, p. 18, footnote 2.

433 Brown, p. 23.

built, 'unsinkable'.[434] Brown's source for this anecdote is a letter from Mrs Finlay. None of the later commentators mentions this case. (Gardner does not refer to any of the cases that Brown is the first to introduce, and was quite possibly unacquainted with her book.)

(RB,2) On boarding *Titanic* Miss **Nora Keane** dropped her rosary and her prayer book. From then on she was convinced that the ship was doomed. Brown's source here is MacKenzie, who claimed that Keane was perpetually saying : 'Glory be to God, I should have never taken this boat. It will never reach New York.'[435] She announced on the evening of the sinking that 'tonight might just be the night of disaster',[436] and, when the *Titanic* stopped dead in the water, said, 'Sure I knew this ship was going to meet a bad end.'[437]

Behe treats the story at some length, taking it further back and saying that Keane wrote a letter to her brother in America, saying that she did not want to sail on *Titanic*, and that a smaller, older boat 'might be the safest'.[438] But he persuaded her to take *Titanic*. As the tender approached the ship in Queenstown, moreover, her nephew is said to have noticed under her name the numbers '3909 04', which as a mirror image may be read as 'NO POPE'. In later years Keane said that she felt that the message that the numbers conveyed indicated 'future bad luck for the

434 Brown, p. 11.

435 Brown, p. 13.

436 Brown, p. 28.

437 Brown, p. 33.

438 Behe, pp. 32-35 (**GB,cc,33**).

ship', and that it would not reach New York. Behe, too, says that Keane's cabin-mate, MacKenzie, claimed that Keane referred several times to her misgivings during the first three days of the voyage. He comments that MacKenzie subsequently said that Keane repeated her prediction of doom so many times that it became quite annoying to listen to it, although none of her 1912 accounts of the disaster mention Keane's repeated forecast. He speculates that MacKenzie may have added an emphasis that was absent in her original memories.

Behe also believes that Keane's forebodings seem to have originated from a combination of several superstitions (a mild form of 'maiden voyage phobia', a feeling that people were so proud of the 'unsinkable' ship that 'something would happen to show people that God is not mocked', and a belief that the 'NO POPE' message boded ill for *Titanic*'s future). He stresses that, in conversation with her nephew, Keane never mentioned having a premonition about the number, which, in any case, was definitely not *Titanic*'s official number. Behe does concede, however, that a possibility exists that 'Miss Keane may have experienced a genuine premonition of danger', which created a feeling of unease made more acute by the three superstitions. He quotes her great niece's report that Nora had another premonition later in her life, and believes it unfortunate that there is no *proof* that she had a premonition prior to and independent of the superstitions listed. Classifying Norah Keane's experiences as no more than a 'curious coincidence', he claims that 'for the time being' any psychic experience must be regarded as 'merely the result of coincidental events to which she attached a sinister meaning'.

Méheust follows Behe in his references to Nora Keane.[439] He stresses the religious side to her worries, and sees her case as another of his 'long-lasting' premonitions, but he otherwise adds nothing significant and classes the case as only one-star-plus.[440]

(RB,4) Brown received a letter in 1974 from one Richard Donnell, who told her that his aunt, **Mary A. Tripp** became violently ill four days before the sailing of *Titanic*. The day before the voyage she read her tea leaves to predict any improvement in her condition: 'Instead of imaging better health, the leaves formed a sinking ship. She immediately cancelled her reservation.'[441] None of the later commentators mentions this case.

(RB,6) One of MacKenzie's dining companions, says Brown, sent a cablegram to his wife, **Mrs Milling**, on 14 April, and – at a time and date unspecified – she wrote a reply from Denmark addressed to New York, to be held for her husband's arrival. In it she 'expressed fear that something horrible would happen to him'. He died in the *Titanic* disaster.[442] None of the later commentators mentions this case.

(RB,8) Brown relates that as they were leaving Southampton, a perfect stranger asked **Mrs Henry Harris**, 'Do you love life?', and, when she nodded, said, 'Well, then

439 Méheust, pp. 106, 122 **(BM,44)**.

440 Méheust, pp. 187-188.

441 Brown, p. 14.

442 Brown, p. 18, footnote 1.

get off this ship at Cherbourg, if we get that far.'[443] Harris could 'vaguely understand' why the man was upset, as the very beginning of *Titanic*'s voyage had been 'a bit ominous'.

Behe, classifying the case as just a curious coincidence, has the stranger standing next to Harris at the time of the *New York* incident, saying, 'This is a bad omen', and telling her that he was leaving *Titanic* at Cherbourg, 'if we get that far'. He comments that it is not known who the man was, or whether he did heed the omen.[444] Méheust does not refer to this case.

(RB,9) Brown says that Mrs Dorothy Pettet of Cornwall was taken to see *Titanic* leaving Southampton, and recalls how **Pettet's father** and the other grown-ups said to each other of the *New York* incident that 'the near accident was a bad omen – that the crew wouldn't like it either.'[445] None of the later commentators mentions Mrs Pettet.

(RB,10) Brown briefly mentions that **Alfred Vanderbilt** 'may have had bad vibrations about this maiden voyage', as he cancelled his passage on *Titanic* the night before sailing (though his 'psychic feelings' were not on target concerning the *Lusitania*).[446] Behe also records the cancellation, but says, somewhat more cautiously, that Vanderbilt did not explain his reasons publicly.[447] Méheust does not refer to the case.

443 Brown, p. 19.

444 Behe, pp. 30-31 **(GB,cc,29)**.

445 Brown, p. 19.

446 Brown, pp. 19-20.

447 Behe, p. 24 **(GB,cc,14f)**.

(RB,11) Brown records that the evening before the fashion writer and buyer, Miss Edith Louise Rosenbaum (who became, and is most commonly known as, **Edith Russell**) boarded *Titanic* 'a fortune teller had prophesied disaster'.[448] In any case, she had misgivings from the moment she set eyes on *Titanic*. These were accentuated by a 'very jumpy gangplank'. So much so that she asked if she could transfer herself and her luggage to another ship. Being told that, while she could sail on another vessel, all her luggage would have to stay on *Titanic*, she decided to stay with it, since she had not only her own very fashionable wardrobe on board, but also designer wardrobes of wealthy clients. She had a letter posted in Queenstown, telling her secretary of her strong feeling of uneasiness and impending disaster.[449] Brown also says later that Elwood Ullman wrote in an article that Edith's intuition was usually right about foreseeing accidents. He had access to her diaries, and claims that she escaped a shipwreck on the French liner, *Général Chanzy*.[450] Brown points out that the diary equally registers that Russell cancelled her reservation on the *Lusitania*: 'it would seem her intuitive powers were at work again.'[451]

Presumably referring to the same incident as Brown, Behe says that Russell visited a clairvoyant in Paris, on the evening of 9 April, and was advised: 'Don't take the boat

448 Brown, p. 92.

449 Brown, p. 21. Russell's letter includes the comment: 'I cannot get over my feeling of depression and premonition of trouble'.

450 Brown, p. 92.

451 Brown, p. 93.

you are planning to take'.[452] She was told she would lose 'all of her jewellery, all of her possessions and even her voice.' About to embark, she saw the gangplank moving, and told a White Star official, 'I'm not going on that ship. I want to get off.' She was 'frankly afraid', and deciding to stay on board because of her luggage, she asked an official to insure her merchandise when he returned to Paris: 'I've got a feeling. I've got a feeling.' She said later, 'I had this dreadful feeling that I never would arrive in America in that ship', but she was saved, along with her famous pig mascot.

Behe believes that the warning that Russell would lose everything 'may well have had a genuine precognitive origin' (though he makes no reference to the prediction that she would lose her voice). But he goes on to express uncertainty about Russell's own presentiments, arguing that she may have worked herself into a state of anxiety, then interpreted this as a psychic presentiment of danger. In a later book, *A Death on the Titanic*, Behe claims that 'It is known that Mrs Russell was not averse to embellishing some of her latter-day accounts in order to make them more colourful'.[453]

Méheust cites Behe's account, but, without any further references, adds some extra details, saying that in January 1912, in Algeria, Russell had been told by a clairvoyant reading in the sand that she would be involved in a serious maritime accident. He suggests that this prediction affected her right up to her embarkation on *Titanic*, and

452 Behe, pp. 100-102 **(GB,po,17)**.

453 *A Death on the Titanic* (2011), p. 370.

claims that she saw the rolling of the boat taking her on board as a bad sign.[454] In Part III of his book he speculates that the original prediction may have awakened something deep inside her. He classes the case as two stars.[455]

(RB,14) Brown describes how a **stoker** climbed up inside the fourth funnel (which was used only to ventilate the ship) at Queenstown and stuck his head out of the opening, thereby leading to an addition to the 'bad omen' list. A passenger boarding *Titanic* saw his face, black with soot, and screamed, 'It's the angel of death!'[456] The stoker meant his appearance to be funny, but nobody seemed to think it was.

Behe says that some of the people who saw the black face, thinking that the funnel was full of heat and smoke from the furnaces, believed no mortal man could survive in it, and thought the incident an omen. He, too, thinks that the stoker's actions were meant 'as a lark'.[457] Méheust says the stoker pretended to be the Devil, but otherwise adds nothing to the case and does not take it up again in Part III of his book.[458]

(RB,15) Brown says that Mrs Cardeza's maid, **Anna Ward**, had a 'definite fear of disaster on this particular voyage, and kept telling her mistress, "This will be the last time I'll ever travel on the ocean."'[459]

---

454 Méheust, pp. 84, 103-104 (**BM,12**).

455 Méheust, p. 172.

456 Brown, pp. 22-23.

457 Behe, p. 32 (**GB,cc,32**).

458 Méheust, p. 105 (**BM,41**).

459 Brown, p. 23.

Behe, whose source is the *New York Times*, claims that Ward was persuaded by her family to accompany her employer to Europe, despite having developed a 'sudden strange fear of again crossing the ocean'. Her father claimed that she feared something was going to happen, but she could not explain what. Ward did not publicly discuss this after being rescued from *Titanic*.[460] Behe makes no comment on this case here, although in the book that he wrote with Goss there is the suggestion that perhaps Ward had come to feel that each successive voyage brought her closer to the possibility of shipwreck. Yet the authors stress that her father's view that she displayed 'particular irrational fear of *this* voyage' deserves to be taken seriously, although they also imply that Ward's fear could have been 'a subconscious reaction to all the sea travelling undergone in Mrs Cardeza's employ'.[461] Méheust does not mention this case.

(RB,16) Brown claims that **Lady Duff Gordon** mentioned to her husband that she had an uneasy feeling that she couldn't manage to shake off. She cites an article published in *Coronet* in June 1951.[462] None of the later commentators mentions this specific case, although Behe relates Lady Duff Gordon's concerns in a different context.[463]

460 Behe, p. 94 **(GB,po,6)**.

461 Goss and Behe, pp. 241-242. They raise the case at p. 228 **(G&B,3)**.

462 Brown, p. 23. John Wilson Foster quotes Lady Duff Gordon as writing, in *Discretions and Indiscretions*, that 'I am even now loath to call this feeling of acute fear which I experienced a premonition, yet the fact remains that though I have crossed the Atlantic many times both before and since I have never had it on any other occasion. Something warned me, some deep instinct, that all was not well.' ('The Titanic Disaster: Stead, Ships and the Supernatural', 2004, p. 41.)

463 Behe, p. 24 **(GB,po,14h)**.

(RB,17) Brown says that an article in the *National Magazine* in October 1912 ('Lest We Forget') claims Miss Marie Young persuaded the ship's carpenter, **Hutchinson**, to let her pay a visit to the French poultry she was shipping home. When she tipped him lavishly, Hutchinson remarked: 'It's good luck to receive gold coins on a first voyage.'[464]

Behe suggests that Hutchinson took Young below to check on the welfare of the chickens each day, and that he said it was good luck to receive gold on a first voyage.' Hutchinson died on *Titanic*.[465] Méheust does not mention the case.

(RB,18) Brown registers that MacKenzie told her that **a young steward**, saying how well he got on with all of his mates, despite the fact that they had never worked together before, also claimed: 'it seems to me we're all too happy for it to last'.[466] Unlike Méheust, Behe briefly mentions this case, but he adds nothing to Brown's account.[467]

(RB,19) Brown records **Mrs William Bucknell** as saying to her friend Mrs J. J. ('The Unsinkable Molly') Brown on the evening of 14 April: 'I felt nervous when we boarded at Cherbourg and I still feel that way. I don't know what it is, but ever since I got on this ship I've felt premonitions of disaster.' Brown also says that, in an interview in the *Denver Post*, dated 30 April, 1912, Molly Brown noted that in Paris, before they started out for

464 Brown, p. 23.

465 Behe, p. 36 (**GB,cc,35**).

466 Brown, p. 26.

467 Behe, pp. 38-39 (**GB,cc,42**).

Cherbourg, Bucknell claimed: 'I'm deathly afraid to go aboard that ship. I feel sure something terrible is going to happen'. And that at Cherbourg itself Bucknell grasped her arm and exclaimed: 'Oh, I dread, I really dread going aboard that ship. It is doomed. I feel it! I know it!'.[468]

Behe repeats what Molly Brown said Bucknell told her. And, like Brown, he records that Bucknell said, 'Didn't I tell you? I knew it', when the two were on deck and in lifebelts.[469] (Both Bucknell and Molly Brown were rescued.)[470] Behe stresses that Bucknell relayed her fear *before* the disaster, but also that it was Molly Brown who revealed the story to the press, since Mrs Bucknell is not known to have commented publicly. He cites both Gracie's book[471] and the *Denver Post* newspaper as his source, and, without further comment, classifies the case as a probable psychic experience.

At first, Méheust follows Behe's account closely,[472] but when he returns to the case he refers to an incident on the evening of 12 April, when Bucknell also tells a doctor from Philadelphia that she has had the presentiment of a disaster ever since embarking.[473] In Part III of his

468 Brown, p. 26, and footnote 1.

469 Behe, pp. 128-129 **(GB,pr,13)**.

470 According to Senan Molony (www.encyclopedia-titanica.org/riddle-of-the-sphinx.html), Molly Brown herself had her palm read in Cairo in March 1912, when an Arab fortune-teller pronounced 'Water, water, water' and painted a portrait of 'a ship sinking amid a carpet of corpses'. Molony gives as his source a news article from April 1912 in a Brown family scrapbook. None of our five authors mentions this case.

471 Archibald Gracie, *Titanic. A Survivor's Story* (2008).

472 Méheust, p. 102-103 **(BM,40)**.

473 Méheust, p. 115.

book he suggests this is another case where one suspects 'subliminal inference', with Mrs Bucknell externalising her fears. Yet he is struck by the insistence and powerfulness of the feelings she experiences, and by the fact that she foresees imminent danger 'one hour before the collision'. Yet Méheust rates the case as only one-star-plus.[474]

(RB,22) Brown says that on the evening of 14 April Norah Keane declared to Edwina MacKenzie, '"Glory be to Heaven, this ship is never going to reach New York and tonight might just be the night of disaster"', claiming to have heard a Cornish woman, whose name later turned out to be **Nellie Hocking**, say that she had heard the sound of a cock crowing at nightfall. Brown suggests that, according to folklore in Cornwall, this was definitely 'a sign of impending disaster'.[475]

Behe also dates Hocking's experience to the evening of 14 April, referring to her as Mrs Elizabeth Hocking. He, too, points out that a long tradition in Cornwall holds that to hear a rooster crow at an unusual time of day presages approaching danger.[476] Méheust argues that the case of the crowing cock shows the influence of the cultural background on some premonitions, agreeing that in Cornwall hearing a cock crow at an unexpected time 'may presage death'.[477] But he is reluctant to see this as a case of genuine premonition,

---

474 Méheust, p. 184.

475 Brown, p. 28.

476 Behe, p. 39 **(GB,cc,44)**. Behe also records an incident as Hocking was boarding *Titanic* **(GB,cc,27)**.

477 Méheust, p. 178. He mistakenly refers to a crow ('corbeau'), presumably confusing the noun and verb forms of 'crow'.

declaring it 'undecidable', and rating it (together with Hocking's earlier worries)[478] as only one star.

(RB,23) Brown records that Eva Hart said that her mother, **Mrs Esther Hart**, from the initial planning stage did not like the idea of an ocean voyage at that particular time, and that when her family's passage was switched to *Titanic* she said, 'I feel worse about it now than I did before.'[479] On board she declared that, owing to her strong premonitions, she was not going to go to sleep at night during the entire trip, 'because I feel that whatever is going to happen will happen at night.' Eva pointed out that her mother was a very down-to-earth woman, not given to flights of fancy or superstitions. But when on Saturday night, 13 April, her husband told her that an odd sound was merely a bit of pack ice grinding against the side of the ship, Esther said, 'If we're in pack ice, surely there's a danger of icebergs.' Brown quotes a letter that Esther's daughter Eva wrote to her: 'I feel fortunate that my mother had her premonition and stayed awake every night we were on the *Titanic*. … I shall never cease to be thankful that she had this remarkable warning.'[480]

Behe claims that Esther was 'plagued with a feeling of impending disaster' from the time she learned of her husband's plans to emigrate to Canada with his family. When she learned that they were due to take *Titanic*, she felt worse than ever, saying that the *Titanic*'s 'unsinkability' was 'flying in the face of God' and that the ship would

478 **(GB,cc,27)**.

479 Brown, pp. 29-30.

480 Brown, p. 105.

never get to the other side of the Atlantic. But although she still had a feeling of dread on seeing the liner, she could not explain it and said she did not know whether the ship was going to sink. And even after the collision she did not know that the 'something' happening was an iceberg. Benjamin Hart went down with the ship, but Esther and daughter, Eva, were rescued.[481]

Behe is not surprised that there are no written accounts from 1912 of Esther's premonition, saying that both she and her daughter retained vivid memories of the event. He interviewed Eva in 1984, and while he acknowledges that one might call Esther's fear that God would inevitably prove that his power is without limit 'mere superstition', he points out that her *original* foreboding had nothing to do with a fear of divine retribution. He, too, quotes Eva as saying that her mother was 'not a superstitious woman', and that this was the only premonition she ever had. Behe rates the case as a probable psychic experience. It seems likely that he (and others) would have made rather less of this case had it not been possible to interview Eva Hart. Serious doubt, however, has been cast on the reliability of Eva's testimony (Esther's post-disaster letters apparently mention no feeling of anxiety or any premonition), and, in any case, one wonders how much Eva could contribute to the matter of her mother's precise feelings (she was seven years old in 1912).

Méheust follows Behe closely in his account of this story.[482] He regards it as 'one of the most extraordinary in

481 Behe, pp. 129-132 (**GB,pr,14**).

482 Méheust, pp. 92, 116, 122 (**BM,24**).

the dossier', claiming that it exposes why so many people were afraid to embark on *Titanic*, seeing its claimed unsinkability as an 'insult to God'. From this point of view, since Esther Hart remained prostrate in her cabin, awaiting the punishment, he thinks the case might be seen as 'paradigmatic of conscious or unconscious inference'. But he does not believe it to be so easily reducible, and stresses that she was overwhelmed by a presentiment of a tragedy as soon as her husband talked of emigration.

Méheust points out that Behe does not say when Benjamin Hart made his plans, but thinks it must have been more than a year before embarkation, so that Esther's premonition was a long-lasting one. He says it began as a general fear of an unknown family disaster and became more precise when she had a new reason to explain it, on learning they were due to travel on *Titanic*, although there is no evidence for his assertion that she 'reached the point of specifying the day and the time'. He also emphasises that the premonition is an insistent, all-powerful one, which tips the balance in favour of its genuineness. Once more Méheust suggests, somewhat dubiously, that the idea of a sinking would have been sharper if Esther had modified her account after the event, although he admits that it was 'obviously determined afterwards'. He does not say why the case of Esther Hart does not quite make it onto his list of eight favoured cases of premonition, but rates it as two-stars-plus.[483]

(RB,24) Having mentioned a seaman's superstition that 'When rats leave the ship, you can be pretty sure she's

483 Méheust, pp. 185-186.

going to have an accident of some description, possibly a sinking', Brown notes that, although *Titanic* was a new ship, half a dozen rats were seen by **a crewman** on 13 April, scurrying aft, away from what was to be the point of collision.[484]

Behe names John Podesta and W. Nutbean as seeing half-a-dozen rats running past them on 13 April. Later Podesta realised the rats had been running away from the starboard bow end. He believed that rats can 'smell' danger.[485] Behe rates the case as a curious coincidence. There is no mention of this incident in Méheust's book.

(RB,25) Brown quotes a letter received by Frank Goldsmith in 1965, from **Mr A. Chandler,** who recounts that when Goldsmith's father, with whom he worked, told his colleagues he was going to America, he suggested they give him something to remember them by. Chandler gave him a pair of outside callipers and his mate an inside pair of callipers. Chandler also said to him in fun, 'What's the good of you having them? You'll get halfway across the Atlantic and down will go the ship … and down will go our callipers!' But Goldsmith senior was not disturbed, arguing that *Titanic* was 'practically unsinkable'.[486]

Goss and Behe record the same story, citing a manuscript by Frank J. W. Goldsmith in the archives of the Titanic Historical Society.[487] They categorise the case as one of the 'odd-seeming occurrences' that were 'merely the

484 Brown, p. 38.

485 Behe, p. 37 **(GB,cc,37)**.

486 Brown, pp. 42-43.

487 Goss and Behe, pp. 225-226 **(G&B,1)**. They refer to 'A. Chantler', not 'Chandler'.

result of ironic coincidences being viewed later with 20/20 hindsight.' The conversational exchange was a familiar, casual one, whereby it is as if, in stating the unbelievable, the speaker may ensure that it will not happen.[488] They say that reading more into the case seems as inappropriate as complaining that Chantler's 'prediction' was hopelessly wrong, since the ship did better than getting only halfway to America, and wonder how many other such statements must have been uttered and forgotten. They regard it as 'clear' that no actual premonition of danger was experienced. Méheust does not refer to this case.

(RB,27) Without quoting sources, Brown records that 'at the exact time' Colonel Archibald Gracie went under the water, **his wife** woke with a start in New York, hearing a voice say, 'On your knees and pray.' She automatically got out of bed and picked up a prayer-book, where her eyes fell on the words, 'For those in peril on the sea'. Brown says, 'Her meditation obviously was helpful, as Colonel Gracie did have a miraculous escape from death', although it is not clear that Mrs Gracie was, in fact, meditating, much less that her experience was 'helpful'.[489]

Behe, who rates this case as probably psychic, claims that while struggling to swim back to the surface of the sea, Gracie recalled an experience of telepathy which had occurred in his wife's family and wanted desperately to

488 The authors remind readers that, in an earlier chapter, they have commented on this kind of 'false pessimism', suggesting that 'a species of "preventive magic" may lead us to voice gloomy remarks that latterly – but only latterly – appear precognitive.' They later claim that Chantler's throwaway line sounds like a lucky – or unlucky – verbal hit (Goss and Behe, p. 241).

489 Brown, p. 60.

convey to his wife and daughter the manner in which he had met his death. He later recalled that he thought if he prayed hard enough he might communicate with them. In fact, he felt this was done, 'through mental telepathy', and saw them praying for him in Washington. Behe adds that as Mrs Gracie obeyed the order to kneel and pray, her prayer book opened by chance at the prayer, 'For Those At Sea'. He also says the thought flashed through her mind, 'Archie is praying for me'.[490] Behe thinks it perhaps understandable that Gracie was not clear about the actual location of his wife, and thinks it 'fairly clear' that *some* type of communication took place between Gracie and his wife.

Méheust records the same details, but specifically points out that Mrs Gracie was not thinking of a sinking.[491] In Part III of his book he claims that in this case we must suspect unconscious inference, since all the appropriate conditions come together. But he finds the simultaneity of the events striking, and says he knows from his own personal experience that the risk of drowning releases an 'unimaginable energy' which, in this case, may have encouraged telepathic contact. He thinks that Mrs Gracie's compulsion to fall to her knees, accompanied by the verbal message and her feeling that her husband was praying for her, indicates that the story has not been embellished. He rates the case as two-stars.[492]

The fact that, in addition to a newspaper report, Behe's

490 Behe, pp. 149-151 (**GB,pr,30**).

491 Méheust, p. 125 (**BM,60**).

492 Méheust, p. 192.

source (and thereby Méheust's) is Gracie's own account[493] will strengthen the case for some, weaken it for others. Behe provides absolutely accurate details from Gracie's account, although it should be noted that when Gracie quotes from Mrs Gracie's own 'written words' describing the hours after she heard the voice, these contain a serious inaccuracy. She claims that at 8 o'clock that morning (15 April) her sister brought her a newspaper giving the tragic news that *Titanic* had sunk and providing a list 'of only twenty names saved'. We know that no morning newspaper reported the sinking of *Titanic* on 15 April, let alone gave any list of those saved, and this rather gross error somewhat undermines confidence, at the very least in Mrs Gracie's account.

(RB,36) Brown received a letter from the son of a couple, Mr and Mrs Louch, who were MacKenzie's dining companions. It records that in a letter to them a **Miss Griffin** said, 'God willing you will be spared to return to your work again.' Griffin was given a photograph of Mr Louch about twenty years before he went on *Titanic*, and kept it in a Victorian album, with various pictures surrounding the photos on each page. She was later struck by the scene on the page where the photo of Mr Louch was kept, since it was 'a ship surrounded by icebergs', tearing out the page and giving it to the Louch's son.[494] None of the later commentators mentions this case.

(RB,37) A Mr Andrews wrote a letter to Brown, claiming that on the night of the *Titanic* disaster a hanging

493 Archibald Gracie, *Titanic. A Survivor's Story.* pp.46-47.

494 Brown, pp. 63-64.

oil lamp at his grandparents' house fell from the ceiling and exploded; 'there appeared to be no reason for it to have fallen'. He noted that 'from that time on' they never again heard from their daughter, **Eliza Wellsted** (Andrews' aunt), and that 'it has been firmly believed' that she was a passenger on *Titanic* 'and that the incident of the lamp was a premonition of the tragedy'.[495] Brown admits that Eliza's dropping out of existence simultaneously with the *Titanic*'s demise may be 'purely coincidental', but also says, 'Perhaps it is more than mere coincidence.' It is hardly surprising that none of the later commentators takes up this case, since it is particularly vague and speculative: the family were unable to check whether Eliza was on *Titanic*, since they did not know under what name she lived, and it is acknowledged that the grandparents heard from Eliza only 'infrequently' in any case.

(RB,38) Brown records in a footnote that on 26 April, 1912 the *New York Times* ran a story that **Isidor Straus's favourite driving horse, Bess**, died unexpectedly during the night of 14 April 1912. A vet was unable to determine the cause of the animal's death.[496] Behe comments that this is again reminiscent of a 'stopping clock' story.[497] Méheust makes no reference to the case.

(RB,39) Brown claims, without citing any sources, that, after the disaster but before Wallace Hartley's body was found, **his mother** said 'she knew her son would face death with his violin close by'. She reminds us that Hartley's

495 Brown, p. 78.

496 Brown, p. 94, footnote 3.

497 Behe, pp. 42-43 (**GB,cc,51**).

violin was strapped to his chest when he was found by the rescue ship.[498] None of the later commentators mentions Hartley's mother.

(RB,40) Referring to a chapter, 'The Dying Girl and the Sinking Ship' in a book by Bernhardt Hurwood,[499] Brown says that Rex Sowden, a Scottish Salvation Army captain, related how he was called to the bedside of a dying girl, **Jessie**, on the evening of 14 April 1912. She said, 'Hold my hand, Captain, I am so afraid. Can't you see that big ship sinking in the water? – Look at all those people who are drowning. Someone called Wally is playing a fiddle and coming to you.' Later Sowden heard the latch on the outer downstairs door to the Salvation Army mission click when there was no one there, and yet he was conscious of someone passing by. Jessie claimed that her mother had come, 'to take me to heaven', and Sowden heard the door latch being lifted as Jessie died: 'The mother had departed with her child.' When he went to investigate, the latch was in place. Sowden had known the violinist Wallace Hartley well as a boy, but had no knowledge of his going to sea, or having anything to do with any ship.[500]

Behe has said in an Internet forum that he provided the original account to Rustie Brown, who reproduced it very briefly in her book; he says he himself gave 'a more lengthy – and accurate – account of the incident'. In his book he adds that Jessie was an orphan girl, and says that it was at precisely 11pm that she asked Sowden to hold her hand.

498 Brown, p. 113.

499 Bernhardt J. Hurwood, *Strange Talents* (1967).

500 Brown, pp. 113-114.

He points out that, allowing for the time-difference, Jessie's experience was apparently a precognitive one, and a vision rather than a dream. He suggests that it was clairvoyant, too, since she knew the name of the violinist.[501] He includes the case among his probable psychic phenomena.

Citing Behe, Méheust uses the same facts.[502] In Part III of his book he claims that, if the facts presented have not been distorted (and, therefore, subject to a more extensive investigation), this case is a remarkable one for the parapsychologist and meets almost all of the required criteria. There was no unconscious inference, since neither participant had any link with *Titanic*, and the name of the ship was not mentioned, which shows that the story has scarcely been modified after the event. The fact that Jessie gave the violinist's name is decisive. In her delirium, Jessie might have had an hallucination concerning a shipwreck, but the probability that at the same time she, by pure chance, named a violinist on *Titanic* who had been a friend of the man at her bedside is zero. Méheust classes the case as three-stars.[503] (He presumably considered this the eighth of his best cases, although he mentions only seven in his comments, having said there are eight.)[504]

It is understandable that Behe should regard this as one of his probable psychic experiences, and that

501 Behe, pp. 143-144 (**GB,pr,25**).

502 Méheust, p. 117 (**BM,55**).

503 Méheust, pp. 190-191.

504 It is also odd that he should say that the case is clearly premonitory when he goes on to argue that, with the exception of Kerlor's experience, his eight cases can be classified as telepathic (Méheust, p. 208).

Méheust should include it in his favoured eight instances, since the case is, indeed, a fascinating and apparently a strong one. Méheust suggests that being at the death-bed of a child would inevitably remain in Sowden's memory for ever, and, like Behe, says that, 'according to what is known', Sowden was very marked by the experience, which deeply affected his vision of the world. Yet, if Hurwood collected Sowden's memories half a century after the event, their precise accuracy is, as the only source, somewhat open to question. Moreover, although it is presumably known that Wallace Hartley was known as 'Wally', there is no indication of why Jessie said that he was coming to Sowden. It is perfectly possible that Sowden had mentioned his violinist friend to her on an earlier occasion. And the matter of Sowden hearing a latch open, as well as the speculation that it was Jessie's mother coming to take her away, is entirely irrelevant to the question of premonitions.

(RB,41) Brown suggests that young **Harry Widener** must have had a feeling something was going to go wrong, since just before *Titanic*'s collision he said, 'I think I'll carry this little rare edition by Bacon around with me in my pocket: if I'm shipwrecked, it will go down with me'.[505] Behe, rating the case as a curious coincidence, also says that Widener told his mother, as she was lowered into a lifeboat, 'I have placed the volume in my pocket – the little Bacon goes with me'. He and his father died on *Titanic*.[506] Méheust makes no mention of this case.

505 Brown, p. 123.

506 Behe, p. 28 **(GB,cc,22)**.

(RB,42) In her chapter on 'Mummies, Myths and Superstitions', Brown mentions the fact that *Titanic* 'wasn't even christened' in connection with superstitions that relate to the sea: 'I'm sure people in olden times would have had dire predictions on a number of counts for the seagoing success of the *Titanic*.'[507] It is unsurprising that the fact that *Titanic* was not christened is not mentioned by Gardner, Behe or Méheust, since it was simply not White Star's policy to christen its ships.

(RB,43) Similarly, Brown is the only commentator to argue that 'On another count, the *Titanic* might predictably have come to harm, according to those who believe in following tradition to the letter, because of her high and mighty name,' giving a number of examples of ships with grandiose names that were 'brought low'.[508]

(RB,44) Brown says that, in a letter in 1975, a Mrs Snyder related the story of the newly-wed **Mrs Bishop**, who disclosed that a fortune-teller in Cairo had told her that 'in her life she would encounter a shipwreck and an earthquake, but that her death would ultimately be caused from injuries sustained in an automobile accident.' This encouraged those in the lifeboat to believe they would be rescued. Mrs Bishop later had a steel plate placed in her head after a car accident, but died when she tripped on a rug and hit her head in March 1916.[509] It may be a little surprising that neither Behe nor Méheust refers to this story.

507 Brown, pp. 130-131.

508 Brown, pp. 132-133.

509 Brown, p. 140.

(RB,45) Brown notes that **Graham Greene** recalls in his autobiography[510] that he 'dreamed of a shipwreck' when he was five.[511] Behe does not mention the case. Méheust adds that Greene also says, 'It was the night in April when *Titanic* sank … An image from the dream has stayed with me for more than sixty years: a man dressed in oilskins doubled up beside another man, being attacked by an enormous wave.'[512] But in Part III of his book he also argues that we can take nothing from the testimony of a child of five, and rates the case as just one star.[513]

(RB,47) After following the experiences of **Edwina MacKenzie** (Troutt) almost from the beginning of her life – and especially closely, of course, in relation to her journey on *Titanic* – Brown mentions only very near the end of her book that Edwina (who 'isn't overly superstitious') had what we might call 'psychic experiences'. In particular, she had a vivid dream about an enormous ship years before she knew she would go on *Titanic*: 'The minute I stepped aboard the *Titanic* I knew it was the ship in my dream.' Brown also mentions that it was in their last conversation that MacKenzie revealed: 'I couldn't have drowned because I was born with a caul and people like that never drown.' This causes Brown to wonder how many *more* survivors were born with a caul.[514] Méheust does not take up these

510 Graham Greene, *A Sort of Life* (1984).

511 Brown, p. 141.

512 Méheust, p. 129 **(BM,64)**.

513 Méheust, p. 200.

514 Brown, pp. 143-145.

experiences of MacKenzie, and Behe probably refers to a different dream.[515]

Brown does occasionally engage in theorising about premonitions, almost invariably taking her points from specific books by those believing in the paranormal. Thus she quotes R. DeWitt Miller as feeling that the night of 14 April 1912 was one of 'psychic explosion', when the impact of the psychic does not just seep through into our everyday life, 'rather, it bursts through, and the effect is felt by a large group of individuals.' The individuals concerned may be 'scattered all over the universe', though the 'vortex' of the psychic happening 'manifests in an event taking place in a limited area'.[516] To some extent, this particular theory echoes Stevenson's speculations about collective experiences and the views of C.D. Broad, whom Brown mentions nowhere in her book.

Again, Brown refers to the comment of a 'cosmic friend' of Jane Roberts, related in her book *The Nature of Personal Reality* (1974), that 'No one dies in a disaster who has not chosen to do so. There is always some conscious recognition, however, though the individual may play tricks with himself and pretend it is not there. Even animals sense their dying ahead of time, and on that level man is no different.'[517] And this relates quite closely to the views of some of the authors that Brown quotes at the

515 Behe, p.93 (**GB,po,4**).

516 Brown, p. 62, footnote 3. This is presumably to be found in Miller's *You Do Take It With You* (1955).

517 Brown, p. 63.

beginning of her book. Later musings on 'psychometry' and 'synchronicity'[518] show the same inclination to believe, without detailed discussion, in almost any theory of the paranormal, but are not shown to have any particular relevance to *Titanic* cases.

In fact, there is a certain looseness, even carelessness, about Rustie Brown's treatment of theories and her handling of premonition cases that is not shared by our other commentators. In general, she gives the impression of being much easier to persuade of paranormal incidents, and somewhat dabbles in theories rather than pursuing them with any rigour. Again, no references at all are given in the great majority of premonition instances, sometimes, no doubt, because she is relying on the testimony of Edwina MacKenzie. Where articles and books are cited, full details are often not supplied, and the items are by no means always included in the Bibliography at the end.[519] In more than a third of her cases, she takes her material directly from Stevenson, but some others raise broad doubts about her use of sources. She is almost invariably uncritical of others' statements or views. Her treatment of a dog who 'turned out to be quite a hero', for example, does not fill one with confidence: 'Some think Rigel might be a myth but he is mentioned in two books and consequently I choose to think he is more than legendary'.[520] Brown lists nearly thirty English-speaking newspapers and more than

518 Brown, pp. 142-143.

519 The list of books in the Bibliography (pp. 155-159) lists many items not mentioned in the text, and only one relating to W.T. Stead.

520 Brown, p. 69, footnote 2.

fifteen magazines and journals at the end of her book, but very few of these are attached to specific premonition cases in her text.

In short, a fair summary would be that, while Stevenson opened up the topic in two articles aimed at a relatively specialised readership, but covered only a fairly small number of premonition cases, Rustie Brown adds as many incidents again to the public domain, but popularises the matter rather than reproducing Stevenson's comparatively rigorous methods.

MARTIN GARDNER

Martin Gardner (1914-2010) was an American writer on mathematics and popular science, said to have written, in 1957, the first bestselling book debunking pseudoscience. He wrote a monthly column in *Scientific American*, which ran for 24 years, bringing serious research to new audiences and revolutionising recreational maths. In 1976, together with Carl Sagan, Isaac Asimov and others, he founded the Committee for the Scientific Investigation of Claims of the Paranormal. But his interest ranged very widely and he published more than one hundred books.

Gardner's book, *The Wreck of the Titanic Foretold?*, which he calls a 'strange anthology',[521] is different in kind from the works of our other commentators, in that it consists of three texts and three poems that may be seen as foretelling the *Titanic* disaster, with a general Introduction and

521 Gardner (1), p. 7.

introductory material to each item. Gardner's own input itself takes up approximately a quarter of the book, which has no footnotes, bibliography or index, but gives, in the text itself, details of books and articles referred to, although the publisher is omitted in the case of many of the books mentioned.

Behe talks of Gardner's 'excellent discussion of coincidences, and how they can sometimes appear to be of a psychic nature',[522] and Gardner begins his Introduction by talking of coincidences in general, arguing that most people have experienced a coincidence so extraordinary that 'it seems impossible to believe it was chance'.[523] His key point is that 'in most cases of startling coincidences it is impossible to make even a rough estimate of their probability. They are what mathematicians call problems that are not "well formed"'.[524]

Saying that the precognitive dream is 'the most common type of precognition', Gardner declares that there is no way to evaluate 'the degree to which such a dream runs counter to ordinary statistical laws.'[525] He stresses that it is impossible to know how many of the wealth of 'vaguely defined, unrelated events' in a dream were quickly forgotten, and that in view of the time-lag between precognitive dream and the events – which may be weeks – the task of estimating the probability of one

522 Behe, 'Further reading', p. 173.

523 Gardner (1), p. 7.

524 Gardner (1), p. 7.

525 Gardner (1), p. 8.

single correlation is 'hopeless'.[526] His last point does not appear to apply to cases where the time-gap between dream and event is short (which is probably the case for the majority of recorded precognitive dreams concerning the sinking of *Titanic*), but we need to remember that he is very specifically concerned to demonstrate only that the statistical probability of a match between dream-event and real-life event cannot be measured. Still, it might be argued that the probability of mere coincidence would surely reduce sharply as the degree of detail and accuracy in the premonition increased. It is hard to believe that the precognitive claims of a dream established to have been dreamed the night before the sinking, and containing reference to *Titanic* striking an iceberg in darkness and sinking with great loss of life, would be radically undermined even if the mathematical probability of a chance correlation *could* be demonstrated. Gardner's further point about the extremely high probability of remarkable correlations of dream events and future events occurring in some of the billions of dreams dreamed every night all over the world retains its force but does not actually establish anything in connection with alleged *Titanic* premonitions.[527]

Nevertheless, Gardner's reminder that we have 'no inkling' of the millions of times that people dream of a major disaster and nothing happens is a timely one.[528] And his speculation that there may be thousands of dreams of

526 Gardner (1), p. 8.

527 Gardner (1), p. 8.

528 Gardner (1), pp. 8-9.

earthquakes in California every month, so that when an earthquake does occur many will remember their dream and have an 'irresistible impulse to regard the dream as precognition' is, in itself, convincing.[529] However, once more this is too general to carry much weight in particular cases concerning *Titanic*. It is a broad warning rather than a tool to enable us to sort the wheat from the chaff.

This is equally true of his undoubtedly accurate claim that some people, 'anxious to gain recognition in a community', lie about any major disaster, and that even honest people tend to exaggerate without realising it. He points out persuasively that dreams are hard enough to remember accurately ten minutes after waking, and that one is soon 'recalling not the dream itself but pictures that formed in the mind during previous tellings.'[530] This leads Gardner to stipulate that the only way a precognitive disaster dream can have evidential value is 'when its details are written down before a disaster and dated in a way that can be verified'.[531] Provided that 'written down' is not interpreted too narrowly as meaning 'by the dreamer', the principle is admirable, and one might wish that the other four of our commentators had followed it a little more regularly and stringently.

Gardner returns to coincidences, pointing out that what is believed to be a coincidence sometimes turns out not to be, but claims that cases like this are 'balanced' by cases in which a startling coincidence really is nothing

529 Gardner (1), p. 9.

530 Gardner (1), p. 9.

531 Gardner (1), p. 9.

but coincidental.[532] Again, it is difficult to see how this has much direct bearing on the *Titanic* disaster, but he does go on to argue that 'enormous numbers' of ESP tests go unreported because the results are negative and that, because of the total number of tests made around the world, 'one would expect a certain proportion, by laws of chance alone, to show unusual correlations'. He also argues tellingly, with striking illustrations, that charlatans are able to exploit this fact to their advantage.[533]

Again, Gardner seems to acknowledge that some 'remarkable predictions' have been made by science-fiction writers, but suggests that, considering the millions of stories about the future that have been written, 'it is perhaps surprising there are not *more* lucky hits.'[534] He has no reluctance to accept that many more extraordinary coincidences occur in daily life than are recognised, and even admits that he tends to notice them in his own life more than most people do, but again refers to ESP when he talks of random events often displaying 'clustering, clumping, or bunching'. His point is that if a parapsychologist reports an unusual number of hits (or misses) in a run of 100 trials it is impossible to tell, without knowing how many tests were made around the world, whether this is ESP or normal clumping. Like most other sceptics, he asserts that unless an experiment can be successfully replicated many

532 Gardner (1), p. 10.

533 Gardner (1), p. 11 and p. 14. He shows, for example, why one should not necessarily buy the name of the winner of a third horse race from someone who has already accurately 'predicted' the winner of two (p. 11).

534 Gardner, (1), p. 12.

times, 'the results may be nothing more than a statistical anomaly. Extraordinary claims for new laws of science demand extraordinary evidence.'[535]

Gardner regards all of this as 'background' to the consideration of premonitions of great disasters, and asks how much reliance can be placed on claims to have predicted major earthquakes, floods, fires, volcanic eruptions or assassinations of a public figure, and so on. Discounting the instances of frauds and fakes, he accepts that 'there remain cases where successful predictions actually were recorded', but again affirms that the evaluation of probability is difficult, because we do not know how many predictions were recorded in some manner and failed.[536] He states that Ian Stevenson has been the person 'most influential in spreading the view that there were widespread psychic premonitions of the *Titanic* disaster', and proceeds to examine Stevenson's two articles, looking at his cases in turn.

His view of the non-Stead cases in Stevenson's first article is that anyone who considers them carefully will agree that only Robertson's novel can be viewed as 'extraordinary'. He claims that Stevenson is aware of 'how weak most of his twelve cases are', and points out that he admits they lack 'much that we would wish in the way of further details', especially contemporary affidavits from witnesses that recorded premonitions prior to news of *Titanic*'s sinking.[537] He also says that Stevenson argues that even the 'novels' by

535 Gardner (1), pp. 15-16.

536 Gardner (1), p. 16.

537 Gardner (1), pp. 19-20.

Robertson and Stead (Stevenson, in fact, refers to Stead's 'articles') can easily be considered cases of 'reasonable inference' rather than precognition, but presents his cases 'as though they add up to significant evidence for ESP', although his final conclusion is 'admirably cautious'.[538]

Like Stevenson himself, Gardner devotes rather more space to each of the cases in Stevenson's second article, finding them, in general, 'weak'.[539] Again, he asserts that ('in spite of sceptical remarks here and there') Stevenson thinks his 'nineteen' cases altogether provide impressive evidence for ESP, and quotes him as saying, in an article published in 1970: 'I was able to assemble a considerable number of corroborated reports suggesting that these nineteen percipients had had extrasensory awareness of the sinking of the *Titanic*. Ten of the cases were precognitive.'[540] Gardner stresses that in the same article Stevenson also repeated his view that the reason why there were so many more cases on record of ESP involving *Titanic* than in connection with worse disasters is that the sinking was 'totally unexpected': 'the very unexpectedness of the sinking of the *Titanic* may have generated an emotional shock not present in disasters that are less surprising'.[541] He also points out that Stevenson recognises that anecdotal evidence is less reliable than laboratory experiments, but implies that Stevenson's claim that 'Perhaps the best evidence for precognition derives from the experiments of Soal' was significantly undermined by the

538 Gardner (1), p. 20.

539 Gardner (1), p. 22.

540 Gardner (1), p. 22. Ian Stevenson, 'Precognition of disasters' (1970), p. 205.

541 Gardner (1), p. 22.

discovery, eight years later, that 'Soal had cheated shamelessly on some of his tests, rendering all his research suspect.'[542]

Gardner ends his general Introduction by admitting that his own scepticism about ESP is well known, and says he will leave it to readers to decide whether the evidence for paranormal perception of the *Titanic* disaster is 'strong enough to support such an extraordinary claim or whether we have here the same familiar blend of unreliable anecdotes with coincidences of the sort that are well within the bounds of normal laws of chance.' He regards the 'amazing mystique' that has developed around the sinking of *Titanic* as springing from the ironic juxtaposition of pride that the ship could not be sunk and the unexpected suddenness with which that belief was shattered. He believes the disaster could easily have been prevented had there not been such a combination of human errors (which he does not specify), and says the sinking can be taken as 'a symbol of the crumbling of proud empires with their similar mix of the rich, the middle class, and the poor – all going down together.' He even claims that for the first time in history it can now be taken as a symbol of the fate of the human race if folly should set off a nuclear war.[543]

The only *Titanic* cases that Gardner is the first of our five commentators to bring to public attention are Garnett's story and the poems by Thaxter and Melville, all of which have already been discussed, but both his theoretical arguments and his reprinting of a number of key texts are extremely valuable contributions to the debate.

542 Gardner (1), p. 23.

543 Gardner (1), p. 23.

CHAPTER 5

GEORGE BEHE

George Behe's interest in the *Titanic* began when he was about seven, and he began actively researching the disaster in 1972. He has published a number of books on *Titanic*-related topics and participated actively in Internet forums. Behe is a past vice-president of the Titanic Historical Society. He is one of the most respected *Titanic* commentators.

In his Foreword to George Behe's book, *Titanic. Psychic Forewarnings of a Tragedy* (1988), Edward Kamuda says that from its construction to its sinking stories concerning *Titanic* persisted, 'foretelling of her tragic end', and that talk of the ship's unsinkability gave rise to whispers that 'this was challenging the Almighty and it was certain that the ship would meet an early end,' although he argues that 'It is the same with any historical tragedy.' He claims that newspaper stories are still being unearthed of premonitions and those who failed to board the liner after booking passage. He says that there have been 'a few half-hearted efforts' to reveal the truth of these stories, but gives no details of exactly what he is referring to as the 'small pamphlets accomplished by learned men of paranormal experiences' and the recent book setting out to explain some of these unusual mysteries. He believes Behe's book reveals 'a more in depth, logical and educational approach' to these matters, leaving out the 'emotional and speculative aspects' of the subject.[544]

In his Prologue, Behe himself gives a brief, measured summary of the building and sinking of *Titanic*,[545] before offering an Introduction, then turning in Parts I-V to his five categories of cases:

The curious coincidences
Mistaken accounts and deliberate hoaxes
Phenomena connected with W.T. Stead
Possible psychic phenomena
Probable psychic phenomena.

In his Introduction, which is also brief,[546] he begins by quoting what is by now a well-known – and clearly ironical – piece published in the *Milwaukee Journal* shortly after the sinking, claiming that 'To Date Only About 6,000 Were About To Take *Titanic*, But Changed Their Minds', and that, of the 4,965 who cancelled their reservations,

544 Behe, pp. 7-8.

545 Behe, pp. 9-10.

546 Behe, pp. 11-13.

899 'had premonitions of disaster'. Behe relates that 'it did seem to have some basis in fact', since in the week following the disaster newspapers from across the United States and England carried small articles describing how someone from their region had intended to take *Titanic* but decided to change to an earlier or later steamer. He notes that 'most of the people who cancelled their reservations on *Titanic* did so for prosaic reasons' and that the newspapers usually reported these commonplace cancellations straightforwardly, and 'wrote them off as fortunate coincidences'.

Yet there were other reports about people who 'by word or deed' seemed to have exhibited foreknowledge of the *Titanic* disaster. (It is interesting to note that Behe, without precisely limiting himself, appears to be focusing on newspaper reports, although the quoted sources for some of his cases include journals, books, and personal letters.) Behe claims that by carefully examining the background and context of these reports it is possible to divide them into the five categories listed above. His view is that it is important to examine 'the entire body of reports which comprise these categories', since this enables us to form an overall view of 'the many curious stories which were made public after the sinking of *Titanic*, stories which seemed to have an origin alien to that of normal human experience.' He says that it also allows us to apply 'critical criteria' to these reports, 'enabling us to separate the commonplace accounts from the precious residue of true mysteries'.

He is also careful to record that none of his cases has been classed as a 'definite' psychic phenomenon and that he does not wish to make 'dogmatic pronouncements about the reality of psychic phenomena', claiming that the time-gap of three-quarters of a century has 'spirited these cases beyond our reach', and made ironclad conclusions impossible. He sees the need to avoid both an 'uncritical, fanatical belief in paranormal phenomena' and 'the attitude of the dyed-in-the-wool sceptic', and to maintain 'a healthy, open-minded scepticism', advising the reader to be critical of his cases, but to follow wherever the evidence leads.

Behe's general stance, as described in his Introduction, is admirably sensible, and tangibly different from that of each of the previous commentators, as well as that of Méheust. This, however, by no means amounts to saying that his judgement in the cases he treats is always entirely sound. There are certainly instances where some of our other authors appear to have a better grasp of a particular experience. Moreover, it is important to bear in mind at the appropriate stages the full implications of Behe's significant division of his cases into categories.

It was appropriate to examine in some detail each of Stevenson's cases, not because they all have intrinsic interest or merit, but because together they constitute, in a sense, the foundations of the study of *Titanic* premonitions. The situation is very different, however, when it comes to Behe's book. Partly, this is a question of numbers: there are only 26 Stevenson cases in all, while Behe deals with over 150 experiences in his book. Furthermore, as we have seen, his classification of these includes categories of 'curious coincidences' and 'mistaken accounts and deliberate hoaxes'. For our purposes, most of the former and all of the latter are not worth dwelling on at any length. Behe's presentation of cases in the three categories that now concern us (in his Parts I, IV, and V) is in broad chronological order. Ten cases at the end of his Part I and others in subsequent parts – a number of them dealt with at some length – relate to incidents that definitely occurred after the sinking and are not referred to here.

Curious Coincidences

Behe's explicit claim is that his 'curious coincidences', although seeming odd at first glance, occurred 'as the result of mere chance'.[547] Conceding that each had a 'certain atmosphere of the mysterious about it', he says that the application of a little research, or the fortunate survival of the person involved, shows these reports as having a 'normal origin'.[548] In fact, in setting out his curious coincidences he sees them as falling into a number of general sub-categories: (A) curious statements made by survivors who 'were able to deny that they had experienced premonitions'; (B) curious statements by those who did not survive, which, although we cannot be positive about their reasons for making them, were made in contexts which enable us to be 'reasonably certain' that they were made 'off the cuff, so to speak, and not seriously meant or felt as premonitions of danger'; (C) 'omens' or curious events that were 'undoubtedly coincidental' but

547 Behe, p. 12.

548 Behe, p. 15.

had folk traditions behind them which associated them with approaching misfortune (in this case, 'misfortune and possible tragedy for the maiden voyage of *Titanic*'); (D) some odd occurrences 'curiously ironic in light of *Titanic*'s later loss', which take on added meaning 'only with the use of hindsight'. Behe adds that there is no real way of proving that several of the events discussed are examples of '"synchronicity" (coincidences which can be connected together meaningfully by someone who is sensitive to their possible cause)', so that his first group of cases must remain classified as coincidental occurrences.[549]

In theory, the assumption on which the first two of these latest categories appear to be crucially based – that premonitions have to be 'seriously meant or felt' as such – is questionable, in that it does not seem to be absolutely essential that the percipient should immediately see the experience as a premonition. We can easily envisage a case where someone, say a couple of days before *Titanic*'s maiden voyage, has a dream 'foreseeing' that the ship strikes an iceberg and sinks, with great loss of life, but has no inclination to take this as a premonition, even perhaps being someone who does not believe in premonitions. If such an experience were unequivocally recorded before the disaster, there seems to be no reason why someone else should not regard it, either before or after the event, as a premonition. Perhaps this is clearest of all in the case of dreams. The correlation of experience and event might, of course, have been simply coincidental, but whether or not it was regarded as a premonition at the

549 Behe, pp. 15-16.

time has no significant bearing on this. The problem here is that the criteria for what makes an experience a potential premonition – that is, the 'opposite' of a curious coincidence – have not been properly established.

In fact, three of Behe's four sub-categories envisage interpretation of premonitions only after the event. In both of the first two he refers to statements 'which (after the disaster) were interpreted to have been premonitions of danger'. His fourth category seems to relate to odd *occurrences* rather than premonitions, but once more the question of timing comes into the picture. He appears to be suggesting that if an occurrence before the sinking was not considered meaningful at the time, then seeing it as meaningful only with hindsight somehow reflects on the significance, or otherwise, of the occurrence itself. This is surely a mistake: in general, the moment when one links two experiences has no relevance to the nature or appropriateness of the relationship made.

Behe's third sub-category may also envisage retrospective ascription of significance, but this is uncertain. His point here is different in kind. Begging the question rather, he describes these events as 'undoubtedly coincidental', arguing that the 'folk traditions' behind them are the reasons for the association with approaching misfortune. Yet these facts need to be established in each individual case, to avoid the charge of further unjustified assumptions. On exactly what grounds can the coincidental nature of the event be confidently affirmed? And can it be shown that the folk tradition is the *only* reason adduced for its premonitory force?

It may seem somewhat unfair to scrutinise so closely what Behe sets out only as 'general categories', but the cases in his initial two chapters ('The Curious Coincidences' and 'Mistaken Accounts and Deliberate Hoaxes') – which take up almost a quarter of the book – are, as he himself argues, extremely valuable as contrasts to the later, more serious premonition episodes. It is extremely important to look carefully at the criteria he uses both to include and exclude experiences as premonitions. In practice, less systematically but at least equally tellingly, factors other than those implied in his introduction to Part 1 are used to undermine claims of precognition, like significant lack of information about an occurrence, legitimate inference, and badly inaccurate predictions.

The instances involving Stead, Robertson and Garnett – all regarded as 'curious coincidences' by Behe – are dealt with in our Chapter I. Some others had already been raised by Stevenson and Brown. We will record most of the other curious coincidences only in the most summary way, while dwelling on a few at rather more length. Where Behe has added a 'Comment' section to his account, his views will be noted, and where Méheust takes up a case – on only 6 occasions – his opinion will be registered.

CASES

(GB,cc,2) A time-capsule buried in 1887 at **'Hell-Bent'** in America predicted the sinking of 'a majestic ship of the sea'. Behe comments that the name of the finder and location of Hell-Bent are not recorded, so that the account is 'of unknown reliability'.[550]

(GB,cc,5) Emil Taussig wrote letters in 1908 and 1909 warning of the possibility of a *Titanic*-type disaster, because of insufficient lifeboats: 'this thing will come to pass sooner or later.' Taussig died on *Titanic.* [551]

(GB,cc,6) An employee of **Arthur Newell**, a prominent Boston banker, photographed *Titanic* in Belfast in 1911. Newell himself died on *Titanic*.[552]

(GB,cc,7) In August 1911, just before **Alexander Robins** sailed with his wife to England on *Olympic*, he remarked to friends that he did not think he would 'ever live to see America again'. They both died on *Titanic*. Behe comments that the bulk of the evidence seems to indicate that Robins originally intended to stay in Britain, and that his remark only took on added meaning in the light of the disaster.[553]

(GB,cc,8) John George Phillips, wireless operator on *Titanic* told a friend at Christmas 1911 that he had a great fear of icebergs, and that he would rather be on a smaller vessel than a big ocean liner. He died on *Titanic*.[554]

(GB,cc,9) On 1 January 1912, **A.J. Pierce** predicted that in the course of the year 'A ship not far from port will sink with all on board', going on to say that the ship would

550 Behe, pp. 16-17.

551 Behe, p. 19.

552 Behe, pp. 19-20.

553 Behe, p. 20.

554 Behe, p. 21.

be off New York, 'probably not very far'. Behe comments that Pierce's prediction was 'not very close to the mark'.[555]

(GB,cc,10) Early in 1912, **Captain Smith**, who had already been told he was to captain *Titanic*, reacted to the prophecy published in England that the spring of 1912 would see the largest vessel in the world go down with heavy loss of life by saying, 'Well, if the largest liner in the world goes down, I shall go with her.' (Present when Smith was told of the prediction, the wife of an officer due to be transferred to *Titanic* – and who eventually died on the ship – became very apprehensive about the future safety of her husband.) Behe comments that there was nothing clairvoyant about Smith's remark, and that one can almost hear him chuckle on making it.[556]

Méheust's treatment of Capt. Smith's casual remark basically repeats – and credits – what Behe says.[557] He, too, records that the wife of a sailor who would lose his life on *Titanic* saw the prophecy at the time as a bad omen, but he includes no reference to this case in his dossier in Part III of his book.

(GB,cc,11) When **Reverend Robert Bateman** left his home to sail to England, his wife wrote to their son, asking him to make sure to see his father in Baltimore, as he might never see him again.[558]

(GB,cc,12) At an official luncheon on board *Titanic* in Belfast, on 30 March 1912, **one of the tables collapsed**,

555 Behe, p. 21.

556 Behe, pp. 21-22.

557 Méheust, p. 82 **(BM,8)**.

558 Behe, p. 22.

and several people voiced the hope that no mishap would befall *Titanic*.[559]

(GB,cc,13) Many people regarded the postponement of ***Titanic*'s sea trials** on 1 April 1912 owing to high winds as an ominous event.[560]

Following the sinking, there were a number of reports that people's belief that to sail on board a liner on her maiden voyage was unlucky prevented them from booking passage on *Titanic*.[561]

(GB,cc,14a) An **unnamed man** postponed his departure with his family, feeling it somehow 'wiser for me to wait for the tried ship'.

(GB,cc,14b) M. Forster cancelled his passage, being 'a little afraid of new machinery'.

(GB,cc,14c) A **man from Penzance** declined to book passage on *Titanic*, preferring to wait for her second voyage.

(GB,cc,14d) The **father of a friend of Marion Grimm** cabled his wife, telling her to cancel passage on *Titanic* and take a later boat.

---

559 Behe, p. 22. Without quoting any sources, J.P. Eaton and C.A. Haas (*Titanic. Destination Disaster. The legends and the reality* (2011), pp. 100-101) record that the table collapse took place on the *Mackay-Bennett* on 30 April, 1912, but that 'at least one reporter decided to change it to a *Titanic*-related omen and wrote his report of the incident so that the table collapse occurred during a reception aboard the liner before her Southampton departure', but Behe's source (the *Belfast Evening Telegraph*), dates from 17 April, 1912.

560 Behe, pp. 22-23.

561 Behe, pp. 23-25.

(GB,cc,14e) Edward Bill's wife, who had never objected to his plans before, urged him not to book on *Titanic*, although she didn't know why. Behe comments that Bill was imprecise in describing his wife's fears, and that a hotel manager claimed that Mrs Bill had said that she did not like to travel by a boat making a maiden voyage. In any case, Bill eventually gave in to his wife and booked on another ship.[562]

Méheust repeats the story,[563] but in Part III of his book he attaches no particular weight to her worries, suspecting inference and arguing that her fear of a 'prototype that had never yet crossed the Atlantic', and a company offering 'aggressive propaganda', is reasonable. He rates the case as only one star.[564]

(GB,cc,14g) The **mother of Mrs George Vanderbilt** declared that the maiden voyage of any ship was dangerous and persuaded her daughter to cancel the passage on *Titanic* that she had booked with her husband (although their footman's reservation was retained and he went down with the ship). Behe classes this as a typical case of maiden voyage phobia.[565] Méheust has nothing at all to add concerning the Vanderbilts, and agrees with Behe, seeing the case as one of conscious inference, and classing it as only one star.[566]

(GB,cc,14h) Lady Duff Gordon said that she would not care to cross the Atlantic 'on a new ship', but her

562 Behe, pp. 23-24.

563 Méheust, p. 96 **(BM,31)**.

564 Méheust, p. 179.

565 Behe, pp. 24-25.

566 Méheust, pp. 96, 180-181 **(BM,32)**.

husband agreed to accompany her on *Titanic*, to ease her mind. They were both rescued.[567]

(GB,cc,14i) The **mother of Edward Ryan** told him that he should avoid *Titanic*: 'You never know what may happen to a new ship'. He sailed nevertheless and was one of the few men in steerage to survive.[568]

(GB,cc,14j) Shortly before the family left Sweden, **Mrs A.G. Anderson** wrote to a sister in Canada that all might not be well sailing on a new vessel which had not yet crossed the ocean. With her husband and five children (and another sister, brother-in-law and baby) she was lost on *Titanic*. Behe makes the comment that 'maiden voyage phobia' was a 'general, all-inclusive type of superstition', not directed specifically at *Titanic* in any of the above cases.[569]

(GB,cc,15) Confectioner **Ernest Farenden** was superstitious of *Olympic*, and was glad to learn that he was being transferred to *Titanic*. He went down with the ship.[570]

(GB,cc,16) **Mrs Joseph Leeford** and her sister feared ill luck if they sailed on Good Friday and decided to wait for *Titanic*. Mrs Leeford died when the ship went down. Behe comments that her name does not appear on *Titanic*'s official passenger list.[571]

567 Behe, p. 24.

568 Behe, p. 25.

569 Behe, p. 25.

570 Behe, pp. 25-26.

571 Behe, p. 26.

(GB,cc,17) Just before **George Clifford**, who had a great fear of crossing the Atlantic, sailed from America his wife persuaded him to increase his life insurance to $100,000. He died on *Titanic*. Behe comments that Clifford's fear seems to have been of a general nature and was not focused specifically on *Titanic*.[572]

(GB,cc,18) Mrs **Mary Mack** seemed to dread her passage on *Titanic*. She used to beg her daughter to give up her job as a stewardess, saying it was 'too dangerous'. Mrs Mack died on *Titanic*. Behe comments that she suffered from a fear of the sea in general, a fear not centred on *Titanic*.[573]

(GB,cc,19) When **Helen and Susan Fitzpatrick and their brother John** drew lots to decide which shipping line they would travel on, Anchor Line beat White Star Line.[574]

(GB,cc,20) Three days before *Titanic* sailed, a **crewman** and his wife made a recording of themselves singing. The crewman, who sang *True Till Death*, died on *Titanic*.[575]

(GB,cc,21) Shortly before *Titanic* set sail, the friends of the bass viol player, **Fred Clark**, were joking with him. He said, 'Well, you know it would be just my luck to go down with the ship …' Like the other musicians, he died on *Titanic*.[576]

---

572 Behe, p. 26.

573 Behe, pp. 26-27.

574 Behe, p. 27.

575 Behe, p. 27.

576 Behe, p. 27.

(GB,cc,23) On 9 April, while steward **Arthur Lewis** was preparing himself for his duties as a steward on *Titanic*, the White Star insignia being fastened on his cap 'fell all to pieces'. His wife said, 'I don't like this', but he thought it of no consequence and joined the ship. He was saved, manning one of the lifeboats.[577]

(GB,cc,24) On the day before *Titanic* sailed, **Sidney Collett** wrote to his parents: 'In the event of anything unforeseen happening to me in my journey to you, please open the enclosed letter addressed to me.' But, after his rescue, Collett denied having had a premonition: 'It was an ordinary precaution'. Behe comments that, if Collett had died on *Titanic*, it might well have appeared that he had experienced a genuine premonition.[578]

(GB,cc,25) On the evening of 9 April **George Wick** selected number 13 in a sweepstake: 'I have always held that number 13 was my lucky number.' He lost his life on *Titanic*.[579]

(GB,cc,26) The **boat train from Waterloo Station** to Southampton developed mechanical difficulties and stopped as it pulled away from the platform on 10 April 1912. Behe comments that this was the kind of occurrence that later took on an 'omen-like quality' for some people.[580]

(GB,cc,27) **Elizabeth Hocking** suddenly exclaimed to her daughter, as they prepared to board *Titanic*, 'I'm not going in that ship. It's too big.' She also disliked the

577 Behe, p. 28. See also **(GB,po,25)**.

578 Behe, pp. 28-29.

579 Behe, p. 29.

580 Behe, p. 29-30.

ship's name, but was persuaded to go aboard anyway.[581] She survived the sinking.

Citing Behe, Méheust tells the same story in Part II of his book,[582] later claiming in Part III that it is a 'classic case where inference is obvious'. He finds the fact that Hocking did not like the ship's name 'revealing', arguing that it probably means she was bothered by its mythological connotations, by the challenge to God that it issues: 'Another illustration of Christian resistances'. (In Part III he also amalgamates this case with the story of the crowing cock, which he has not mentioned in Part II of his text, awarding Hocking's case as a whole only one star.)[583]

(GB,cc,28) A **member of the kitchen staff**, apparently seeing *Titanic* prematurely slip her mooring lines, refused to go on board the ship, because of a seamen's superstition that this was bad luck. Behe comments that the origin of this report is unknown and that there is no evidence that *Titanic* did slip her moorings prematurely, or that a crewman refused to embark for that reason.[584]

(GB,cc,30) On *Titanic*'s way to Queenstown, Mr **Charles Clarke** wrote to his parents, promising to tell them of the *New York* incident, 'if we reach New York'. Behe comments that Clarke, who died on *Titanic*, probably meant his remark as 'a humorous reference to the near-collision'. He died in the sinking.[585]

581 Behe, p. 30. See also **(RB,22)**.

582 Méheust, p. 96 **(BM,30)**.

583 Méheust, p. 178.

584 Behe, p. 30.

585 Behe, p. 31.

(GB,cc,31) While waiting for *Titanic* in Queenstown, and discussing the huge numbers that would be on the ship, a **Mr Duane** remarked what an awful thing it would be if she sank with all her passengers. Behe comments that, with the ship due to be so crowded, it was like 'putting all your eggs in one basket'.[586]

(GB,cc,38) On 14 April a picture in the home of **Mrs Daughtrey** slipped from the wall and crashed to the floor. She remarked, 'My goodness, a ship will go down tomorrow.' Her husband had been disappointed not to be posted to *Titanic*, but all of his friends went down with the ship. Behe comments: 'This event seems related to cases of the stopping of a clock upon the death of its owner, and similar reports.'[587]

(GB,cc,39) On 14 April 1912, the **Reverend Charles Brown** asked his congregation to pray for the safe return of two absent members, and that the two women be 'conducted in safety through the perils of the great deep'. Barely twelve hours later, the two women were saved as *Titanic* went down. Behe comments: 'In close-knit church congregations, prayers are often said for the safe return of absent, travelling members.'[588]

(GB,cc,40) On 14 April 1912, **Reverend John Chew** told his congregation of a true story told to him by Bishop Potter, concerning the narrow escape of a ship from a collision with an iceberg, 'a remarkable story of telepathy and prayer connected with the deliverance of the ship'. Chew

---

586 Behe, p. 32.

587 Behe, p. 37.

588 Behe, pp. 37-38.

observed that this was the time of the year for such disasters and that some ship might be in similar danger now.[589]

(GB,cc,41) During the Sunday religious services on board *Titanic*, the **Reverends Thomas Byles and Joseph Peruschitz** each spoke, at a mass for steerage passengers, of the 'necessity of man having a lifeboat in the shape of religious consolation at hand in case of spiritual shipwreck'. They both died when the ship went down.[590]

(GB,cc,43) A **French engineer** suddenly commented to two French passengers that the ropes for the lifeboats were too short. Behe comments that the engineer was mistaken.[591]

(GB,cc,46) On 14 April, **Reverend Ernest Carter** organised hymn singing in the dining saloon. One participant was struck by how many passengers requested hymns dealing with dangers at sea. Carter pointed out that this was the first time hymns had been sung on the ship and trusted that it would not be the last. He and his wife died on *Titanic*.[592]

(GB,cc,47) The happy atmosphere of a party in steerage on the night of 14 April was briefly interrupted when a **rat** darted across the floor. Behe comments that this incident is reminiscent of Podesta's encounter with rats.[593]

(GB,cc,48) A fortune-teller told **Constance Willard** when she was very young that she would die when she was approaching 21 years of age. After the collision she

589 Behe, p. 38.

590 Behe, p. 38.

591 Behe, p. 39.

592 Behe, p. 40.

593 Behe, p. 41.

claimed to have had a 'peculiar sensation that something had happened which I had been expecting', and suddenly remembered the fortune teller's prophecy. Behe comments that sources give different ages for Willard, and that in any case she lived until 1964.[594]

(GB,cc,50) Behe claims that fireman **Fred Barrett**, in lifeboat 13, noticed a thin crescent moon rising above the horizon and said: 'A new moon! Turn your money over, boys! That is, if you have any.' He also commented: 'Well, I shall never say again that 13 is an unlucky number. Boat 13 is the best friend we ever had.'[595]

(GB,cc,52) Giving the *Vancouver Daily Province* (2 May, 1912) as his source, Behe records that in **Suva**, Fiji, on (or after) 16 April 1912, the officers of the liner *Marama* were told by the inhabitants that *Titanic* had gone down with heavy loss of life. Two days after their departure for Honolulu, *Marama* received a wireless message saying that *Titanic* had struck an iceberg, but was being towed to safety. The officers could not explain how Fiji knew about *Titanic*'s *loss* two or three days before the first reports of the *collision* reached this area of the Pacific. Behe comments that this is indeed a puzzle, though there is probably a 'completely normal explanation' for it. He believes it may always remain a mystery.[596]

Citing Behe, Méheust follows his account of this incident (although he mistakenly refers to the *Marana*).[597]

594 Behe, p. 41.

595 Behe, p. 42. Brown (p. 143) records Barrett's second comment, but attributes it only to a 'survivor'.

596 Behe, p. 43.

597 Méheust, p. 133 (**BM,70**).

In Part III of his book he says that if the information is exact this is 'one of the strangest cases in the dossier'. The 'incomprehensible' phenomenon makes him wonder whether it is a question of 'means of communication characteristic of ancient peoples'. He points out that in the accounts of missionaries, and early ethnographic literature, stories of this kind are very common. He thinks that an historical inquiry ought to be able to establish when exactly news of the loss of *Titanic* and passengers reached the Pacific, and asserts that if this was on 18 April we have a striking case of 'metacommunication'.[598]

While it is noticeable that Méheust's rating of the case as two-stars-plus contrasts with Behe's categorisation, it has to be said that there is a vagueness about the account of this incident that rather undermines its significance (What was the exact date of the incident? How long was *Marama* in Suva? Where exactly was it when it received the wireless message? When – and how – did news actually reach Fiji? And so on.)

(GB,cc,53) Several months before his death, **Captain Smith** had spoken about his bad luck at sea with a businessman, J.P. Grant. He felt that he had been jinxed and said he would resign if he had another accident with a liner. Behe comments that Smith intended to retire after *Titanic*'s maiden voyage, although this is by no means certain.[599]

Méheust suggests that a series of accidents to *Olympic* 'must have' weighed heavily upon Smith, who came to

598 Méheust, p. 201.

599 Behe, pp. 43-44.

wonder, in a discussion with Grant, whether 'the die had not been cast for him'.[600] He does not return to this vague and inconsequential story in Part III of his book.

In many cases Behe's reports of curious coincidences are either too vague or too general to be seriously considered as genuine premonitions. And, in saying that his ten examples of 'maiden voyage phobia' were not directed specifically at *Titanic*,[601] he reminds us that in some cases the very connection with *Titanic* is extremely tenuous in any case. Other instances more directly concern *Titanic*, but are entirely inconsequential, having no obvious predictive significance at all.

Altogether, there are many different reasons for taking little account of most of Behe's curious coincidences as psychic premonitions: only a few of his cases are worthy of detailed comment in their own right in the present context. It would be wrong, however, to pass on from Behe's curious coincidences without registering the fact that in a few cases he is reluctant to rule out altogether the possibility of a psychic phenomenon, suggesting or implying that further research *may*, at some future date, increase the likelihood of such an explanation. None of this quite contradicts Behe's opening account of what constitutes 'curious coincidences', but it hints at a predisposition to believe in the reality of psychic premonitions – something that comes out much more clearly in later sections of his book.

600 Méheust, p. 85, (**BM,14**).

601 Behe, pp. 23-25.

Mistaken accounts and deliberate hoaxes

These cases, taken up in the brief Part II of his book, seem, according to Behe, to have 'some paranormal element, but […] are not what they first appeared to be'.[602] Yet at the beginning of Part II itself, Behe appears less than absolutely convinced that these are not instances of the paranormal, saying that his first two (of three) accounts 'at first seem to have mysterious overtones', but are 'almost certainly hoaxes', presenting the first (which is 'either a hoax or a spectacular case of life after death') 'for the reader's consideration'.[603] Since all three experiences occur after the sinking of *Titanic*, they fall outside our terms of reference. They concern Captain Peter Pryall who claimed to have seen Captain Smith in Baltimore in July 1912;[604] Gordon Cosgrave ('the victim of a hoax'), who in 1936, on six occasions received messages in Morse code, which appeared to be distress calls and other messages exchanged between *Titanic* and *Carpathia* twenty-four years earlier;[605] and Doris Williams, who was said to have regressed, under hypnosis, to a previous life, in which she was a passenger on *Titanic*.[606]

In the present context, the interest of Part II of Behe's book lies in the processes and criteria that he uses in (virtually) rejecting the suggestion that particular

602 Behe, p. 12.

603 Behe, p. 50.

604 Behe, pp. 50-51.

605 Behe, pp. 51-53.

606 Behe, pp. 53-57.

experiences are paranormal, although a little care is needed, in that none of the three is allegedly a case of premonition. It is worth noting that he links the paranormal with 'mystery'. But, crucially, he implies that both of his first two instances illustrate the point that 'So powerful is the emotional impact of the *Titanic* saga that many people wish to somehow become involved with it, to become a part of it.'[607] In fact, his third case bears this out most strongly of all, despite the fact that he emphasises, rather puzzlingly, that it is 'the result of an honest mistake' on the part of an honest researcher. In other parts of his book, too, it can be seen that Behe has in mind in treating his cases the possibility of an excessive wish to be involved, even if there are experiences where one wishes that he had taken it more seriously. Indeed, with Pryall, although Behe clearly believes that he made up his account, he does make a point of saying that 'He had no conceivable motive for fabricating an unlikely story like this, and his reasons for doing so remain a puzzle.'[608] His scepticism regarding Pryall's account seems to arise simply out of its 'unbelievable' and 'unlikely' content.

Behe's reasons for rejecting his second and third cases as paranormal are based on close scrutiny of the claims themselves. He finds enough 'internal inconsistencies' and straightforward errors in the messages received by Cosgrave to make him certain that they did not originate on *Titanic* and *Carpathia*.[609] And close examination of the

607 Behe, p. 50.

608 Behe, p. 51.

609 Behe, p. 52-53.

information that Doris Williams 'recalled' shows it to be 'either demonstrably false or readily explainable'. Behe is particularly struck by the fact that Williams neglected to mention that she had written to the Titanic Historical Society requesting information nine months before her hypnotic regression, but also believes she had absorbed details from her reading of Lord's *A Night to Remember*. He even goes further in suggesting that Williams's recollection of the name of Stephen Blackwell – said to be her identity on *Titanic* – was 'an example of cryptamnesia – the emergence into the conscious mind of information once buried in the subconscious'.[610] This last theory is again well worth bearing in mind as one looks at Behe's treatment of cases elsewhere in his book.

(Behe's handling, of the **'Phenomena connected with W.T. Stead'** in his Part III is dealt with in our Chapter 2.)

Possible psychic phenomena

Here is how Behe initially describes this category of cases in the general Introduction to his book:

> *These are accounts which have many characteristics of probable psychic phenomena, but which lack a vital piece of information necessary to class them as such. With additional information, some of these accounts might be explained as having normal causes. Others, however, may turn out to have*

610 Behe, pp. 56-57.

> *a probable paranormal origin. Pending further research, these accounts must be classed in a category between the two extremes.*[611]

This is marginally modified in his introduction to Part IV, where he claims only that 'many' of the cases 'lack certain vital information', and that several 'may well be examples of genuine psychic phenomena'.[612] He does, however, suggest three sub-categories into which the accounts which lack information fall: (A) names of the people involved are not mentioned, thus precluding further research, though this does not ('in most cases') cast doubt on the truthfulness of the accounts; (B) the percipient died on *Titanic*: 'His words or actions before the disaster suggest that he *may* have experienced a premonition of danger, but his death precludes a definite conclusion'; (C) the percipient survived, but never commented publicly on his possible psychic experience. There is the possibility of researching these cases further, through family members.

He also suggests three sub-categories into which the 'remaining reports' fall: (D) predictions made by 'professional psychics'. Since genuine psychic phenomena 'seem to have a rather sporadic, spontaneous nature', caution seems advisable in dealing with 'individuals who claim the ability to routinely utilise psychic phenomena'. Although some of the latter made extremely accurate predictions, all of their reports should be grouped together as *possible* psychic events; (E) cases which occurred 'long

611 Behe, p. 12.

612 Behe, p. 88.

after the *Titanic* disaster'. These cases are provocative, but need further research; (F) a 'couple of cases' previously classed as genuine, but where new information raises serious questions about their true nature. (Behe adds that two cases may well be examples of precognition, but cannot be considered as *probable* psychic phenomena, because the names of those involved will never be known.)[613]

These comments raise a number of extremely important issues and deserve careful consideration. The first point is that the allocation of the six categories into two groups of three, with only the experiences in the first group apparently lacking vital information, seems a pretty significant departure from Behe's opening comments on 'possible' cases. Category (E) is at least consistent with these comments, but (D) – classing all predictions made by professional psychics as possibles – is radically different. Approximately a third of the cases discussed in Part IV of Behe's book fall into this category. And (F), concerning instances where *new* information has come to light, is barely compatible with the criterion of lack of vital information. Once again, it might be argued that categories (A)-(F) should not be taken too literally, but Behe might have done better not to set them out at all than to create inconsistencies.

His remarks about newspapers ('Most of the anonymous accounts were published in British newspapers') also deserve some attention. His view that the reporters 'wanted to let the public know that these curious events *did* take place, and yet still preserve the

613 Behe, pp. 88-89. The two cases are **(GB,po,15)** and **(GB,po,16)**.

privacy of the people involved' and that 'the newspapers did not wish to intrude upon their grief by publicising their names' is a generous one. It may certainly be questioned whether this generosity is justified, and Behe's view contrasts strongly with the stance of Gardner, who is dismissive of cases where names are omitted. Moreover, there are undoubtedly instances where names are simply not known. All of this rather strengthens the worry that, in general, Behe is somewhat over-dependent on newspapers in his book as a whole.

Both (B) and (C) seem to imply that comments made by percipients *after* the disaster may (greatly) strengthen the case for premonitions, but it is important to remember that this is by no means necessarily so. Indeed, there are examples of survivors whose claims to have had premonitions are tangibly weakened by their comments after the event. And, of course, Behe's earlier critical remarks about the use of 'hindsight' also bear on this matter. Furthermore, it has to be pointed out that the dangers of reliance on the later recollections of members of the percipient's family are considerable. In fact, unless these are supported by written records (preferably registered by the percipient), it is quite hard to imagine in what circumstances one might upgrade a case to probable just on the basis of what family members remember of earlier discussions.

Category (D) obviously raises the question of whether the decision to regard all predictions by professional psychics as only possibles is justified. Especially as Behe has taken some trouble to expose in some detail the fraudulent measures used by some psychics, caution here seems entirely appropriate. But, remembering that Behe himself is anxious not to classify any of his cases as 'definite' psychic phenomena, it might have been more helpful had he distinguished between the strengths of his different professionals' claims by locating them in separate categories, rather than grouping them *en bloc*. Much more important here, however, is the assertion that 'Genuine psychic phenomena seem to have a rather sporadic, spontaneous nature which cannot often be summoned at will'. In addition to having negative implications for the whole matter of scientific experiments on the paranormal (which are not mentioned anywhere in Behe's book), this is a rare attempt on Behe's part to characterise psychic phenomena in general terms. It is, needless to say, a view widely shared, and one to which Behe adheres consistently in his treatment of individual cases (which very frequently includes the terms 'sudden' and 'suddenly' in descriptions of experiences).

Categories (E) and (F) are of less significance. Behe acknowledges that only a 'couple of cases' fall under (F). And, in practice, those under (E) are scarcely more numerous: Behe seems to imply that they have come to light *so* recently that there has been no time for them to be looked into carefully.

The following list does not constitute the whole of Behe's sequence in this section. Some of the experiences he records in Part IV actually occurred too late to be considered as premonitions of the *Titanic* disaster. And a few have already been discussed as Stevenson's or Brown's cases, since they were the first to raise them.

CASES

(GB,po,1) In 1907 a gypsy fortune-teller told the American doctor and surgeon, **Dr Minahan**, that he would die while on a steamer on his second trip abroad. In 1911 Minahan's sister was told by another fortune-teller that within two years misfortune would befall two members of her family, at least one of whom would die. Behe notes that both predictions were fulfilled, since Minahan was returning from his second trip to Europe when he died on *Titanic*, and another sister accompanying him had been very seriously ill with appendicitis in Europe. He finds the specificity of the first prediction 'striking', speculating that, in spite of the fact that 'the lines in a person's hand have nothing to do with his future', the clairvoyant may have 'tuned in' with Minahan 'in a psychic manner' while reading his palm. But he believes that the second prediction might be put down to coincidence.[614] The caution that Behe exercises in reporting on all professional clairvoyants probably explains why he regards this case as only a *possible* psychic phenomenon, but, although he uses five different newspapers as his sources, details are somewhat lacking.

Méheust follows Behe very closely in this instance,[615] adding that Minahan increased his life-assurance before embarking on his second cross-Atlantic journey.[616] In

614 Behe, pp. 89-91.

615 Méheust, pp. 78-79 **(BM,3)**. The warning given to Minahan's sister, Mary MacCormick, may be regarded as a separate premonition in Méheust's book **(BM,4)**, where he adds that we do not know whether she passed this warning on to her brother.

616 Méheust, p.81.

Part III of his book he emphasises that death at sea is a prediction commonly made by fortune-tellers. He thinks that the available information is insufficient to enable us to decide whether the succession of events could be attributed to chance, and classes the cases of Minahan and his sister together as only one-star-plus.[617]

(GB,po,2) In 1911 a gypsy fortune-teller read the palm of an **officer of the steamship *George Washington***, saying 'on the sea lies your work and next year the greatest ship in the world will sink – sink!'. The officer (who had 'no real connection' with *Titanic*) and his wife are greatly amused, but the gypsy weeps, seeing 'sadness – death – sinking – sinking!' Behe stresses that the gypsy was accurate in saying that the greatest ship in the world would sink, despite the fact that the sinking was 'a very remote possibility'. If the woman was just guessing 'it was a guess which was extremely unlikely to come true'.[618]

Méheust astutely points out that Behe does not say whether the officer was in uniform, arguing that, if he was, there is nothing extraordinary about the gypsy's predictions, which may well have been a vengeful reaction to the officer's amusement: 'what she says to the officer is less a prediction than a curse'. But he concedes that it is possible that a real prediction was also involved, acknowledging that the case would be more disturbing if the officer could not be identified as a sailor. He rates the case as just one star.[619]

617 Méheust, p. 167.

618 Behe, p. 91.

619 Méheust, pp. 79-80, 167-168 **(BM,5)**.

(GB,po,3) A friend of John Hume, a violinist in *Titanic*'s orchestra, told a reporter that **Hume's mother** begged him not to go back to life on the sea after *Olympic*'s collision with *Hawke*, saying that she had had a premonition (a dream 'of some sort') that 'something would happen to him' on *Titanic*. But Behe acknowledges that we do not know when Mrs Hume had her dream, or exactly what it entailed, pointing out that the friend's statements are 'slightly at odds with each other' (he first said that Mrs Hume thought something would happen to her son on *this* trip, then that she believed no good would come of it if he went back to sea). Nevertheless, he finds it significant that Hume was so deeply impressed that he told several people about his mother's dream.[620]

Méheust relates the same story, citing Behe.[621] But he is not convinced, and in Part III of his book rates it as only one star.[622] Like Behe, he emphasises that the mother's concern for her son was entirely normal. The whole case, apparently based on a single newspaper report, is particularly insubstantial.

(GB,po,4) The case of Edwina Troutt (**Edwina McKenzie**) is even more elusive and unconvincing. Behe says that it involves a dream that happened 'either around 1907 or 1911-12' and was related in the 1980s. Only the ending of the dream stuck in Miss Troutt's memory: 'She dreamed that someone had tapped her on the shoulder while speaking to her. His final words were, "… and it

620 Behe, p. 92.

621 Méheust, p. 84 **(BM,13)**.

622 Méheust, p. 170.

was the largest ship in the world"'.[623] Behe's source for this case is a personal letter from Don Lynch. It is hard to understand why he considers it 'unfortunate' that we will never be able to clarify the incident any further, and no surprise that Méheust does not mention it at all.

(GB,po,5) Behe includes the original **prophecy** of a sinking mentioned in one of his 'curious coincidences' as a separate case in his category of possible psychic phenomena, saying that he has been unable to find any additional information on the prediction, but regarding its accuracy as 'uncanny'. He now argues that the prophecy itself may be a 'genuine case of precognition', though he allows that it cannot be classed as such without further particulars on the circumstances surrounding its origin.[624]

Méheust adds that the prediction circulated in maritime circles, but does not include this in the cases in his dossier in Part III of his book.[625]

(GB,po,7) The famous clairvoyant, **Madame de Thèbes**, apparently made a number of (accurate) political predictions concerning 1912, and also forecast a 'great marine disaster'. In April 1912, she told an American woman not to sail on *Titanic*, since her palm yielded signs of danger. Later, she denied warning Astor that he would lose his life at sea, but agreed that she had told Stead more than once that danger by water threatened him.[626] Behe, who discusses the warnings to Stead elsewhere in his book,

623 Behe, p. 93.

624 Behe, p. 93 **(GB,po,5)**. See **(GB,cc,10)**.

625 Méheust, p. 82 **(BM,8)**.

626 Behe, pp. 94-95.

wonders here whether these were 'mere guesswork'. He speculates that she may have had occasional 'precognitive insights'.

Méheust points out that we do not know the identities of the *two* American women, or whether the warning to them was heeded.[627] In Part III of his book he claims Madame de Thèbes's other predictions may have been deductions and her foreseeing of a maritime catastrophe based on statistical probabilities. He claims the story of the American women is second-hand, and rates the case of Mme de Thèbes as just one-star.[628]

(GB,po,8) Miss **Caroline Endres**, a nurse who cared for Astor's young wife, accompanied them to Europe despite the fact that, for some unknown reason, she 'dreaded the thought' of taking this particular trip. After the sinking, she never publicly elaborated on her fear.[629] Méheust does not refer to this case.

(GB,po,9) In January 1912, **one of the daughters of Mr and Mrs Mark Fortune**, **Alice**, had her palm read in Cairo by an Indian fortune-teller: 'You are in danger every time you travel on the sea, for I see you adrift on the ocean in an open boat. You will lose everything but your life. You will be saved, but others will be lost'. Despite this unpleasant prediction, in April Alice persuaded a friend of the family, W.T. Sloper, to travel with them on *Titanic*, only to point out the next day that she was a 'dangerous person' to travel with, because of the fortune-teller's prediction.

627 Méheust, pp. 81-82 **(BM,7)**.

628 Méheust, p. 176.

629 Behe, p. 95.

In saying goodbye to Sloper after the disaster, Alice again reminded him of the fortune-teller. Mrs Fortune and her three daughters were saved, as was Sloper, but Mark Fortune and his son were lost on *Titanic.*[630] Behe – whose source is a book privately published by Sloper (in 1949)[631] – describes the prophecy as 'accurate in every sense of the word', although, since Alice's mother and Alice's two sisters were saved with her, she cannot be described as having lost everything but her life. He believes that if the fortune-teller had read the fortunes of the rest of the Fortune family (and their friend Sloper), this would have solved the question of whether or not she was guessing, but this seems to be a considerable over-simplification.

Like Behe, Méheust, who follows the fate of the family stage by stage,[632] notes in Part III of his book that there is more in the prediction than the usual fortune-tellers' generalities, saying that it continued to trouble Alice 'until the fatal moment', but he also remarks that it is fulfilled only 'in part'. He does not regard the case as wholly convincing and rates it as two stars.[633]

The oddity of the fact that, in this story, Alice seems in many respects to play the part that her mother might be expected to have played (asking for the fortune-teller, then paying him; asking Sloper to change his return reservation from *Mauretania* to *Titanic*, only to say that she was sorry he had done so; appearing with a tear-stained face at the

630 Behe, pp. 95-97.

631 *The Life and Times of Andrew Jackson Sloper* (1949).

632 Méheust, pp. 82-83, 94, 123, 133 **(BM,9)**

633 Méheust, p.172.

cabin door on *Carpathia* and telling Sloper they would be met by friends) may be explained by a particular interest that Sloper had in Alice, who appears to have been his dancing partner.

(GB,po,10) The businessman **George Wick** was advised by a colleague in New York not to go to Europe with his family: 'I have a feeling that this trip is not going to do you any good. Better stay here'. Wick went down with *Titanic*, but his family were saved.[634] Behe very weakly speculates that the colleague might have had a more specific fear for Wick's personal safety, but was too embarrassed to express it. Méheust makes no reference to the case.

(GB,po,11) It was rumoured that the famous novelist **Jacques Futrelle** had a premonition of danger before *Titanic* sailed, and that that was why, in March 1912, he made arrangements for the administration of the estates of his wife and himself, and for the future care of their children: 'You can never tell what will happen'. He went down with the ship, but his rescued widow never commented on her husband's state of mind.[635] Surprisingly, Méheust, who has a great deal to say about writers' premonitions, makes no reference to Futrelle.

(GB,po,12) It was rumoured that the **wife of the Reverend Stuart Holden** had a presentiment that *Titanic* would not reach America. They were due to sail on the ship but did not, because Mrs Holden was ill.[636] They never

634 Behe, p. 97.

635 Behe, p. 98.

636 Behe, pp. 98-99.

commented publicly on the circumstances. Méheust does not take up this case.

(GB,po,13) Using a 1945 book by W.O. Stevens as his source, Behe notes that an **unnamed woman**, in 1912, after observing 'glowing, shining letters on the wall of her home which spelled the words "Beware Titanic"', deliberately missed *Titanic*, on which she had booked a passage.[637] He comments that it is 'unfortunate' that the account was not more thoroughly documented, and hopes that more information may come to light. There is no record of this in Méheust's book.

(GB,po,14) Behe uses a newspaper report as his source for noting: 'It was said that an **unknown woman** approached Andrews before sailing day and solemnly warned him that, if he sailed on *Titanic*, calamity would befall him.'[638] He records that there is no corroboration of this account, and no further detail. The incident is not mentioned by Méheust.

(GB,po,15) In March 1912, the **mother of a young farmer** from Athenry in Ireland dreamed for three nights in succession that *Titanic*, on which he was due to emigrate to America, sank in mid-ocean, with all on board. She was so affected by the dream that she eventually persuaded her son to cancel his passage.[639] Behe refers to an American newspaper as his source, and, despite the fact that names were withheld (he claims that this 'does not cast doubt on the reality of the mother's experience'), considers it

637 Behe, p. 99. W.O. Stevens, *Unbidden Guests* (1945).

638 Behe, p. 99.

639 Behe, pp. 99-100.

'pretty clear that the dream was of a precognitive nature'. The reasons he gives are 'the repetition of the same dream and the deep impression it made on the woman'. In introducing this section of his book he picked out two cases, of which this is one, that 'may well be examples of precognition relating to *Titanic*', saying that it is only because the names will never be known that the story is not classed as a *probable* psychic phenomenon. He ignores the inaccuracy of the mother's prediction that all on board *Titanic* will die.

Méheust is not concerned by the lack of names (though he notes the absence of a written record), but is struck by the *insistent* nature of the dream, suggesting that, in Ireland, a dream occurring three times is considered premonitory. But he again stresses the normality of the mother's concern for her son, rating the case as only one star.[640]

(GB,po,16) On 9 April 1912, a well-known solicitor was visited by a **wealthy businessman** who wanted him to agree to be a guardian to his two little boys, saying: 'Tomorrow I and my wife are sailing on *Titanic*. I cannot tell why, but I feel that something is going to happen, and that we shall never see our children again.'[641] Once more, the names were never revealed (the source is a Cornish newspaper). Despite acknowledging that it is unknown whether the businessman or his wife survived (there is, of course, no proof that they even sailed on *Titanic*), Behe asserts that the man's premonition of danger was 'very

640 Méheust, pp. 87, 174 **(BM,18)**.

641 Behe, p. 100.

real'. Surprisingly, this was the second case he singled out that 'may well' be an example of precognition. Méheust makes no reference to this case.

(GB,po,18) A **Southampton steward** told his wife, just before leaving her to board *Titanic*, that he wished he had never signed on for the ship.[642] Behe feebly remarks that the tone of his comment suggests that he felt uneasy about the ship! The press did not reveal the man's identity, and we presumably do not know whether he survived, or even sailed on *Titanic*. Méheust does not mention the case.

(GB,po,19) A **greaser** turned around and walked back down *Titanic*'s gangway, saying that he would not sail on the ship because his 'missus would only worry'.[643] Behe wonders why the unemployed greaser would turn his back on a profitable berth, and asks whether the wife had a premonition. Méheust makes no reference to the story.

(GB,po,22) On 14 and 15 April 1912, **Mrs M. von Walden** experienced a 'strange psychological nervousness' and heard the 'voice' of her brother calling for help. She tried to discover whether he was on *Titanic*.[644] Although it is not known whether the brother was actually on the ship, or what the outcome was, for some reason Behe concludes that Mrs von Walden 'may well have had a genuine psychic experience regarding some misfortune which may have befallen him'. Méheust does not mention the case.

(GB,po,23) A **newspaperman with the *Houston Chronicle*** woke out of a sound sleep on the night of 14-15

642 Behe, p. 102.

643 Behe, pp. 102-103.

644 Behe, p. 107.

April 'oppressed by a feeling of horror'. He later recalled, 'I had a sense of disaster on me', and said he was 'impressed with the thought that something evil had fallen one near and dear to me' [*sic*]. It seemed as if he could hear 'frantic voices calling from a very great distance'. When he learned in the morning papers of *Titanic*'s collision with an iceberg, he was sure that some of his friends were on the ship. He did not believe the reassuring reports that *Titanic* was still afloat, but was concerned that there had been a great tragedy 'and that one or more of my friends had shared in it'. On 16 April he read that a couple whom he had known affectionately for years had been involved. The wife had been saved, but the husband had died. The newspaperman was sure that the man had sent him a message 'while he fronted death on the sinking wreck'.[645] Interestingly, Behe denies this, saying that, because of the time-difference, *Titanic* had sunk two-and-a-half hours before the newspaperman woke at 2am. He is nevertheless impressed with the awareness of a tragedy in which friends were involved and the certainty that this was the *Titanic* sinking.

Using Behe as his source, Méheust modifies a few details in the account,[646] but in Part III of his book he echoes Behe's point about the time-difference (although he says it was two-and-a-half hours, then three hours), concluding that there was no direct telepathic communication. He still believes that this was 'very probably' an experience of a paranormal nature, and one which matches perfectly

645 Behe, pp. 107-109.

646 Méheust, p. 130 (**BM,66**).

what is known about telepathic 'hallucinations', saying that information sometimes takes a certain time to rise from psychic depths. He classes the case as three stars.[647] But when discussing his eight favoured paranormal experiences, Méheust claims that the journalist had 'the vision of an indeterminate sinking'.[648]

(GB,po,24) After the early optimistic reports, **Stead's son Alfred** greatly doubted – 'the opinion of the experts to the contrary not withstanding' – that *Titanic* had remained afloat.[649] Behe admits that Alfred never commented publicly on his doubts, but says that is was 'suggested at the time' that his belief that *Titanic* was lost had originated during his sleep on 14-15 April. He argues that his subconscious mind 'may have received knowledge of the sinking in a telepathic manner,' and that after he awoke that knowledge existed 'only as a haunting recognition of something that remained just below the threshold of consciousness.' Behe says that it may not have been recognised at all, but still influenced his consciousness, producing a belief he could not explain logically. But Behe's elaborate speculation has no particular justification at all and seems out of proportion, given that we have no knowledge of Alfred's reaction. Méheust does not mention this case.

(GB,po,25) The **wife of steward Arthur Lewis** had to wait until 20 April to learn that her husband was safe. She said, 'I knew all along he would be safe. A voice kept

647 Méheust, p. 196.

648 Méheust, p. 208.

649 Behe, pp. 109-110.

telling me he would be all right.'[650] Behe admits that Mrs Lewis did not go into detail concerning her last comment, but suggests that she may have meant exactly what she said and heard a 'voice' telling her there was nothing to fear. He regrets that she was not questioned further on this point. Méheust makes no reference to the case.

Probable psychic phenomena

Behe first describes his cases of 'probable psychic phenomena' as accounts which 'stand up well to critical examination, seem incapable of being explained in "ordinary" terms, and *may* be genuine examples of paranormal phenomena.' Anxious not to make 'dogmatic pronouncements about the reality of psychic phenomena', he adds that 'the most we can say' is that the cases in his final category are 'highly suggestive of psychic phenomena, and that the evidence now available seems to preclude their being explained in "normal" terms.'[651]

In his introduction to Part V he says that these cases are not 'general misgivings about crossing the ocean on just any ship, but were directed specifically at the upcoming voyage of *Titanic*.' Serious premonitions told many people that something ghastly was going to happen on *this* voyage, even though the ship was considered unsinkable and a disaster on her maiden voyage a 'ludicrous impossibility'. Without making this a criterion of premonitions, Behe

650 Behe, p. 110.

651 Behe, pp. 12-13. He does later record that in one of his cases, **(GB,pr,23)**, there is very persuasive evidence that a particular dream was 'a true example of precognition'.

emphasises that some of the passengers who 'suddenly' had forebodings of danger were profoundly impressed and deeply affected, especially as several had never had such a presentiment before. He also believes that for a crew member to give up his berth on *Titanic* merely because of a feeling, 'one must assume that these forebodings were quite strong, too strong to be an ordinary feeling, too strong to be ignored'.[652] Although he limits the scope of this last point – almost arguing in a circular fashion – by focusing on crew who decided not to sail, the very *strength* of forebodings is something on which he will insist on many occasions in examining particular cases. Indeed, this often seems to be the only – or certainly the main – reason why he classifies them as probables. However, the apparent assumption that premonitions are *feelings* should not go unnoticed.

It is a measure of Behe's great contribution to the topic of *Titanic* premonitions as a whole that of his 35 'probable' cases no fewer than 29 are ones that he is the first of our authors to bring to light.

CASES

(GB,pr,1) Mrs **Jennie Hansen** said to her brother before undertaking a trip from Wisconsin, 'I dread taking the trip to Denmark, for I have a feeling that I will never return alive. I just know the boat will sink or something awful happen to me either going over or coming back.' She felt sufficiently strongly to make funeral and other

652 Behe, pp. 118-119.

arrangements. Her husband and his brother went down with *Titanic*, but she was saved.[653] Behe points out that she *was* a victim, though not quite in the manner she feared, but this is surely to underestimate the inaccuracy of her prediction.

Méheust recounts the same story.[654] But in Part III of his book he says he believes that not enough is known to decide on this case, especially as there is no written account from before the event. Yet he rules out 'subliminal inference', since Mrs Hanson did not know before leaving America on which ship she would return. He rates the case as one-star-plus.[655]

(GB,pr,2) Mr B.O. Shepherd booked his return passage on *Titanic* two months in advance. At an unspecified time, **his wife**, in Nebraska, had a frightening dream in which she saw *Titanic* sinking. She wrote a letter to her husband asking him not to travel on the ship, then sent a cable repeating her plea. Mr Shepherd transferred to another White Star steamship.[656] Using one newspaper (*New York Tribune*) as his source, Behe stresses the strength of the wife's certainty, although he admits that she may not have known that he had actually booked on *Titanic*, and only wanted to make sure that he was not considering doing so. Méheust does not mention this case.

(GB,pr,4) In March 1912, Miss **Helen Bell** suddenly saw a picture formed between herself and a newspaper

653 Behe, p. 119. Behe mistakenly spells the surname 'Hanson', as does Méheust.

654 Méheust, pp.85-86 **(BM,15)**.

655 Méheust, p. 173.

656 Behe, p. 120.

carrying an article describing *Titanic*. The picture showed 'a night scene with what I took to be jagged and pointed rocks, with the hull of a boat sticking out of the water'. With it came a voice saying, 'This will be on its first voyage', but when she asked 'Why? What is the matter with the boat', the reply was, 'Nothing; *that* is all right, but it will be on its first voyage'. Bell said she had not sent her experience to the newspapers before the disaster because no paper would have printed it.[657] Behe comments only that Miss Bell sent her experience to the spiritualist publication, *Light*, at the end of August 1912. Again he says nothing of the inaccuracies in the picture and voice (the jagged rocks and the suggestion that there is nothing wrong with the ship).

Méheust does not rate this case at all highly (one star), emphasising that the account appeared only after the sinking, and suggesting that the voice seems too good to be true.[658]

(GB,pr,5) Mr C.S. Battle had a 'strange feeling' that all might not go well if he sailed on *Titanic*, and booked his passage on *Olympic* instead.[659] Behe makes no substantive comment. Méheust does not mention the case.

(GB,pr,6) On seeing *Titanic*, on which Richard Rouse had booked a passage, **his wife, Charity**, said, 'that ship is too big. I have a bad feeling that it will never reach America. Please don't go! Please don't get on the boat'. She pleaded with him all week before the sailing, but Richard

657 Behe, p. 122.

658 Méheust, pp. 88, 175 (**BM,20**).

659 Behe, p. 123.

assured her that it was said that the ship was unsinkable. He went down with *Titanic*.[660] Behe received a letter from Rouse's daughter, who clearly recalls the events, but he also cites two newspapers. However, he makes no substantive comment on the episode.

Méheust sees this as another case where we cannot decide whether it was a true premonition or a 'subliminal inference', believing that working-class people in 1912 did not automatically associate great size with greater safety.[661]

(GB,pr,7) Fred Smith, who was responsible for Archdeacon Madden's visit to America to lecture in Carnegie Hall, instructed him to change his passage from *Titanic* to *Mauretania*, saying it 'would save time and get here earlier'. He said later that he had had 'a very strong feeling that the Archdeacon ought to come earlier'.[662] Behe thinks Smith may have meant that Madden could leave home three days later (*Mauretania* sailed on 13 April, later than Smith expected) and still arrive on time. He simply reiterates that Smith had 'a very strong feeling' that it was in the Archdeacon's best interest to miss *Titanic*'s maiden voyage. Méheust makes no reference to the case.

(GB,pr,8) Miss **Margaret Devaney**, who was due to emigrate on *Titanic*, had a 'premonition that something was going to happen', but took passage on *Titanic* because she thought it would be safe and could not sink. She was confident in *Titanic*'s safety even after the collision, and was one of the few Third Class passengers to find a place in a

660 Behe, pp. 123-124.

661 Méheust, pp. 92, 180 (**BM,23**).

662 Behe, pp. 124-125

lifeboat.[663] Behe thinks Devaney's 'definite, but unfocused, foreboding' is very reminiscent of that experienced by Major Butt: both thought they were avoiding danger by travelling in the safest ship in the world.

Méheust briefly echoes Behe's treatment of Devaney's feelings,[664] but fails to include Devaney when he examines his own dossier case by case in Part III of his book.

(GB,pr,9) Mrs Frank Adelman had a sudden premonition of danger regarding *Titanic*, shortly before sailing day, and wanted to take a later ship with her husband. She won the toss when they flipped a coin to decide, and they sailed later on *Kaiser Wilhelm der Grosse*.[665] Behe comments only that the premonition must have made a very deep impression on Mrs Adelman. He cites four newspaper sources for this especially flimsy story. Méheust does not mention the case.

(GB,pr,10) Having made three sets of golf clubs for an American visitor, **Mr Steer**, a Blackpool golf professional, had the 'sudden, strange feeling that he should urge the man not to travel on *Titanic*', but did not do so.[666] Behe says that Steer related this story to his son 'in later years'. The name of the American is not recorded, so that we do not know whether he survived the sinking (or even sailed on *Titanic*). Méheust does not refer to this story.

(GB,pr,11) William Klein, a friend of the theatrical producer Henry Harris, was filled with a 'strong feeling of

663 Behe, p. 125.

664 Méheust, pp. 91, 123 **(BM,22)**.

665 Behe, pp. 125-126.

666 Behe, p. 126.

impending danger' on learning of Harris's booking to return to America on *Titanic*. He cabled Harris asking him not to sail on the ship, but plans had already been made. Klein even approached another friend of Harris, asking him to send a cable. Harris's wife was saved, but he died on the ship.[667] Behe comments only that Klein's premonition must have been very strong. Méheust makes no mention of the case.

(GB,pr,12) When steward **Mr W. Ward's young son, Jackie**, told him not to sail on *Titanic*, because 'the ship was going to roll over', Ward did not change his mind about taking up his first post with White Star. In the days following the disaster there was no news of Ward, but Jackie dreamed 'three times in a row' that he and his father and mother went to the cinema together and was convinced his father was alive. On 19 April a cable arrived from Ward, confirming that he had been rescued.[668] Behe concedes that Jackie's three dreams could have been 'merely due to wishful thinking', but finds his warning that *Titanic* would roll over harder to dismiss (even though 'rolling over' is not a natural description of what happened to *Titanic*). He argues that it was the suddenness of Jackie's fear that made his warning reasonable to those concerned. Méheust makes no reference to this case.

(GB,pr,15) Before boarding *Titanic* **Isaac Frauenthal** had a dream: 'It seemed to me that I was on a big steamship which suddenly crashed into something and began to go down. I saw in the dream as vividly as I could see with open eyes the gradual settling of the ship, and I hear the cries

667 Behe, pp. 126-127.

668 Behe, pp. 127-128.

and shouts of frightened passengers.' He became worried when he had the identical dream a second time, but felt there was no reason to be alarmed or apprehensive about anything when he was on *Titanic*. He was rescued, with his brother and sister-in-law.[669] Behe considers that the *vivid* nature of the dream (and its repetition) makes it probable that the two dreams were 'of a precognitive nature'.

Méheust has Frauenthal worried by his dream throughout *Titanic*'s voyage,[670] and records that after the collision he boasts to his brother: 'Well, Henry, I wasn't so mad, was I?'[671] He is once again impressed by the insistence and powerfulness of the dream, which prevents him from 'totally' rejecting the case, which in Part III of his book he nonetheless classes as only one-star-plus.[672]

(GB,pr,16) Stephen Jenkin was so uneasy when his cross-Atlantic booking was transferred to *Titanic* that he returned to his parents' home to leave his watch and chain and other articles of personal jewellery with them, in case he never returned. He died on *Titanic*.[673] Behe comments only that Jenkin's presentiment of danger must have been strong indeed for him to leave such a necessary article as his watch behind.

Méheust tells the same story.[674] He claims that the details suggest that the premonition did in fact precede

---

669 Behe, pp. 133-134.

670 Méheust, p. 115 **(BM,53)**.

671 Méheust, p. 122.

672 Méheust, p. 190.

673 Behe, p. 134.

674 Méheust, p. 95 **(BM,29)**.

the events, and that the feelings of fear were very intense. But he says that the hypothesis of 'inference' is very strong in this case, and classes it as only one star.[675]

(GB,pr,17) On 9 April 1912, **Colonel John Weir** developed a 'funny feeling' about his passage back to America on *Titanic* ('I'll be hanged if I'll go tomorrow'). He claimed to his hotel manager that he would not go if he received a business message that evening. His foreboding was fuelled by the discovery that a water pitcher had inexplicably broken in his room overnight, and even on the morning of 10 April he told his secretary that he might send a wire from Queenstown if he did not feel like continuing his journey. But he stayed on *Titanic* and went down with her.[676] Behe comments that the presentiment experienced by Weir seems to have been a 'vague, but very real, sense of impending danger connected with his upcoming voyage to America'.

Citing Behe, Méheust modifies a couple of details in the story.[677] He is struck by the strength and sudden nature of the presentiment, but thinks that Weir's feeling is like the sudden conclusion of an unconscious process, which he says is confirmed by Weir's conversation with the hotel manager. If we knew that the feeling preceded Weir's decision to travel on *Titanic*, this would make the genuineness of the presentiment more plausible, but the hypothesis of 'unconscious inference' is the more likely. Méheust finds the superstitions that Weir conjures up

675 Méheust, p. 178.

676 Behe, pp. 134-135.

677 Méheust, p. 94-95 (**BM,28**).

interesting, but stresses that we do not know why he finally decided to travel on *Titanic*. He classes the case as one-star-plus.[678]

(GB,pr,18) According to his mother, says Behe, one of the three **Slade brothers**, trimmers from Southampton, had a dream about *Titanic* the night before they were all three due to sail on her. He afterwards said he had a 'dread' of the ship. They joined up with three shipmates in a pub on the morning of 10 April, but when two of these skipped across the tracks in front of a train shortly before 12 noon, the three brothers stood waiting, saying 'Oh, let the train go by', as the train passed in front of them. Podesta and Nutbean joined *Titanic* in time, but the Slade brothers were turned away as too late to board her.[679] Behe says that it appears that the brothers were intent on boarding *Titanic*, despite their dread of her.

Méheust, however, claims they were 'dragging their heels'. He believes, without mentioning any sources at all, that they forgot the time in the pub. Surely mistakenly on all counts, he says that a passenger train 'stopped' in front of them, recording that Podesta and Nutbean jumped on the train, but that the brothers let it go and returned home.[680] He is surprised that the dream (which he specifies was Bertram's) took on so much importance to them, and that they made such an effort to miss *Titanic*. He classes the case as one-star-plus.[681] Unless Méheust has

678 Méheust, p. 179.

679 Behe, pp.136-137.

680 Méheust, pp. 94, 98 **(BM,27)**.

681 Méheust, p. 182.

some uncited source for this story other than Behe's three (one of which is Beesley's book),[682] this is a good example of how alleged premonition stories can become distorted in the telling.

(GB,pr,19) Harry Burrows had been especially keen to work aboard *Titanic*, but returned to his mother's house on 10 April without having signed on. She later told the press that he had changed his mind 'at the last minute'. She could not explain why: 'some sort of feeling came over him, he told me'.[683] Behe says Burrows's feeling must have been very strong indeed, since he had waited in Southampton for an entire month in order to sail on *Titanic*, but he does not mention that Burrows himself did not apparently comment on his change of mind. Méheust briefly relates the story,[684] but does not include it in his dossier in Part III of his book.

(GB,pr,20) Citing four newspapers, Behe says that before leaving South Africa for England **Mr T.W.S. Brown** experienced a bad dream, but he refused to say what it was about. Then, his wife Edith says, he had a 'strange premonition' when he and his family were walking towards *Titanic*'s gangway. He later told his wife that he had had a ghastly feeling that 'something was going to happen'. And after the *New York* incident he said, 'That was a bad omen'.[685] Behe finds it 'unfortunate' that we know nothing about Mr Brown's dream, which

682 Lawrence Beesley, *The Loss of the SS Titanic. Its Story and its Lessons* (1912).

683 Behe, p. 137.

684 Méheust, p. 98 **(BM,34)**.

685 Behe, pp. 137-139.

seems to have been connected with his plans to journey to America, but points out that his presentiment before boarding *Titanic* was much more immediate, and that Mrs Brown recognised it as 'pertaining specifically to that ship's upcoming voyage.[686] (Behe also refers his reader to a 'possible' psychic phenomenon when, a year after the *Titanic* disaster, Mrs Brown and her daughter Edith apparently received a message from Mr Brown through a medium in Australia.)

Citing Behe, Méheust recounts the story, suggesting that the meaning of Brown's dream at the end of 1911 may have come back to him near *Titanic*'s gangway.[687] If this were so, it would indicate that this is another case of the recurring, long-lasting premonition. In Part III of his book he classes the case as two stars.[688] (Interestingly, in a memoir on his mother's life, Edith's son David records Brown's feeling of faintness and panic on approaching *Titanic* as a repetition of a feeling when the booking was made – he also registers the 'bad omen' incident and the Australian medium's message – but makes no reference whatever to any dream Brown may have had in South Africa.)[689]

(GB,pr,22) On the night of 10 April 1912, **Patrick O'Keefe**, due to board *Titanic* in Queenstown the next day, had 'an unsettling dream in which he saw *Titanic* going down in mid-ocean'. He survived the sinking and

686 Behe, pp. 110-113.

687 Méheust, pp. 99-100, 123 **(BM,37)**.

688 Méheust, p. 181.

689 David Haisman, *'I'll See You in New York'. Titanic. The Courage of a Survivor* (1999).

wrote a letter to his father mentioning his dream.[690] Behe states that the newspaper reports went into no detail regarding the contents of this letter, so that we know only that O'Keefe dreamed of the tragedy before it happened. Méheust does not mention the letter, but briefly recounts the story of the dream, though he does not include this case in his dossier in Part III of his book.[691]

(GB,pr,23) A survivor, Bertha Mulvihill recorded that when *Titanic* left Queenstown, Eugene Ryan – also from Athlone in Ireland – told her he had dreamt that *Titanic* was going to sink, 'And every night we were at sea he told us he had dreamt that *Titanic* was going down before we reached New York. On Sunday night, just before he went to bed, he told us *Titanic* was going to sink that night. It was uncanny.' Elsewhere she related that in his dream Ryan 'had plainly seen the collision with the iceberg'.[692] Behe thinks Mulvihill was actually referring to **Eugene Daly** (something that has subsequently been confirmed), but points out that, although Daly survived, he never spoke publicly of his dreams. He wonders whether Daly's dream repeated itself each night or whether he dreamed it once and kept reiterating the warning to his friends. In any case, Daly finally told his friends on Sunday evening that the ship would sink *that night*, even talking of collision with an iceberg. Behe is so impressed by how specific the dream was about what would happen and when that he regards it as 'the most impressive case

690 Behe, p. 141.

691 Méheust, pp. 105, 125 **(BM,42)**.

692 Behe, pp. 141-142.

on record concerning the sinking of *Titanic*' and 'a true example of precognition'.

Although Méheust refers to Eugene *Daly*, he mistakenly claims that Daly was lost. He emphasises that on the Sunday evening Daly very specifically foresaw that *Titanic* would sink during the night after striking an iceberg.[693] In Part III of his book he finds the story very striking, but says it does not have the guarantees that he seeks, since we know of it only via a survivor. He says, rather mysteriously, that even if the account is reliable and the dream really did precede the tragedy, there is nothing to exclude the possibility of an 'unconscious process at work'. If this was a dream that was actually repeated, moreover, it comes under the Irish belief that something dreamed three times is indeed premonitory. Méheust assumes that Daly was Catholic and claims that he was, consciously or unconsciously, expecting 'divine punishment'. Yet, although he does not go quite so far as Behe, he acknowledges that the insistence of the dream and the 'emotional potential' are disturbing enough for us to put this case 'on the paranormal side'.[694] He rates it as two-stars.

Méheust's implication that some doubt must attach to the accounts of survivors is unsatisfactory and far-reaching, but the fact that Daly never subsequently recorded anything about a dream that was allegedly so powerful and insistent is puzzling, and, as elsewhere, Behe's reliance on two newspaper reports does not inspire full confidence.

693 Méheust, p. 116 **(BM,54)**.

694 Méheust, p. 187.

(GB,pr,24) On 11 April 1912, **William Rodgers** of Stockport, was attending a meeting of fellow spiritualists – 16 people were present – when he had the curious experience of seeing 'a very large liner with four funnels sailing, then saw it strike what seemed to me white cliffs and gradually sink, bow first'. Another gentleman present said that he sensed the white cliffs were in reality an iceberg.[695] Behe admits that, since the names of the other sitters are unknown, no corroboration is now possible, but he considers Rodgers's statement 'believable'. He finds it 'truly striking' that Rodgers 'saw' in his mind's eye a four-funnelled liner sinking only three days before *Titanic* went down, especially as he was not 'trying to take credit for a completely accurate "vision" of the future', and acknowledged that someone else had a different interpretation of the event.

Méheust adds no details to the case.[696] In Part III of his book he says he finds the evidence for the case to be poor and that the 'usual objections' of subconscious inference, influence of the newspapers, and so on, apply. He claims there is nothing to indicate that it may not have been drawn up after the event, although the reference to white cliffs gives it a dreamlike quality and suggests that it was not subsequently revised. If there had been a written record from before 14 April, this vision would be one of the most notable examples of precognition. As it stands, it remains in the realm of the 'undecidable', and he rates the case as one-star-plus.[697]

---

695 Behe, p. 143.

696 Méheust, pp. 107-108 **(BM,45)**.

697 Méheust, pp. 179-180.

(GB,pr,26) On their way home on the evening of 14 April 1912, **one of Mrs Guggenheim's daughters, Benita**, urged her mother to buy a newspaper: 'Mama, please buy that newspaper. I *know* that something happened to that ship!' Her father, Benjamin Guggenheim, died on the *Titanic*.[698] Behe concedes that it is not known at exactly what time Benita had her sudden foreboding of danger to *Titanic* (though it may have been about two hours before the collision), but claims that it was so strong that she assumed something had *already* happened to the ship, and that news was already in the newspapers. She had somehow become aware that a tragedy was approaching.

Méheust claims that Benita's presentiment took place at the same time as dinner on *Titanic*.[699] He believes that all the usual comments concerning 'unconscious inference' are valid in this case, but that it still offers some insights into the temporal processes of clairvoyance. He classes the case as one-star-plus.[700]

(GB,pr,27) Soon after 10.30pm on 14 April, seventeen-year-old **Laura Cribb** woke very suddenly in her bunk on *Titanic*, with a shiver, almost breathless ('I have a very powerful instinct'). She sat upright for several minutes and heard the ship collide with the iceberg.[701] Unconvincingly, Behe claims she 'must' have wakened before there was any *physical* stimulus to do so, which leaves only a *mental* stimulus.

698 Behe, pp. 145-146.

699 Méheust, p. 114 (**BM,52**).

700 Méheust, pp. 186-187.

701 Behe, pp. 146-147.

Méheust relates the incident,[702] but says in Part III of his book that it is impossible to prove that this was not a simple coincidence. He rates the case as only one-star.[703]

(GB,pr,28) After the collision, Mrs Churchill Candee asked **Edward Kent** to take care of her locket and other valuables. Kent did so, but was reluctant, telling her he had a 'feeling that fate would be against him in the coming crisis'. The valuables were returned to her after his body was recovered from the sea.[704] Behe comments that when Kent sought Candee out it was not generally known that *Titanic* was sinking. He thinks that Kent's reluctance to accept responsibility for Candee's valuables would be 'natural under any circumstances', but that his feeling that fate was against him gives added meaning to his reluctance. Méheust makes no reference to the case.

(GB,pr,29) In lifeboat 7 Miss **Margaret Hays** told her fellow passengers not to worry, that a ship 'with a name like "C-A-R" was on its way to their rescue. *Carpathia* picked up the survivors several hours later.[705] Behe says that in later years Hays said that the partial name had 'just come' to her, and that she had no 'normal' way of knowing what ships were coming to the rescue. Lifeboat 7 was lowered almost simultaneously with Captain Smith's being made aware by Bride of *Carpathia*'s proximity, but this was on the bridge and not within earshot of the lifeboat. Behe argues that there is no evidence of Hays unconsciously

702 Méheust, p. 119 **(BM,58)**.

703 Méheust, p. 195.

704 Behe, p. 147.

705 Behe, pp. 148-149.

overhearing *Carpathia*'s name being mentioned. No other survivor in lifeboat 7 heard any early mention of the ship. Hence 'all available evidence' suggests that Miss Hays independently came up with a partial name for it. According to her daughter, Miss Hays had several other psychic experiences in her life. Méheust makes no mention of this case, which one might be forgiven for finding especially flimsy. It is hard to establish a negative conclusively (that Miss Hays did not overhear mention of the name).

(GB,pr,31) The **wife of Luigi Gatti**, restaurant manager on *Titanic*, 'suddenly began to experience a strange presentiment of danger' on the night of 14 April 1912. Her foreboding continued on the morning of 15 April and her uneasy feeling went with her to London, where she paid regular visits to the White Star offices to find out whether her husband was safe. He was lost on *Titanic*.[706] Behe insists that Mrs Gatti knew that *something* was wrong on 14 April, although she apparently did not connect her presentiment specifically with *Titanic*. He cites only the *Belfast Evening Telegraph* as his source.

Méheust mentions only Behe as his source, but adds that Mrs Gatti's presentiment dated back to January, when her husband signed on.[707] Yet in Part III of his book he repeats, puzzlingly, that it was 'a strong worry with no apparent reason' and that she did not connect it with *Titanic* sinking. He finds the case 'factually fairly convincing', illustrating the 'classic phenomena that

706 Behe, pp. 151-152.

707 Méheust, pp. 84, 127 **(BM,11)**.

accompany telepathic hallucinations', and rates it as two stars.[708]

(GB,pr,32) Henry Forbes Julian, a British mining and metallurgical expert, uncharacteristically had a presage of coming disaster when he very reluctantly agreed to go to America for his firm. Neither his wife nor his aunt had ever seen him in this mood before. His wife, Hester, had never felt anxiety for his safety while he was on board a ship, but on 14 April she could not sleep, because she was suddenly 'filled with some presentiment of coming evil and felt too anxious to be able to sleep.' She rose at midnight, to read prayers, 'especially those appointed to be used at sea'. Several days later she learned she had been widowed by the *Titanic* disaster.[709] Behe states that Julian 'never stated to anyone' that he was uneasy about his trip, and that the letters he wrote to his wife from *Titanic* contained no hint that he felt any premonition of danger. He finds Mrs Julian's uneasiness 'more striking', coming as it did about two-and-a-half hours before the collision. Her fear that her husband would face danger at sea on 14 April seems to Behe to have been 'precognitive in nature'.

Méheust (who, in Part III takes Forbes to be the surname and talks of Esther rather than Hester) cites Behe in the case of the husband, and relates both stories, treating them separately in Part II of his book, but, like Behe, together in Part III.[710] He thinks the hypothesis of

708 Méheust, p. 198.

709 Behe, pp. 152-154.

710 Méheust, pp. 87, 198-199 (**BM,17**).

inference is ruled out in Henry's case, pointing out that his worries at first are not specifically related to the sea, so that they cannot be said to concern taking *Titanic*'s maiden voyage. There is, however, some vagueness in Méheust's presentation, and some discrepancies with Behe's account. He agrees that, given the time-difference, if the wife's worries were paranormal they were certainly premonitory, although the timing may have been due to chance. He thinks Hester may have been 'contaminated' by her husband's presentiments and considers her case 'undecidable'. Yet he rates the two cases together as two-stars.

(GB,pr,33) On the night of 14 April 1912 **Marcelle Navratil**, wife of Michel, who had – without her knowing – kidnapped their two young sons, and was on *Titanic* with them, had a vivid dream. She dreamed that 'her husband entered the bedroom and silently handed her a letter sealed inside a black-bordered envelope'. In the following days she dreamed of her children and of funerals. Later, these dreams were accompanied by an obsession that she should be wearing mourning, and of herself in a black dress. On 22 April, reading reports of how the two rescued 'Hoffman' children had responded to questions, she became certain that the boys were hers. She was reunited with them on 16 May.[711] Behe thinks that, while Marcelle's dreams of her children, and funerals, as well as her later obsession with mourning, might have been merely the result of anxiety over her missing children, her dream on 14 April is 'remarkable'. He finds the implication of Michel's death in

711 Behe, pp. 154-155.

it 'inescapable'. He names a newspaper report and a book published in English in 1981 as his sources.[712]

Using at least two further (French) sources, Méheust adds a great deal to this account, although only some of it is directly relevant to the dream.[713] Citing Elizabeth Navratil, Marcelle's daughter,[714] he says that in Marcelle's dream of 14 April,

> *At the end of a long white corridor, she notices her husband Michel Navratil. He advances towards her, staggering, ghostly, his face pale. Suddenly, the corridor slopes, the man totters and sticks out his arms to hold onto the walls. The corridor is now sloping steeply; the man in distress manages to climb up it and gives her a letter. Marcelle holds out her hand to him and brushes her husband's hand. It is frozen. As for the letter, it is the announcement of a bereavement, bordered in black. At this moment, the corridor disappears and is replaced by a petrified landscape.*[715]

Méheust claims that Michel had posted a letter to his wife from England, informing her of his decision to take their children to start a new life in America, and that Marcelle learned 'almost simultaneously' of the death of her husband

712 *New York World* (24 April, 1912) and Sidney Tyler, *A Rainbow of Time and Space: orphans of the Titanic* (1982).

713 Méheust, 118, 124, 134 **(BM,57)**.

714 Elizabeth Navratil, *Les Enfants du 'Titanic'* (1998).

715 Méheust, p. 118.

and the kidnapping of her children, thus understanding the meaning of her dream.[716] In Part III of his book he argues that the absence of a reference to *Titanic* or to a maritime disaster prevents us from suspecting that the dream was reconstructed after the event. But the structure of the dream and its main themes constitute an obvious reference to death and an indirect reference to a sinking. Marcelle's nightmare resists all reductive arguments. He rates the case as three stars, includes it in his favoured eight, and considers it 'one of the most remarkable in the dossier'.[717]

After going through his dossier of cases in Part III of his book, Méheust says that, as often happens in accounts of psychic phenomena, Marcelle's dream representation translates in a striking way something of the concrete situation that it conjures up; some information forces its way through the symbols. One cannot fail to think, he claims, that the slippery, sloping corridor is exactly what hundreds of second- and third-class passengers experienced as the ship began to sink. Méheust also regards it as 'highly unlikely' that Marcelle's dream was just a matter of chance.[718]

However plausible – or otherwise – Méheust's reading of the dream may be, it has to be noted that the extra detail that he imports into it is of questionable value, especially as one of his sources, Elizabeth Navratil's book, is as much fiction as fact – which she herself has acknowledged – and belongs to a collection for young people.

---

716 Méheust, p. 134.

717 Méheust, pp. 192-193.

718 Méheust, pp. 204-205.

(GB,pr,34) When, on 15 April 1912, someone told **Louise Logsdon** about the accident to *Titanic*, she immediately felt certain that her brother Harry Homer, a professional gambler, was on board. Harry survived the sinking.[719] Despite the fact that there was a remote possibility that Homer might sail on *Titanic*, Behe comments that Louise was so *sure* of it that she told her neighbours of her conviction before trying to find his name in the newspapers. Méheust does not mention the case.

(GB,pr,35) After several days of waiting at the shipping office for news of her husband George, Mrs Prangnell returned home one evening to find that her **babysitter** had something to tell her. The old woman had suddenly had a 'vision' in front of the fireplace, in which she 'saw' George clinging to the side of a life-raft. She was sure that this meant he was still alive. A cable finally arrived telling of George's safety. He had fastened his braces to the side of a life-raft and hung on until he was picked up.[720] Behe says that the babysitter had no reason to raise possibly false hopes in Mrs Prangnell, and that it is 'more reasonable' to assume that she told her exactly what she had 'seen' in the flames and what she thought it meant. He cites two local newspapers from 1979 and 1980 as his sources, but interviewed George's daughter and states that the account has been preserved in the Prangnell family since the event occurred. He adds that it was on the third day of Mrs Prangnell's wait that the incident happened, and that the news of George's safety arrived the next day.

719 Behe, p. 156.

720 Behe, pp. 156-157.

Méheust relates this story,[721] but says in Part III of his book that Mrs Prangnell and the community so much wanted George to be safe that the case is 'undecidable'. He argues, very oddly, that, since so little was known to the family of the circumstances, the 'improbable' details of George's survival seemed a 'likely' scenario to them. He concludes that the 'coincidence' between the reality and the babysitter's hallucination is perhaps due to chance, and classes the case as one-star.[722]

It is noticeable that, not only does the amount of detail in Behe's 'probable' cases fluctuate very considerably, his degree of conviction is also variable. He commits pretty strongly to one or two instances in particular, but often leaves us wondering why he has included others in this category at all, since he gives no reason for doing so. His assertion that he finds a statement 'believable' hardly helps persuade us, and a few experiences are so insubstantial that the reader is left genuinely puzzled that Behe should rate them so highly. Together with the fact that a number of 'possible' cases appear more plausible, this rather undermines Behe's classification scheme as a whole.

In a final, fairly brief section of his book, entitled **'Discussion and conclusion'**, Behe claims that the talk of unsinkability makes the many predictions of *Titanic*'s loss all the more impressive, although others have argued, to the contrary, that it is part of what generated such predictions.

721 Méheust, p. 134 **(BM,71)**.

722 Méheust, pp. 199-200.

He stresses that the experiences concerned 'ran the gamut from unshakeable feeling of approaching danger all the way to specific dreams that *Titanic* would sink on *this* voyage,' and suggests that they came 'unbidden to perfectly ordinary people, and were something outside their normal range of experience.' He goes on to point out that sceptical investigators see no need for a paranormal explanation of his cases, and that it is their belief that 'normal coincidence can account for all supposed foreknowledge of danger to *Titanic*.'[723] He lists six approaches that their explanations may take and comments sympathetically on each. Once more, it is worth noting, for the sake of accuracy, that not all of the approaches he lists are, in fact, explicitly shown to rest on a belief in 'normal coincidence', although this may lie behind the warnings of unreliable evidence.

(1) *Lies or exaggerations may be perpetrated by a 'professional (or phoney) psychic'*.[724] Behe admits that in many or even most instances involving a professional psychic this may well be true, but affirms that his probables category includes ordinary people who 'had nothing to gain by lying'. However, apart from the obvious point that this does not address the matter of exaggeration (which he takes up to some degree under (2)), his claim is difficult to accept when one considers that people often lie to themselves or deceive themselves for reasons that are hard to discern. Moreover, Behe's further statement that percipients told others about their experiences *before* the

723 Behe, p. 158.

724 Behe, p. 158. The italics in these six approaches are my own and do not represent actual quotes from Behe unless quotation marks are used.

event by no manner of means always applies to potential premonitions, and establishes only that some premonitions could not have been wholly fabricated after the event. That is, it relates to the timing of certain experiences, rather than their source, nature or quality. The fact that Behe is commenting on a reason for rejecting psychic events does not prevent aspects of the criteria that he himself adopts from emerging and, in this instance, proving somewhat wanting. At this stage, as at others, it appears that, while Behe is discussing sceptics' arguments, he is focusing very strongly on his own cases, especially those classified as probable.

(2) *Behe says that anecdotal accounts are not very reliable. Even honest people tend to exaggerate in constantly repeating their story and describing a memorised version of the dream.*[725] But it is far from clear why he switches from 'accounts' to 'dreams' in describing this particular sceptical explanation, especially as it seems applicable to *all* accounts of psychic episodes. In any event, he again stresses the point that in his cases the precognitive occurrences were recounted *before* the sinking of *Titanic* (which does not quite cover the issue of *repeated* tellings), and states that after the sinking percipients were still able to relate their experiences accurately, and witnesses to recall the circumstances in which they were told.

The relevance of the very last point, however, is not clarified, and we have no measure at all by which to judge the accuracy of the percipients' subsequent memories. Perhaps partly to overcome this, Behe asserts that 'One

725 Behe, p. 159.

characteristic of a true precognitive dream is its *vividness*, coupled with the powerful influence it has on the dreamer after he awakens.' He adds that percipients are aware that these dreams are not 'normal' nightmares, and that their very vividness ensures that their content is accurately recalled. It is probably true that, in general, 'precognitive' dreams are vivid, although there may be exceptions, so that vividness cannot be said to be a necessary condition. Yet there seems to be no reason at all to say that this ensures the accuracy of their telling, much less of their *re*-telling. Some of the points made by Gardner concerning how many details of dreams we forget come back to mind here.

(3) *'To be used as actual evidence of precognition, a dream should be written down and witnessed by unbiased persons before the predicted event takes place.'*[726] Agreeing that this would be the ideal situation, Behe argues that percipients were less concerned with later public verification of their forewarnings than with questions of physical safety. And even if his point that *all* percipients hoped that their forebodings would be proven false is a slight exaggeration, it has some force. But it remains an extremely weak response to the inadequacy of the available evidence to reiterate that percipients 'could only' repeat their stories after the event and have witnesses collaborate that they had told of their forewarnings before the sinking. And Behe's assertion that 'without a doubt' all of the premonitions he has examined 'took place as described *before* the *Titanic* went down' is much more

726 Behe, pp. 159-160.

than one step too far – even if one takes it to refer only to his probable cases.

(4) *'Under the law of averages, a certain number of dreams will probably correspond closely to actual future events.' Only hits are remembered, with misses conveniently forgotten.*[727] Acknowledging that this is true as far as it goes, Behe urges that occasional hits should be randomly distributed among an infinite number of topics, and that there is no 'normal' explanation for the overwhelming number of premonitions concerning *Titanic*. In principle, his reservation is wholly justified, although it is noticeable that Behe here slips from talking of dreams to referring to premonitions as a whole. Nevertheless, the question he raises of what it was about *Titanic* that made so many people certain that *something* was going to happen to her retains its force.

(5) *Someone connected with any ship that sets sail might 'easily' dream of a future sinking. An occasional dreamer will sometimes be proven correct.* Behe finds this assumption 'not unreasonable', but again suggests that such results should be randomly distributed among all the passenger liners of the day, whereas in the case of *Titanic*, where nervous fears for her safety should have been at an absolute minimum, these fears were very numerous, building toward a peak as sailing day approached. In fact, a 'startling number of people' – many of whom had never had feelings of foreboding before – experienced premonitions of danger regarding the ship. Moreover, in some of these cases they were non-passengers, so that their own safety

727 Behe, p. 160.

was not at stake. In all instances 'their forebodings must have been powerful enough to take precedence over their own rational assessment of that possibility.' This category, and Behe's comments on it, are so similar to (4) that we seem to be dealing with one category, rather than two.

(6) *'The more time which elapses between a precognitive-seeming dream and a corresponding future event, the greater the probability that the event will eventually come to pass, due strictly to chance.'*[728] Behe agrees that chance might occasionally account for the eventual fulfilment of a predicted event, but argues that 'when *large numbers* of *similar* predictions occur *independently* in a *short period* of time and are focused on a *specific* upcoming event, the initial probability of the predicted event must be examined.'[729] Assuming that an event which seems impossible will be predicted only very rarely, Behe finds the likelihood that someone would predict not only that *Titanic* would sink, but also on which voyage very remote. Yet a 'significant' number of people correctly predicted this 'impossible' disaster. He cites two of his 'probable' cases in particular,[730] saying – without obvious justification – that the odds against these two people being correct are 'beyond human comprehension'.

Behe concludes his book by asking how many predictions of an 'impossible' event, followed by its immediate fulfilment need to occur before mere chance must be ruled out, and foreknowledge accepted as a

728 Behe, pp. 161-162.

729 Behe, p. 161; italics original.

730 Behe, p. 162. The cases are **(GB,pr,21)** and **(GB,pr,23)**.

more likely explanation, repeating that precognitive warnings of the sinking of *Titanic* are 'more numerous and better documented than those of any other event', and that the sheer number of people who 'knew' that they or their loved ones would face danger on *Titanic* is 'almost overwhelming'. He believes the weight of evidence in favour of psychic phenomena must eventually force the sceptic to seriously consider 'the possibility of their reality', stating that, in his opinion, 'the accounts we have examined here are numerous enough, and contain enough detail, to be accepted as probable psychic foreshadowings of the greatest peacetime disaster in maritime history.'

'Discussion and conclusion' provides a slightly unsatisfactory conclusion to Behe's book as a whole. For one thing, he seems to have in mind throughout only his cases of 'probable psychic phenomena', since many of his comments clearly do not apply to those covered in other parts of his book. But even limiting the application of his comments in this way leaves him vulnerable to the charge that on more than one occasion he goes too far in generalising about his cases. Furthermore, structuring his final remarks around sceptics' reasons for rejecting paranormal explanations does not work out particularly well, especially as only a couple of the six stated reasons obviously depend on 'normal coincidence', as Behe suggests they all do. Then, there is the puzzling fact that, while five of the reasons set out include crucial reference to dreams (which figure in only eight or so of Behe's 35 probable cases), almost all of his comments focus on premonitions as such. This is an important mismatch, which does nothing to strengthen Behe's general contentions. Moreover, his claims regarding the number of predictions and the number of times they turned out to be correct contain some exaggeration, or at least over-generalisation. These claims also appear to lead him to a conclusion slightly more positive about premonitions than one might have expected, although, looked at very closely, they stop just short of the 'dogmatic pronouncements' that he eschewed in his Introduction, since his view is only that sceptics will be forced to *consider* the *possibility* of the reality of psychic phenomena, and that the weight of the evidence dictates only the acceptance of *probable* psychic premonitions.

GOSS AND BEHE

Near the beginning of the chapter in *Lost at Sea. Ghost Ships and Other Mysteries*, where they deal with thirteen 'premonition' cases in all,[731] Goss and Behe emphasise that despite the apparent 'unsinkability' of *Titanic*, there definitely were people who 'for some unexplained reason' were absolutely certain that something was going to happen to the ship on her maiden voyage. Some had no direct connection with the vessel, others had booked a passage on the liner, and several of the latter took their presentiments so seriously that they cancelled their passage. The authors argue that the sinking of *Titanic* was the birth of a whole album of legends that claimed

731 Chapter 6. 'RMS *Titanic*: The Unsinkable', pp. 223-252.

that the loss of the ship was, if not foreordained by some power punishing humanity's hubris, then at least rendered foreknowable 'to a randomly chosen few'. They talk of 'a bundle of human documents' suggesting that awareness of the disaster preceded the event, or public announcement of it. The chapter is said to contain a 'mere sample' of *Titanic* premonitions, a 'representative mixture': 'the moderately well-known and the obscure, the highly dramatic and the near-banal'. It is accepted that they are 'not all equally convincing, not all equally evidential'.

In fact, Goss and Behe stress that it would be 'unwise' to categorise all apparent premonitions of the *Titanic* disaster as having had a psychic origin and argue explicitly that their first case is one of a number of odd-seeming occurrences which were merely the result of ironic coincidence being viewed later 'with 20/20 hindsight',[732] although their following case is said to belong to a small category of those that are 'not quite so clearly the result of coincidence'.[733]

It is not easy to say whether commitment to a belief in the paranormal is any weaker or stronger here than in Behe's earlier book, or exactly where the authors' comments as a whole stand in relation to Behe's original five-fold categorisation of his own cases. In any event, classification as such falls by the wayside as Goss and Behe go on to link one instance with the next in a number of ways, both thematic and incidental.

Of their thirteen cases in the chapter, eight have not been mentioned by the four previous commentators or

732 Goss and Behe, pp. 224-225. See **(RB,25)**.

733 Goss and Behe, p. 226.

referred to earlier in this book; two concern Stead, and two were already covered in Behe's book.[734] All thirteen are now handled in a slightly different way from in Behe's earlier book, being described in a somewhat more leisurely and detailed manner, and without a 'Comment' section marked as such in each instance. Nevertheless, the authors do relate a case and then comment on it, as well as subsequently looking at all cases together and making further comments. **(G&B,12)** is the only one of the following cases taken up by Méheust.

CASES

(G&B,2) Sophia Laitinen, a Finnish woman had three possible premonitions that are not clearly the result of coincidence. She had booked her passage on *Titanic*, and entrusted some borrowed money to a friend, saying: 'If I should go to the bottom of the ocean on my way, then pay it back.' The authors comment that only because Sophia did drown on *Titanic* does her remark seem more than 'ephemeral to the point of forgettable'.[735] But, before departing, she dreamed that she fell into cold water in a well. Though Sophia's friends later wondered if this was a premonition, Goss and Behe, conceding that the content of the dream is not strikingly similar to Sophia's death, admit that it is 'entirely possible' that the dream had a normal

734 **(G&B,6)**, **(G&B.10)**; **(IS,12c)**, **(RB,15)**.

735 Goss and Behe, pp. 226-227. They later comment that Laitinen's remark about repaying her loan would conceivably seem like a lucky – or unlucky – verbal hit but for her two subsequent warning dreams (p. 241).

origin. They do, however, point out that Sophia was sufficiently impressed or disturbed by it to relate it to her friends, and that there is also the possibility that dream-based precognition does not involve literal perception of coming events, but a 'more figurative or metaphorical process'.

Moreover, still before leaving Finland, Sophia had a second dream, the 'message' of which was 'specific, leaving absolutely no room for misinterpretation'. After the death of an old woman in the house in which she worked, she had a dream ('centred on herself and the other members of the household') that 'a second (older) person would die soon, followed by a third (younger) person'. Another older member of the family did indeed die after the dream, and it turned out to be Sophia herself who became the third, younger member of the household to lose her life. The authors believe it does not seem too imaginative to see a sort of dreadful irony here. They suggest that Laitinen could not see that the warning was meant for herself, and 'seems to have been unaware that her own death would fulfil the conditions of her dream'. They later suggest that Laitinen's two dreams resemble the 'ambiguous, disorderly parade of images we connect with the word'. Without knowledge of the fate of *Titanic* to give us the benefit of hindsight, her dream of falling into a well appears 'incapable of decipherment', and the precognitive element of her second dream is 'far from blatant' without that same information.

The ultimate source for this potentially impressive case seems to be a Finnish newspaper, so that it is open to the kind of objection that might be raised, in general, to such a source. But the authors make some important points about dreams as premonitions, to which we will return

(G&B,4) Elizabeth Sims, whose family knew that she often had 'fey premonitions' about future events, was absolutely convinced that *Titanic* would be 'a tragic ship' and insisted that her son Tom remain on his present vessel instead of being transferred to *Titanic*, even going to London to have his name withdrawn from the ship's crew roster.[736] Goss and Behe, giving as their source 'a British newspaper from near Southampton', in 1985, admit that we do not know in what way she foresaw or suspected *Titanic*'s fate would be tragic, nor, indeed, how accurate her previous premonitory experiences had been. They later point out that we have to take Elizabeth's fey premonitions 'on trust'.[737] She may have reacted, rationally, to the general unease that *Titanic* was 'daring Fate, God, or both,' although they also imply that Sims's worries about her son could be seen as just a 'strong feeling'.

Goss and Behe suggest that in this case 'the paranormal interpretation is justified merely by the fact of the accident', a formula – 'actions attributable to some nebulous (but not precognitively precise) sense of disquiet over the new and much vaunted ship subsequently "confirmed" as paranormally prescient by the (accidental) fact of the sinking' – to which 'any number of *Titanic* premonitions might be reduced'.[738] Referring to the 'vagueness' of certain predictions, they note the part played by Mrs

736 Goss and Behe, pp. 228-229.

737 Goss and Behe, p. 242.

738 Goss and Behe, p.229.

Sims's commitment to a belief in the paranormal, raising the general question of whether, when someone has a previous record of fulfilled predictions (although the point, presumably, equally applies to *subsequent* predictions), we should disregard this personal factor as non-evidential or accept it as corroboration that this particular prediction is authentically precognitive. They suggest that much 'surely' depends on the proven accuracy of the other premonitory experiences. At this point the authors shelve 'until later' any questions as to how 'a commitment or predisposition towards belief in the paranormal may affect the telling of a story', saying that these questions 'invade' several of their subsequent (nine) cases.[739]

(G&B,5) On 26 March 1912, **Angus McCormack**, visiting a spiritualist's house, asked about a photograph hanging on a wall. He was told that it was of a woman he knew, whose husband was starting on a new voyage, and who was 'always naturally anxious at such times'. McCormack became depressed and agitated when he learned that the husband was going on *Titanic*, saying that there was 'something wrong' about the ship, 'something the matter with it'. He acknowledged that it did not seem very serious and that something would happen 'before it gets out of port'. He repeated that he did not like the ship, and that there was 'a hole right through the skin of it'.

After the disaster he stated that he was 'almost certain' that the husband would be found among the saved. Eventually, the crewman's name – he is simply known

739 Goss and Behe, p. 229.

here as 'Mr K' – appeared on the list of survivors.[740] Understandably, the authors raise the possibility that McCormack knew a lot more of the crewman and his wife than this account implies, even if he had forgotten what he knew. They add that he may have been voicing the 'general malaise concerning the unsinkable and awesomely huge new ship.' But they are more impressed by his predictions regarding what happened to *Titanic*. They admit that McCormack's original impressions seem very wide of the mark, but claim that they were '100 percent accurate', since the *New York* incident 'fills the bill exactly', is 'right on the money'. They ask whether, in the light of his comment on a 'hole right through the skin' of *Titanic*, it is possible that he was 'picking up' and confusing two separate impressions about *Titanic*: one concerning the *New York* incident and the other the fatal collision with the iceberg. This, however, seems a generous reading of McCormack's vision. It may be true that something happens to *Titanic* 'before it gets out of port', but 'there's something the matter with it' does not fit the *New York* incident particularly well. And McCormack's comment that 'I don't think it's serious. Mr K… will get back all right' seems to apply to that incident. Moreover, the speculation that McCormack had 'another impression concerning the fatal collision with the iceberg' is arbitrary and has no obvious justification.

Goss and Behe say that the names of the people involved were not made public in the original report (in the *Occult Review*, in May 1912), and that they are using pseudonyms. At this point, they do not express any

740 Goss and Behe, pp. 229-232.

misgivings concerning reports by committed spiritualists. They say later that the way McCormack expresses his fears rather resembles the style of a medium 'thinking out loud', and there was a predisposition towards accepting the paranormal in the Henderson household. But the facts that McCormack himself may have been a spiritualist and that his account appeared in a magazine devoted to publicising the supernatural do not, they say, prevent his story from being credible.

(G&B,8) At Southsea Beach in Portsmouth, as the Rev. **Estelle Barnes** ('as she signs herself') was watching *Titanic* steam by, with her fiancé on board, 'a woman in a golden brown dress with a matching hat and parasol' suddenly appeared to her left and then to her right. She told Barnes to call the police and the White Star line and tell them to order the *Titanic* to return to port, explaining that unless the ship turned back now, 'tragedy would overtake the ship in just a few days' time.' When Barnes looked back towards the woman, there was no one there. She returned to the Apartment Hotel in Portsmouth and told her fellow guests about the warning she had just received. But she did not notify the police or the shipping line. Her fiancé died on *Titanic*.[741]

Goss and Behe comment that the account (in the archives of the Titanic Historical Society) may possibly be 'too dramatic to be strictly or literally credible'. They also admit that 'Barnes's standing as a spiritualist may be forced into the reckoning': this is 'the most theatrical and, to be honest, the least acceptable in terms of conventional

741 Goss and Behe, pp.235-236.

thinking' of all their cases. They later argue that Barnes's encounter had a decidedly theatrical flavour, but then 'apparitional encounters not infrequently do'. Again, suggesting that the woman in golden brown was just an hallucination scarcely removes the oddity, or the story's suggestiveness, given the tragedy that followed. The authors point out that the source of Barnes's evidence is actually a letter by Barnes herself dated June 1973.[742] They acknowledge that it is the letter of a committed spiritualist, who 'does not question one iota of the events she describes'. The letter apparently ends with the claim that her warnings have saved no fewer than four U.S. presidents (and could have saved Lindbergh's baby son).

(G&B,9) During the night of 13 April 1912, **M. Abrahams** dreamed he was in the dress circle of a theatre, when he saw the side of a ship where the theatre's wall should have been. His nephew was by the ship's side, with a white and haggard face, raising his arms imploringly towards his uncle. Abrahams could see his nephew only from the waist up. On four previous occasions in his lifetime he had had vivid dreams which had come true shortly afterwards. Abrahams had not known that his nephew was on *Titanic*, but later learned that he had died on the ship.[743]

Goss and Behe do not initially comment on this case, but they later argue that it 'carries a certain credibility', although we do not know whether some 'especially close link' existed between the two people. Nevertheless, they suggest that Abraham's personal fear was about losing his

742 This seems to be the source of the Chantler story, too. See **(RB,25)**.

743 Goss and Behe, pp. 236-237.

nephew. They also later note that Abrahams sent his dream vision to *Light*, 'then a weekly spiritualist newspaper whose news items would not always satisfy the most astringent evidential demands of scientific psychical research.'[744]

(G&B,11) During the night of 13 April 1912 **Bert John** experienced a vivid dream that *Titanic*, on which he was a third-class passenger, was sinking, and then that he was in a casket carried up to the boat deck. He finally released himself from the coffin and leaped desperately from the deck into a lifeboat. He spent the following day wondering what the dream might have meant. On the boat deck after the collision with the iceberg he unsuccessfully tried to enter several lifeboats, before finally jumping down into one being lowered and hence surviving the sinking.[745]

The authors suggest that the way in which Bert dreamed of escaping death (represented by his struggle to escape the coffin) parallels the way in which he did actually escape his real death on *Titanic*, and wonder whether he might have recalled his dream and realised that it had shown him the only way in which to survive. They later claim that John's experience in his dream seems oddly direct.

(G&B,12) In the early hours of 15 April 1912, the psychiatrist **Alfred Adler** (whom Goss and Behe later describe as a 'confirmed sceptic')[746] woke up from a vivid dream in which a huge ship was going down in mid-ocean. He eventually realised that his dream had occurred at the same time as the *Titanic* disaster, but convinced himself that

744 Goss and Behe, p. 249.

745 Goss and Behe, pp. 239-240.

746 Goss and Behe, p. 249.

his dream merely reflected his anxiety for the manuscript of his new book, on its way to America by ship.[747] The authors say only: 'And perhaps he was right.' They later say that Adler's dream is specific rather than symbolic and that its substance is clairvoyant in its aptness to *Titanic*'s fate.

Méheust claims that Adler was developing his version of the theory of the unconscious at this time, and that, although telepathy was 'probable or certain' for him, he wondered about the personal reasons that connected him to the *Titanic* event.[748] In Part III of his book he says that inference is 'improbable' in this case, since Adler had no link with *Titanic*, and that he may have dreamed of a shipwreck 'by chance'. He notes, nonetheless, that Adler considered his dream an 'authentic telepathic phenomenon', and that the experience posed a theoretical problem for him. He rates the case as only one star.[749] Méheust's reading of the event is slightly different from that of Goss and Behe, although this is the only case where he cites their book as a source.

(G&B,13) When nineteen-year-old **Edward Dorking**, who had been ordered away from a number of lifeboats 'at the point of a revolver', was desperately struggling in the water towards an overturned lifeboat, a black cloud suddenly seemed to enshroud him and he found that he could see his people at home before him. But the vision disappeared when someone on the boat grabbed him.[750]

Goss and Behe concede that Dorking's vision was

747 Goss and Behe, p. 240. They stress this perceived link with *Titanic* later, at p. 244.

748 Méheust, pp. 130-131 **(BM,67)**.

749 Méheust, p. 200.

750 Goss and Behe, pp.249-251,

'probably' an hallucination, but say it might possibly have been an 'out-of-body experience'. Could the dying young man have actually been 'seeing' his family? But if he ever tried to confirm the details of his vision of his family at home, he did not record the results of his inquiries. In fact, Dorking does not appear to have mentioned his vision at all on a number of occasions when he was describing his experience in some detail in public in May 1912.[751]

Slightly oddly, it is after presenting 12 of their 13 cases, that Goss and Behe conduct a general review,[752] saying that, while they feel obliged to 'examine the evidence, to note its limitations', they will not come down heavily on one side or the other. Stressing that their cases merely represent the 'vast store of paranormal episodes' concerning *Titanic*, they begin by looking 'most critically – and perhaps least sympathetically' at the six cases where the paranormality 'rests solely upon remarks taking on a sombre and precognitive significance in the light of events that followed'. Although they are, quite rightly, wary of the term 'coincidence', saying that we do not know what it really amounts to, and that for most of us it is no more than a term of convenience, this does raise some questions about Behe's crucial use of the term in his earlier book.[753]

751 See www.encyclopedia-titanica.org/edward-dorking-ship-wreck-survivor-appears-at-star-theatre.html and www.encyclopedia-titanica.org/titanic-survivor/edward-arthur-dorking.html

752 They do not explain why their review is offered at this precise point, though in introducing case 13 they rather stress the point that the experience took place 'even as the great liner was making her final plunge to the seabed' (p. 249).

753 Goss and Behe, pp. 240-243.

Goss and Behe acknowledge that there is no way of distinguishing between a genuine premonition and a strong feeling, even when the latter seems borne out by subsequent events. They believe Shaw Desmond's conviction and the ambiguous reactions of Butt bear this out. They also suggest that, in the face of all the boasting about *Titanic*, some people may have experienced 'a primitive suspicion of divine retribution', and that, in the cases where there were also personal worries, a few may have acknowledged the possibility of retribution as a strong feeling or premonition. Such a feeling, moreover, might be a visualisation of the more pessimistic of numerous possible outcomes, perhaps even 'a magical, prerational mode of trying to avert the worst through an act of admitting that it *is* possible.' Rather unhelpfully, they suggest that even if the 'seers' were proved right, it is 'as usual, a matter of private opinion' whether they had supernatural aid.[754]

Admitting that the dreams and visions in their 12 cases have 'superior narrative interest', they still judge that these are 'more conclusive', 'more evidential'; 'they are patently more dramatic, explicit, and memorable', if only because they seem more likely to compel readers' attention than strong feelings. Goss and Behe argue that, although the division between 'dream' and 'vision' is artificial, there can be said to be five warning dreams (Laitinen (x 2), Abrahams, John, and Adler), and three 'spirit visions' (McCormack, Barnes, and Chase). But not all precognitive dreams relating to *Titanic* are strongly symbolic. The

754 Goss and Behe, pp. 241-243.

dreamers may have focused on one possibility relevant to themselves selected from hundreds or thousands. The authors claim that what little we know of psychic events suggests that an emotional bond between percipient and subject increases the likelihood of an impression being formed. The 12 cases include a number where friendship or even blood ties are involved, but none of this validates the evidence for dream precognition in these instances.[755]

Furthermore, the authors assert, the possibly more damaging issue of how these stories came to be told, or who recorded them, and why, must enter into the review. Accepting that some sources (like the British and American Societies for Psychical Research) composed of accredited parapsychologists tend to carry more weight than others, they point out that newspaper items may be open to charges of bias, since they are tailoring their material to suit particular tastes – a view not obviously expressed or taken into account in Behe's earlier book. And certain specialist publications 'may be accused of utilising unreliable material not for direct financial gain but to promote a defined view or belief system favoured by the editors and/or the readers.'[756] These reservations on the part of Goss and Behe are very timely, and, with the reservations in mind, they follow up three of their cases – McCormack, Barnes, and Chase – in some detail.

Emphasising that 'people need outlets for their unusual experiences', they suggest that a paranormal story must not only justify itself by being striking: 'if it proclaims

755 Goss and Behe, pp. 243-245.

756 Goss and Behe, p. 245.

itself a *true* story, it must evince evidence to back up that peculiar claim.' Granted that the narrators of these cases felt they warranted telling outside a personal circle of family and friends, one question is whether the editors of the journals that accepted them did so 'in the hope of promoting a particular set of beliefs or (which amounts to the same thing) of meeting the interests and beliefs of a specific audience.' The authors' tentative answer to this question, and whether the writers approached the editors with this mind, is '"Yes" and "No"'.

Goss and Behe concede that 'some spiritualistic accounts suggest that a believer is less prone to criticise a subjective experience than other folk, overemphasising its "evidential" aspects'. In the early twentieth century 'what looked suspect to a severe rationalist was quite orthodox to a proponent of the truths of spiritualism'. How we react to a particular account, they sat, derives largely from how we react to spiritualism itself.[757]

Somewhat unconvincingly, the authors conclude, before treating the Dorking case, by affirming that all the percipients could have done better, had they wanted to work on the susceptible reader's conviction. They also claim that 'the mechanism that provokes paranormal precognition does not function in an obvious fashion', and their further comment that any paranormal experience relating to *Titanic* will have a 'personal, ambiguous quality' adds nothing to the debate.[758]

757 Goss and Behe, pp. 247-248.

758 Goss and Behe, p. 249.

CHAPTER 6

BERTRAND MÉHEUST

Bertrand Méheust, born in 1947, is a former philosophy teacher who now specialises in parapsychology and enjoys a good reputation in France as a researcher in paranormal matters. He has a doctorate in sociology and is on the management committee of the Institut Métapsychique International (IMI).

In the short Introduction to his book, Méheust makes some general observations on the *Titanic* tragedy (and some critical remarks on the British press) before announcing his intention to explore systematically the 'parapsychological dimension' of the catastrophe.[759] He argues that the works of fiction he examines fit into a broader picture, and goes on to characterise the ways in which 'tens' of people in England, Europe and the United States also foresaw or 'saw' *Titanic*'s demise 'through a

759 Méheust, pp. 9-13.

whole range of spontaneous experiences of a prophetic or premonitory kind, whether it be dreams, bursts of unmotivated anxiety, or hallucinations experienced in the waking state'. He says that the feeling of a maritime catastrophe, which often involved people close to them, imposed itself brutally upon percipients 'with a procession of emotions and images', and all of that within a very narrow time-frame, before the news of the sinking was widely known. The images seen, often fragmentary but sometimes very precise, showed the sinking of a huge ship, rarely identified explicitly, but portrayed with sufficient precision. The vessel was vertical, slowly sinking into the sea. Some people heard it break apart, others saw their relatives among those struggling in the water. Méheust admits that, while certain reports can be dated from before the sinking, most were obviously recorded after the event, but he claims that in certain instances the facts and details allow cross-checking which leads to the conclusion that the accounts preceded the event. Although both Robertson and Stead have received some public attention, Méheust argues that the paranormal dossier relating to *Titanic* is known mostly to specialists and remains unknown to the general public. His triple purpose in the book is to bring the cases together, to complete the corpus if possible, and to analyse and comment on it, using his thirty years of experience with paranormal material.

Méheust's comments on the literary cases of premonition in his Introduction are relatively unexceptionable, if over-simplified, but the section in which he describes other cases contains a number of generalisations that are far from justified, or are unacceptably vague. While reference to a 'whole range' of premonitory experiences is appropriate, mention of a very narrow time-frame is much more restrictive than the spectrum of cases that he himself later considers. Similarly, his description of what people saw consists simply of a series of examples, rather than a genuine characterisation of *Titanic* premonitions. Above all, his remarks on the crucial matter of the dating of premonitions are entirely unconvincing as they stand. It is an unenviable task to represent the whole body of *Titanic* premonitions in a few sentences, but, given the detailed scrutiny of particular cases required, and the variety of judgements on them that he will make, Méheust might have done better to avoid generalisations that his later text will falsify.

He claims that it is impossible to describe the premonitions and comment on them at the same time, and says that while the first two parts of his book present a chronological record of the experiences and coincidences, the third and fourth parts analyse and comment on the data. And, indeed, as Méheust goes chronologically through a segment of Stead's life (Part I), and then through the history of *Titanic* (Part II), he records the cases of premonitions with virtually no critical comment on them, reserving his judgements as such for later in the book. He can be said to play down (and, in some cases, ignore) the instances where premonitions prove wrong, either completely wrong or mistaken in some significant detail.

There are 9 instances where cases in Méheust's book are mentioned by none of the previous authors, and one that he is the first to treat separately.

CASES

(BM,1) A *Titanic* **draughtsman** notices, in 1909, that the hull number allocated to *Titanic*, 390904, when reflected in a mirror, can be seen as reading 'NOPOPE'. This causes Catholic shipworkers in Belfast to send a delegation to the directors and later provokes the 'Godless' into hanging streamers on the side of the ship, saying 'NO GOD, NO POPE', and so on.[760] Méheust regards the draughtsman's perception as the starting-point of *Titanic*'s involvement in the sectarian conflicts in Ireland, and clearly takes it seriously. He quotes Eaton and Hass as his source,[761] but fails to mention that they – like many others – stress that the story of the number 390904 is no more than a legend, since Harland and Wolff did not issue hull numbers to its ships. (Elsewhere in his book Méheust acknowledges this.)[762] He does not return to this case in Part III.

(BM,2) A young **cabin boy** who was lost on *Titanic* wrote to his parents, saying that he was convinced that the ship 'will not reach America because of the odious blasphemies covering its sides'.[763] Méheust gives no details of the letter concerned, and goes on to say that various rumours that circulated concerning *Titanic* (including the one that workers had been imprisoned in the hull) show the stressful political and cultural climate in which

760 Méheust, pp. 77-78.

761 John P. Eaton and Charles A. Haas, *Titanic. Destination and Disaster. The legends and the reality* (2011), p. 56.

762 Méheust, p. 188.

763 Méheust, p. 78.

the ship was built. He concludes by saying that the idea that *Titanic* was cursed because its builders offended the Creator is one that goes right back to its construction. This last point is an unjustified logical jump in a story that is wholly lacking in credibility and coherence. He does not return to it in Part III of his book.

(BM,4) According to Méheust, in February 1911, **Mary MacCormick** – sister of Dr Minahan – has her cards read by a fortune-teller, who tells her that in less than two years she will pass through a great test: at least one person she knows will die. Méheust quotes Behe in connection with this case,[764] but adds that we do not know whether she passed on this warning to her brother.[765] He returns to the case when discussing and grading that of Dr Minahan in Part III of his book, without rating it in its own right.[766]

(BM,25) On 10 April 1912, **Mrs A.**, known among her acquaintances to have clairvoyant gifts, had a 'sort of vision' at a lecture in London, in which she saw a number of catastrophes take place: a train accident, a house on fire, a mine explosion, and 'a steamer with four funnels colliding with a mountain of ice'. It was dark, and the ice shone in the darkness. She could not remember the name of the ship exactly, but it was 'something like the *Tintac*'. She also heard the name 'Southampton' in her head.[767]

---

764 **(GB,po,1)**. Behe mentions the prediction for MacCormick in connection with the case of Dr Minahan.

765 Méheust, p. 79.

766 Méheust, p. 167.

767 Méheust, p. 93.

Méheust gives no source at all for this incident, but claims that Mrs A. had given evidence of her clairvoyant powers on other occasions. He stresses that she had no links with *Titanic* and 'apparently' did not know of its existence, so that there is no case for invoking inference on the part of her unconscious. The approximation of *Titanic*'s name conforms, he says, with the known processes of telepathy: distortions of details are common in the messages passed on by clairvoyants. Similarly, the voice pronouncing 'Southampton' is a classic telepathic phenomenon. If Mrs A. had correctly named *Titanic*, her performance would have been 'much less convincing': one might have suspected 'the people who reported her account' of having modified it after the sinking: 'Here we are facing a case where a half-error is more persuasive than a complete success'.[768]

Méheust concedes that we cannot completely rule out the possibility that Mrs A. had somewhere heard talk of *Titanic*, forgotten this, then unconsciously elaborated a scenario of divine punishment, but claims that a 'paranormal factor' seems to enter her vision, in that she saw the sinking as caused by an iceberg and taking place at night, something that is more intriguing in the case of a spontaneous experience than in that of a fiction developed over a period of time, like Robertson's. He argues that we cannot be entirely sure that this is an instance of genuine premonition, but notes that the processes involved are closely related in all respects to it.[769] Rated as two stars plus, this case obviously comes very close to being included

768 Méheust, pp. 176-177.

769 Méheust, pp. 176-177.

among Méheust's favourites, but it has to be said that his account is not entirely coherent, and that the complete lack of documentation weakens it severely for his readers.

(BM,26) On 8 April 1912, John Jacob Astor IV received a telegram from an old friend, **Colonel Long**, who was very involved in the psychic sciences. It claimed that *Titanic* would come to a bad end, and advised Astor not to sail on her. But Astor's wife did not take the warning seriously, saying: 'If some misfortune happens to us, we'll die together. What more could you wish for?'[770] Méheust points out that the premonition definitely preceded the sinking, but, as so often, can be ascribed to inference. He says that the idea that *Titanic* was cursed was already circulating in psychic circles in New York before the maiden voyage, and suggests that there should be further investigation of who circulated the idea and what reasons were given. But he cites no source for this story and rates the case as one star only.[771]

(BM,33) Citing Robin Gardiner,[772] Méheust claims that **George Beedem** felt ill at ease in his Southampton hotel the evening before joining *Titanic* as a seaman. Among other things, the 'atmosphere' of embarkation bothered him and he was afraid of being bored on the ship. He wrote to his wife, saying, 'I feel depressed. There is nothing to do on board. How I would love to see this blessed boat at the bottom of the sea.'[773] He died with *Titanic*. Méheust regards this as a classic case of inference,

770 Méheust, p. 94.

771 Méheust, p. 177.

772 Robin Gardiner, *L'Énigme du 'Titanic', mystères et dissimulations* (1998).

773 Méheust, p. 97.

suggesting, as Behe often does, that it looks premonitory only after the event. He classes the case as one star.[774]

(BM,35) As Mrs Hodge, a chambermaid, was embarking on *Titanic*, her daughter **Rosalind Hodge** cried out, sobbing: 'Don't go, mama, I know that you won't come back, you will all die, the ship is going to sink.' She tells her mother of a dream she had two days before, in which she saw a ship rise up out of the ground, with people running around in panic on it. The ship broke in two with a dreadful cracking sound, then was swallowed up in the ground. Mrs Hodge died on *Titanic*.[775]

Méheust argues that the case is not compelling, since Rosalind had a 'direct reason' to fear a catastrophe, and that there is no written account of the dream. (He does not draw attention to the oddity of the daughter waiting two days before telling her mother of the dream.) He is nevertheless struck that the structure of the account (for which he gives no source) suggests something out of the ordinary. What is reported has the strangeness of a dream, but also contains an unexpected factual element of the sinking: the breaking-apart of *Titanic*. Méheust is impressed by this 'coincidence', since *Titanic* is the only transatlantic liner to have broken in two before sinking. He rates the case as two stars.[776]

(BM,36) When **Mrs Hakesworth**[777] was seeing off her husband and brother-in-law on *Titanic*, she suddenly

774 Méheust, pp. 177-178.

775 Méheust, pp. 98-99.

776 Méheust, p. 181.

777 A Mr William Walter Hawkesworth is listed as an Assistant Deck Steward on *Titanic*. His older brother, James, was a Second-Class saloon steward.

began crying, and told her young son: 'This ship will never get to New York, dear.' They both died on *Titanic*.[778] Méheust cites no source for this case, and does not take it up again in his dossier in Part III of his book.

(BM,43) *Titanic*'s Chief Officer, **Henry Tingle Wilde**,[779] posted a letter to his sister in Queenstown, saying 'I really don't like this ship ... I have a queer feeling about it'.[780] Méheust again cites Robin Gardiner as his source, but the book concerned records Wilde as also saying, 'I still don't like this ship ...', and expresses some surprise at the 'still', since Wilde did not join *Titanic* until early morning on 10 April. Méheust rightly claims that too little detail is known for us to form a clear opinion, and that inference is an obvious possibility. He stresses that Wilde was well positioned to see that the vessel was not fully prepared for its maiden voyage, and wonders whether Wilde shared the superstitious side of many sailors. He rates the case as one-star-plus.[781]

(BM,56) Madame Maréchal fainted on 14 April, and when she came to announced that a great misfortune had just taken place on *Titanic*. Some days before, the news that her husband was to travel on the ship caused her great distress. She even said: 'I don't know in what respect, but I sense that misfortune will characterise this journey.'[782] In Part III of his book Méheust sees elements in favour

778 Méheust, p. 99.

779 Misleadingly, Méheust refers to him as 'second officer on the ship'.

780 Méheust, p. 106.

781 Méheust, p. 183.

782 Méheust, p. 118.

of both inference and the paranormal in this case. He acknowledges, without citing any sources, that indications of the timing of the fainting are imprecise, and suggests that its coincidence with the sinking may be a matter of chance. Yet he is struck by the indeterminate and insistent nature of the distress that oppressed Mme Maréchal, which argues that this is not a question of inference. And the vagueness of Maréchal's predictions – she does not speak of a sinking – at least suggests that the account was not modified after the event. But none of this is decisive: Méheust rates the case as one star plus.[783]

Although, obviously, the ten cases that Méheust is the first of our commentators to introduce are not grouped in his book, it is legitimate to look at them together. They do not constitute an especially impressive array. Or, at least, his treatment of them does little, in general, to make them a convincing list. The first two are particularly weak, he cites no source for more than a half of the cases, and on three occasions does not bother to come back to the story in Part III of his book. It does not seem that Méheust's major contribution to the topic of *Titanic* premonitions lies in the new cases that he brings into the open.

It has to be said, moreover, that there are a number of peculiarities concerning Méheust's material in general and the structure of his book.[784] Although his distinction between recording and commenting broadly stands, it is striking that the first and last parts of his book (comprising roughly

783 Méheust, pp. 191-192.

784 For the Table of Contents to Méheust's book, see Appendix 2.

117 pages, out of 312) focus very largely on Robertson and Stead, apparently giving a literary frame and emphasis to his inquiry. Part I is entitled 'The *Titanic* and Literature: Morgan Robertson and W.T. Stead, Mediums, Writers and Prophets in Spite of Themselves'. However, its Chapter 3 is called 'W.T. Stead and the *Titanic*, or the Chronicle of a Predicted Death', suggesting – as scrutiny of the chapter itself confirms – greater emphasis there on predictions of Stead's death (some 17 pages) than on his fictions (fewer than 5 pages).[785] It is true that the fictions receive much more detailed attention in Part IV of Méheust's book, but even there the thrust of the argument, as is the case in the treatment of Robertson, is to position the fiction firmly within the context of the writer's life as a whole.

Following Part I on literary premonitions and forewarnings of Stead's death, Méheust goes through his list of other cases twice, in the two most substantial parts of his book: firstly in the eight sections of Part II, where he records the story of *Titanic* chronologically, from the 'first premonitions' before the maiden voyage to the 'visions and hallucinations' of the days after the sinking,[786] then again – this time with evaluation – in Part III, Chapter 6 ('Examination of the Dossier'),[787] which is also broadly chronological, although the order in which the cases are presented now varies somewhat from his first

785 The chapter also incorporates 5 pages on Stead's 'appearances' *after* his death, as well as nearly 10 pages on Stead in general.

786 Méheust, pp. 77-131. There are some inaccuracies – and unjustified assertions – in Méheust's general account of the history of *Titanic*, taken from other commentators.

787 Méheust, pp. 167-205.

run-through. Questions remain, however, concerning the precise range of Parts I, II, and III and the status of Méheust's 'dossier', since only slightly more than two thirds of the premonitions treated in Parts I and II recur in Part III. With the – unexplained – exception of Garnett, the literary cases as such are omitted from the dossier in Part III, being dealt with in some detail in Part IV.

Again, in Part II, without explaining why, he refers to just 5 of the 24 premonitions of Stead's death treated in Part I.[788] He returns to all 5 cases in his dossier in Part III, adding – once more without explanation – 2 more from Part I.[789] The net effect of all of this is that while the total number of non-literary premonition cases in Parts I and II is 92,[790] only 65 of these in all are treated in Part III,[791] although there are also a number of instances where – very unsatisfactorily – in Part III he amalgamates under one name premonitions mentioned separately in Part II.[792] Other oddities are noticeable in Méheust's numbers.[793]

When, in introducing his dossier in Part III (Chapter

788 By Cheiro, Wesley Adams, Witt Hopkins, Turvey, and Pardoe Woodman.

789 By Kerlor and Desmond. The case of Mrs Tweedale is included in this dossier, but has not previously been referred to at all in Part I or Part II – presumably, just an inadvertent omission on Méheust's part.

790 24 premonitions of Stead's death in Part I, plus 68 other cases in Part II).

791 This excludes the case of William Reeves, which occurred in 1935, and takes account of the fact that the list in Part III includes two separate entries for what is one and the same case: 'E.M.' (p. 194) and 'M.M.' (p. 200), **(IS,13)**.

792 For example, he amalgamates the Kerlor cases to rate them in Part III; he treats the cases of Henry and Hester Forbes Julian separately in Part II, but together in Part III; and similarly with Mary MacCormick and Dr Minahan.

793 There is, for instance, no obvious explanation for the fact that his figures late on – 35, 18, 8 – add up to only 61 cases (Méheust, p. 207), while 67 are treated in Part III, Chapter 6.

6), he claims that he formed it by combing the lists of Stevenson and Behe and adding cases picked up here and there in the literature on *Titanic*, he adds that he has eliminated the cases about which 'information is lacking', but he gives no details of the latter process, and does not say whether it is the explanation of the discrepancies between Parts I and II on the one hand and Part III on the other.[794] In any case, one implication of the omissions is that those cases (including the Stead cases) that Méheust includes in Part I and Part II, but does *not* also include in his dossier in Part III receive very little by way of evaluation and certainly no star-grading anywhere in his book.

Before evaluating and grading one by one the cases in his dossier in Part III, Chapter 6, Méheust discusses a number of theoretical issues. In some brief introductory comments he says that the idea that the *Titanic* disaster gave rise to a combination of premonitory and telepathic phenomena must itself be regarded as an hypothesis which needs to be subjected to methodical examination. He claims that his own analysis extends the work of Stevenson and Behe: he is setting out to separate the wheat from the chaff, the cases that are really unexplained from those that can more easily be explained rationally. This will entail, first, examining the errors to which the human mind is subject when seeking to think objectively about such strange phenomena, and reviewing the criteria that parapsychologists have used in judging spontaneous facts of a premonitory nature.[795]

794 Méheust, p. 164.

795 Méheust, p. 139.

In the first chapter of Part III, entitled 'The Dossier of Telepathic Hallucinations',[796] he points out that the paranormal manifestations that seem to have anticipated and accompanied the sinking are part of a body of telepathic hallucinations much studied by parapsychologists for more than a century. He claims that everyone has heard accounts of people suddenly having the feeling, when dreaming or going about their daily lives, that someone close to them is in danger of dying. This feeling may manifest itself in many ways. In dreams the mental images superimpose themselves over the normal dream processes and impress the subject by their intensity, their gratuitousness and their precision. And in waking life the premonitions impose themselves irresistibly upon people. This kind of event, he says, is experienced 'universally', and goes way back in time, although the scientific investigation of it dates back only to the end of the nineteenth century. The pioneers of the Society for Psychical Research used rudimentary statistical tools and other means, but subsequent research has shown their hypothesis to be justified. It enables us, with contemporary means of communication and refined criteria, to better define a certain dimension of psychical activity.

Méheust argues that the fact that spontaneous telepathy is closely related to the extrasensory perception displayed by gifted subjects in experimental situations leads one to believe that psychic faculties are latent in all human beings and that the death of someone close can open them up. Going on to dwell at some length on a particular

796 Méheust, pp. 140-143.

case concerning French twins, he says it illustrates how far spontaneous telepathy can reach between two people who are close, and shows that in general it is situations of imminent death or of grave threat that generate the phenomenon. Hence the idea that the sinking of *Titanic* gave rise to stories of 'visions' comes as no surprise to parapsychologists. The quantity and the convergence of these stories is more astonishing, and may be explained in two ways. Either we are dealing with genuine visionary or premonitory experiences, and the scale of the disaster acted as a kind of catalyst, or it is the publicity given to the event that contributed to a re-reading of the stories after the event. Méheust says these two hypotheses are not entirely incompatible and that he will clarify them and decide between them.

Although he mentions premonitory experiences at the end of this brief chapter, Méheust's focus is very much on telepathy, as the chapter's title indicates. With the next chapter being squarely on the topic of premonitions, it looks as if he regards the distinction between the two as particularly important. Yet the thrust of the first chapter very strongly suggests that he has the whole range of paranormal experiences recorded in Part II in mind, and it is not clear why he gives the term 'hallucinations' so much prominence. Equally, the narrow emphasis on sensing danger for someone close is somewhat hard to understand. It is true that the chronicle in Part II includes a number of such cases, but they hardly constitute the great quantity that he implies, and it is even more dubious whether they can reasonably be said to display significant convergence.

Méheust's next chapter, 'Precognition Criteria',[797] is again brief and two thirds of it is devoted to two examples entirely remote from *Titanic*. He begins by specifying the 'precise' criteria used by parapsychologists for distinguishing premonitions. The first, and most difficult to satisfy, is that the experience must have left a definite trace fixed before the event in question. If there is no written record, indirect testimony affirming that a certain person said something may be taken into account, on condition that *this* is properly registered in writing, although even then it will have inferior and only complementary value in evaluation. Written records and witness statements created after the event may also be taken into account, provided they support other documents or provoke reflection in some way, but they will not be conclusive. This last category is the one into which most evidence concerning *Titanic* falls, he says, having appeared long after the sinking.

Although Méheust has so far outlined only one criterion, he claims that if 'these criteria' are tough, this is because if precognition were established it would change our whole view of the world. Moreover, the natural mechanism of memory leans towards error, since time is the dimension that slips out of our grasp. Memory deforms and reconstructs memories according to the needs of the present and according to later events. There is no reason why the *Titanic* dossier should escape these revisions. These are the reasons why visions of the future encounter systematic prejudice, which has constructed a

797 Méheust, pp. 144-150.

barrier of arguments almost impossible to overcome. The objections are often valid and it is difficult to prove that they are not always so. Most alleged premonitions fail to meet the fundamental criterion – or necessary (though not sufficient) condition – of an earlier written record. Yet Méheust says there are genuine premonitions, and he dwells at length on the case of a young French nun, Yvonne Aimée de Malestroit in the 1920s, which does nothing, of course, to strengthen the case for *Titanic* premonitions as such.

Méheust begins his following chapter – 'Precognition, Chance, Inference'[798] – by stating that, even when the condition of an earlier written account is fulfilled, it is still necessary to eliminate chance and inference. Hence a prophecy can count as a premonition only if it was not possible to arrive at it by a predictable process of reasoning. He again asserts that if many cases fall at this hurdle a number meet the criterion. He once more cites the case of Malestroit, saying that to go beyond the limits of inference a prediction must include special details that chance could not provide. Méheust also dwells in some detail on the example of Alexis Didier, a French clairvoyant on whom he has written a book,[799] arguing that the criteria for clairvoyance are the same. He then offers another French example of precognition.

It is fair to say that a great deal more might have been expected of Méheust in this brief chapter. It is already somewhat unsatisfactory to give a major example of

798 Méheust, pp. 151-155

799 Bertrand Méheust, *Un voyant prodigieux: Alexis Didier (1826-1866)* (2003).

clairvoyance, then simply to slip in the assertion that the criteria are the same as for precognition. If there is an abundance of examples of precognition, why not offer one of these? And the criteria cannot be exactly the same, since the question of anteriority does not arise in the case of clairvoyance, which, in its narrowest meaning, is a matter of perceiving *objects* that cannot be perceived by the normal senses. There is a general problem with the term 'clairvoyance', since it is also commonly used to mean the obtaining of information about objects, persons, locations, physical events and actions by extrasensory perception, which obviously covers precognition. In *distinguishing* between 'clairvoyance' and 'precognition', as he does here, Méheust must be using the former in its narrower sense. But, far from bringing some precision to the use of these terms, in this chapter and probably in his book as a whole, Méheust uses the terms rather loosely, often employing them as if they are interchangeable and only occasionally distinguishing between them. In this chapter, moreover, in spite of its title he sometimes treats 'chance' and 'inference' equally loosely, bringing them together in unjustified ways. Serious and extended consideration of both is obviously required in connection with the criteria for precognition.

In the next chapter – 'The Three Levels of Clairvoyance'[800] – Méheust unexpectedly uses the French term 'voyance' in the wider sense in which 'clairvoyance' is often used in English. In some contexts 'extrasensory perception' would be an appropriate translation, but here

800 Méheust, pp. 156-158.

it is preferable to employ the term 'clairvoyance' itself. He distinguishes between 'low-level', 'middle-level', and 'high-level' clairvoyance. The first category, which he characterises in brackets as 'false clairvoyance', contains phenomena that can be explained within the limits of our normal knowledge. He says that the 'rationalist consensus' is that all forms of clairvoyance should be reducible to this first type, while those believing in psychic phenomena believe that we need to be able to analyse experiences in the first category to make genuine clairvoyance objective.

His description of 'middle-level' clairvoyance relies heavily on the concept of metaphor. He says – mysteriously – that it is characterised by metaphorical approaches to a target. Unhelpfully, he offers the example of a subject being given an envelope with a bankbook in it for him/her to identify, and listening to the subject talking of a squirrel and miserliness. His suggestion is that we would be doubtful of the subject's powers at first, but recognise that they could not be attributed to chance if the subject repeated this approach to other objects and in other situations. Acknowledging that middle-level clairvoyance is difficult to prove, he finds it very interesting to study because of its metaphorical aspect.

High-level, or genuine, clairvoyance occurs when the subject succeeds in identifying unequivocally the target towards which he/she is being directed, and where this involves special features which radically exclude the possibilities of chance and inference. Méheust concedes that clairvoyants capable of this level of precision are rare, but he names seven and gives a detailed example of Stefan

Ossowiecki's powers. He says that, strictly speaking, only high-level clairvoyance can furnish proof of the reality of extrasensory perception, concluding that, to clearly establish paranormal phenomena connected with *Titanic*, it will be necessary to locate high-level clairvoyance in the dossier. Middle-level clairvoyance will come into play above all as a complementary factor in the analysis of the processes involved.

This chapter is extremely unsatisfactory in most respects. Said to be based on Méheust's long experience, the threefold division of the phenomena of clairvoyance contains a number of serious obscurities. Nothing earlier in the book has prepared us for the sudden injection of metaphor into the picture, which does not advance the argument. And the three levels of clairvoyance brought out here scarcely figure at all in subsequent sections, although he does claim – in a sequence ruined by the failure to mention high-level clairvoyance at all[801] – that his grading system by stars in Part III, chapter 6 corresponds to the three levels described. Furthermore, the terminology and examples Méheust uses more or less exclusively involve cases where a subject is *challenged* to identify *something* by paranormal means: this could hardly be further from premonitions concerning *Titanic*, and from his previous strong emphasis on the notion of the spontaneity of alleged paranormal phenomena.

At the beginning of chapter 5 – 'Adjusting the Criteria for the *Titanic* Case'[802] – Méheust rather surprisingly

801 Méheust, pp. 163-164.

802 Méheust, pp. 159-166.

describes his dossier as 'selected by the English and American parapsychologists'. He also slightly revises his earlier statements in saying that if a prediction could have been the result of a chain of reasoning, it may still count as a premonition if the percipient has also foreseen a series of particular facts that it would not have been possible to deduce rationally. He says this applies equally to laboratory experiments and spontaneous phenomena, but that the principle needs to be discussed and refined for the *Titanic* case.

Méheust suggests that Stevenson advanced two arguments for the paranormal hypothesis. The first is that the reputation of unsinkability enjoyed by *Titanic* makes the idea of an inference to the contrary very unlikely. The second is the convergence of the alleged premonitory accounts. He claims that English parapsychologists have not gone far enough in their analysis on this last point. His own argument is that, while, under the influence of religion, many were shocked by the claims of unsinkability and saw the disaster as a punishment or divine warning, it is entirely rational to have doubts about a prototype with new technical features on its first voyage. With *Titanic*, religious superstition was supported by common sense and rationality. Rightly or wrongly, Méheust believes that women in particular were simply scared to travel on the ship, and he adds, rather arbitrarily, that a number of worrying facts about the ship and its crew were unknown to the public.

He conjectures, therefore, that White Star's publicity concerning *Titanic*'s unsinkability had the reverse effect on a number of people, who consciously or unconsciously began to anticipate a disaster. Those scheduled to board the ship or having someone close to them due to do so were especially affected, and all this is sufficient to explain many alleged premonitions without reference to the paranormal. It might explain the convergence of visions noted by Stevenson, but Méheust believes that the weakness of existing analyses is that they have neglected *unconscious* inference. He argues that it is well-known by psychologists that in the unconscious the contrary of everything formulated is also formulated, so that the image of the ship defying the gods was inverted in people's unconscious minds into a challenge to the devil, and the implacable forces of nature were called upon to exact punishment. Unconscious inference is said to weaken Stevenson's two arguments and turn them against him: if it was the very idea of unsinkability that led certain people to imagine scenes of catastrophe, the public announcement of the maiden voyage of *Titanic* focused attention on this event and generated the convergence of visions. Méheust adds that rumours that *Titanic* was somehow cursed began well before the sinking, in Belfast, and probably crossed the Atlantic into spiritualist circles through immigrants or the friends of Stead.

Now stressing that the precision of the special details given by the percipient is the 'major criterion' for distinguishing whether an experience is a genuine act of clairvoyance or not, Méheust says that when the object is known to everyone such precision is suspect, unless accompanied by further unpredictable details. Hence in spontaneous experiences concerning *Titanic* naming the ship is suspect. He says that we seem to be faced with contradictory demands, with the need to square the circle: if a statement is too imprecise, it is unusable, but if it is too precise, it becomes suspect. If this seems abstract, the problems will appear, he claims, as we examine the most striking cases from those already mentioned.

Before setting out the cases in his dossier in Part III, Chapter 6, Méheust offers a few further points.[803] He claims that more women than men claim to have had paranormal experiences, although we should bear in mind that more women survived the *Titanic* disaster. He then goes on to make some interesting observations in relation to gender. He says there is a strong predominance of 'pure presentiments' among women, with the typical percipient foreseeing something happening to a loved one, to her husband and children. But while women fear for someone else, men, in general, fear for themselves. He qualifies this, however, by saying that it is ordinary women at home who worry for their loved ones: the wealthy ladies on board react like men. This is said to mirror the feminine condition of the time: having no decision-making powers, women still experience ancestral superstitions, whereas men *know* things and talk about technical progress. Yet, in reality, this dichotomy can almost be inverted, he claims, with masculine irrationality and its fascination with distance, utopia, abstraction and technological power opposed to feminine rationality, consisting of common sense and concern with closeness.

803 Méheust, pp. 164-166.

Méheust turns next to the timing of premonitory experiences, saying that while they can sometimes be situated precisely, in the majority of cases it is a time-*margin* that is given, which sometimes complicates interpretation. He asserts that – Robertson and Stead apart – the cases stretch over a little more than a year, although the instance of Dr Minahan dates from 1907. Most of the experiences took place during the few days before *Titanic*'s departure, during the night of the sinking, or the next day. Close to the time of the collision it becomes more and more difficult to decide whether one is dealing with a precognition or a phenomenon of vision at a distance. This is undecidable when only an approximate time-margin is offered.

He argues that in the majority of cases, the percipients had a link with *Titanic*, direct or indirect, and goes on to say that the lack of a link is 'very rare'. Rather oddly, he concludes that this is an essential element for parapsychologists, providing a 'criterion for assessing the reality of the experience' and also for understanding the way in which telepathic communications work. Méheust's point at this stage is particularly obscure, and, in general, one feels that far from offering certain 'precisions' concerning the dossier, the whole section consists of generalisations of dubious value. Méheust often quickly modifies or qualifies them in any event, and one is not inclined to refer back to them in scrutinising the cases in his dossier. Nor, indeed, is it clear how they map onto the list of experiences he catalogued in Part II of his book.

After going through and star-grading his cases one by one in Part III, Chapter 6, Méheust says, in his section

'Conclusions', that he has downgraded a certain number of apparently solid cases on the grounds that it is not possible to exclude simpler hypotheses than the paranormal for explaining them. He sets out six types of experience that he has not rated highly, with the great emphasis being on the need for 'special details' in the premonition account.[804] But this idea requires a great deal of further clarification and precision, and the exact importance of the stress on whether percipients have 'a link' of some kind with *Titanic* remains very obscure at this point; from here onwards he seems to believe that anyone with a link can be suspected of auto-suggestion or unconscious inference.[805] Furthermore, there is no obvious correlation between this codification of Méheust's grading of cases and his actual comments as he went through his dossier.

He goes on to argue that, although the criteria he has recorded are in part contradictory, they are not absolutely so. But he adds some confusion in referring back to one of his cases in particular, saying why it does not have to be put aside, when, in fact, he awarded it only one-star-plus![806] He now appears to be regarding his criteria as ones that have to be fulfilled rather than as reasons for downgrading cases, and his general point is that, in spite of their demanding nature, a certain number of cases meet them. He specifies that 35 cases were put aside, on the grounds he has just explained, while 18 seemed to contain

804 Méheust, pp. 205-206.

805 See, for instance, pp. 207-208.

806 **(BM,62)**. This is the case that Méheust records twice in Part III, under 'E.M.' and 'M.M'.

a paranormal element, but were not clear enough to be retained (he refers in particular to the cases of long-lasting premonitions in this connection). 8 cases satisfy, if not all of the criteria (since the ideal case does not exist), then at least most of them.[807] It is puzzling, however, that, when he goes on to discuss briefly his 8 favoured cases, he does not list them, and uses only 7 as examples, not spelling out at any stage that the case of Jessie[808] belongs in this category.

While denying the implication that spontaneous precognition is not a reality, but reiterating that the probability of precognitive experiences being endorsed before the event is very low, Méheust states – and this is clearly vital for our purposes – that precognition as such has, 'as one might have expected', been almost entirely excluded from his 8 favoured cases, the only exception being W. de Kerlor. Once more it is strange that he does not regard the case of Jessie as another exception, since he has claimed that this is an instance of premonition.[809] He says that Kerlor's is 'the only premonition' to have passed over all of the hurdles: it is well endorsed, sufficiently explicit not to apply to any ship, and it concerns a man no one at the time knew would embark on *Titanic*. A complication here, however, is that in Part II he mentioned not one, but four alleged premonitions by Kerlor, two of which make no reference to ships or drowning at all.[810] He

807 Méheust, pp. 206-207.

808 **(RB,40)**.

809 Méheust, p. 191.

810 These four incidents are reported as three cases by Méheust: **(BM,wts,11)**, **(BM,wts,12)**, **(BM,wts,16)**. Stevenson records two of them: **(IS,11a)**, **(IS,11b)**. Behe records all four as three cases: **(GB,wts,9)**, **(GB,wts,10)**, **(GB,wts,14)**, pointing out that the fourth incident also refers back to the second.

mentions only two in his dossier in Part III, but treats them together.[811] This raises the whole question of the value of his gradings: in most cases he is assessing particular cases, but in some instances – apparently – an individual's precognitive powers. Considering the unique status, according to Méheust, of two of Kerlor's predictions, much more care should have been taken in distinguishing between, and dealing with, the four separate incidents.

Méheust claims that the other cases in his list of 8 invoke a time-margin sufficiently narrow for them to count as *telepathic* experiences. The majority – 6 out of 8 – concern women, and almost all took place during a dream. He says that they all have the same structure: the percipients did not know that someone close to them was on *Titanic* and almost all (say, 6?) were alerted by a dream to the fact that that person was in danger of death. Narrowing down still further, he claims that almost all of the dream cases (say, 5?) envisaged a sinking, or at least a maritime disaster, although in one instance it was simply a death. Méheust's whole treatment of numbers at this stage is somewhat cavalier. For instance, at one point he names four cases and adds 'etc'; and at another he talks of 'almost all of the cases' and mentions just two. Even in the best scenario it is clear that talk of 'almost all' cases where we are looking at a total of eight carries little weight.

Nevertheless, he continues with this terminology in suggesting that in 'most' of these cases the structure of the dream is sufficiently indeterminate and involved for us to rule out the hypothesis of a later modification. Returning

811 Méheust, pp. 207-208.

to the question of naming *Titanic*, he asserts that, apart from the cases where percipients had booked passage on the ship, in the whole dossier the ship is named only once. He claims that this strengthens the accounts, since modifications after the event would have included mention of the name. But, as we have already seen, his argument here is speculative in the extreme. He dismisses the possibility that *Titanic* as such was not mentioned in order to give added authenticity to the stories, saying – unpersuasively – that men and women in 1912 did not have the knowledge required of such psychological mechanisms.[812]

Méheust concludes this section by returning to the matter of whether pure chance might be enough to explain (away) the alleged instances of the paranormal. Although the differences in his eight cases contradict the claim, he asserts that this is a group of eight people who, on the same night, within the same time-margin of a few hours, all dreamed of a sinking when someone close to them was enduring just that. He claims that this is not impossible by chance, but sufficiently impossible in practice for us to conclude that the sinking of *Titanic* did indeed give rise to a combination of paranormal perceptions. If this seems an unsurprising conclusion, we need to remember that he began by saying that it could not be taken for granted, but needed to be established. But he does, in fact, go a little further than this, arguing that the eight favoured cases also give support to 'the others', and that it is probable that authentic premonitory and telepathic experiences figure among the downgraded cases, even if we cannot decide

812 Méheust, pp. 208-209.

which ones: 'Our empirical base is probably wider than that formed by the favoured cases.'[813]

Finally, in Part III, Chapter 7, 'Analysis of the Processes', leaving aside the matter of *proving* paranormal activity, Méheust turns to the *processes* involved in his cases; that is, to the question of the channels through which percipients became aware of the *Titanic* disaster, whether precognition or telepathy be at issue. For this review he appears to draw on all of the cases in his dossier, although this seems a slightly odd – almost backward – step to take, since he has spent so much time singling out just eight cases where there was definitely paranormal activity. Exactly how seriously should one take his account of the channels of paranormal processes, when many of the examples that he uses in this chapter were graded as one-star, which he earlier characterised as 'false clairvoyance'?

(1) He claims that the commonest channel for these processes is not dreams, but emotional impact. This acts as an alarm signal warning the subject of the event, or warning of *something*, since the subject often experiences an anxiety without visible cause. The signal sounds in 24 cases in the dossier, Méheust says, predicting a future event in 22 of these (in 20 of which women are the subject). Like many of Méheust's figures, these need to be treated with caution, but, in any case, they reinforce the point that it is odd to go back to the whole dossier at this stage, since in the 8 cases he favours, only *one* is an alleged premonition.[814]

813 Méheust, pp. 209-210.

814 Méheust, pp. 211-212.

(2) But, as has been known since the end of the nineteenth century, dreams are also a major channel for the paranormal, especially for telepathy. He says they occur in 21 cases in the dossier (12 instances of premonition, 9 of telepathy) – here he reiterates that 6 of his 8 favoured cases involve dreams. Méheust claims that it is 'obviously' only later that dreams can be declared premonitory, or not, because the dreamer at first has no means of deciding, although this does not appear to be borne out by many of his earlier cases. Because of his earlier stress on the importance of the emotional effect of alleged paranormal phenomena, it is impossible to believe that he wants to say that dreamers never awake believing that they have had a premonitory dream. From the fact that the *decision* about whether a dream was premonitory or not necessarily comes later it certainly does not follow that dreamers never believe they have just had a premonitory dream.

Méheust goes on to dwell at some length on dream processes.[815] He begins by claiming that, in analysing the *Titanic* dossier, he is only developing the views of those who created the theory of the unconscious, although certain French parapsychologists have worked on the same processes, independently of psychoanalytical theory. His central point is that dreams rarely say anything directly: they generally use allusion, the most complicated and circuitous possible. Méheust believes, unlike Freud, though like Jung and metapsychologists, that this is not the result of repression, but the 'natural means of expression' of dreams. He does not enter into this debate, but notes

815 Méheust, pp. 212-217.

only that the way in which dreamwork uses all kinds of material is illustrated in the *Titanic* dossier, highlighting the cases of Mrs Hughes, Marcelle Navratil, E.M., Mrs Potter, Mrs Henderson, Kerlor, and Morgan[816] – not all of which feature in his favoured eight cases.

Méheust elaborates much further, however, on another example from Alexis Didier. He adds (as if he had been talking of *only* premonitory dreams) that 'these premonitory dreams' have two other characteristics that distinguish them from 'the other dreams': they have an intensity, a real character, and an exceptional emotional charge, and they often have a repetitive nature, being especially insistent. He illustrates these features by reference to the New York wife, the woman farmer from Athenry, Connon Middleton, Mrs Hughes, Frauenthal (badly misspelled here as 'Freudentahl'), and Daly,[817] four of which do not belong in his favoured eight cases.

(3) Méheust next discusses paranormal experiences undergone by subjects in the waking state, saying that the phenomena occurred suddenly, while they were attending to their daily business, and take various forms. Some premonitions were just ideas, like Mrs Marshall's initial notion that *Titanic* would never reach America.[818] In other cases, such as the long-lasting premonitions, there was an anxiety without cause, which took over the subject's consciousness. Or, again, the process was (or

816 **(IS,17)**, **(GB,pr,33)**, **(IS,13)**, **(IS,5)**, **(IS,14)**, **(IS,11a**, **IS11b**, **GB,wts,14)**, **(IS,6)** respectively.

817 **(IS,3)**, **(GB,po,15)**, **(IS,2)**, **(IS,17)**, **(GB,pr,15)**, **(GB,pr,23)** respectively.

818 **(IS,4)**.

became) definitely hallucinatory, taking the form of a vision. The paranormal intrusion might occur without discernible reason, or might fix on something tangible in particular, whether this be having a fortune told or a single image or sound. These processes are especially well known in the context of prophecies, biblical or otherwise, when acts, names, objects or people become charged with associations and symbolic resonance.[819]

(4) Finally, Méheust considers the ways in which language plays a role in the paranormal process. But he merely gives different examples of the *use* of language, without significantly relating these to Freud's elaboration of the meaning of slips of the tongue. He vaguely suggests that two people are sometimes involved, yet entirely fails to elaborate or illustrate this point. Méheust admits that cases in this general category are thought-provoking, but that it is impossible to demonstrate that they manifest the paranormal. Psycho-analytic theory makes much of them, but parapsychologists never regard them as conclusive.[820]

Méheust adds that paranormal processes sometimes unravel in different phases, passing from the general to the more precise. This may be linked with the matter of long-lasting presentiments, which, quite unlike the 'bad feelings' that we all have from time to time, contaminate everything. He believes that long-lasting premonitions have not been sufficiently studied by parapsychologists.[821] We do, however, need to note at this point that they

819 Méheust, pp. 217-218.

820 Méheust, pp. 219-220.

821 Méheust, pp. 220-222.

are by no means easy to reconcile with the notion that premonitions are essentially sudden and spontaneous.

Although there are no obviously pathological cases in the *Titanic* dossier, Méheust claims that the processes involved correspond to, and go beyond, the manifestations of the unconscious, which have been examined by psycho-analysts for a century. Psycho-analytic theory explains only some of these processes and does not provide the key to them. Freud wanted to show only that telepathy reflects dream-work. His aim was to make parapsychology a mere branch of psycho-analysis, whereas Méheust's own analyses suggest that this should be turned around: since dream-work operates on both unconscious and paranormal information, psycho-analysis itself seems like a local branch of a science of the mind of which parapsychology sees the broad lines. It is a matter of going beyond the 'local' and 'individualist' framework within which Freudian theory operates.[822] Needless to say, Méheust's view of the relationship between psycho-analysis and parapsychology is highly controversial, requiring far more careful consideration than he gives to it.

After returning to literary cases of the paranormal in Part IV, Méheust concludes his book with an Epilogue.[823] He repeats that the *Titanic* disaster gave rise to a cluster of apparently telepathic and premonitory experiences, some of which need to be explained in terms of psychic

822 Méheust, pp. 222-223.

823 Méheust, pp. 290-296.

activity, and addresses the question of why this particular drama should have done so. He claims that there is a clear historical and spatial background to the catastrophe, whereas in the subsequent period up to 1945 the apocalyptic circumstances made paranormal phenomena seem futile in an 'ocean of madness'. Furthermore, while it is especially difficult to pick out a target of psychic activity in a period saturated with extraordinary events, *Titanic* was an ideal target, sinking in the middle of the ocean at the end of a time of peace and prosperity. Its sinking was also an unprecedented drama in its nature and its scale, and this was the first time that a catastrophe became known so quickly on the whole planet, as a result of the telegraph, the telephone, and the press. It marked an historical turning-point, and this, he claims, is why it continues to fascinate us.

Méheust points out that while public settings and arrangements for prophecies (like the Delphic oracle) have disappeared, paranormal experiences have come to occur as spontaneous events, or in an often impoverished form in laboratory experiments. He claims that certain collective events, by their scale or their mythical dimension, can establish 'spontaneous arrangements' for the paranormal, having the capacity to generate a critical mass of emotions and visions that favours psychic activity, which they capture and amplify. Méheust says that certain recent research by parapsychologists like Dean Radin and Roger Nelson tends to support this hypothesis. This approach will help, he believes, to close the gap between experimentation and spontaneous psychic experiences, and perhaps give us a new understanding of the psychic at both the individual and collective levels.

Méheust's only Appendix, 'The Tail of the Comet',[824] explores the 'dark legend' of the *Titanic*. He thinks that the potential cult that began to build up around Stead was ended, but that we may yet hear more of Stead himself, although he is less certain about legends surrounding Captain Smith. He gives short shrift to the conspiracy theory that it was *Olympic* that was deliberately sunk, but goes into great detail on the subject of the curse of the mummy, about which he is totally sceptical. He describes, more briefly, the theory of a freemason plot, but devotes too much space to some truly fanciful 'New Age' musings on how *Titanic*, or the iceberg, was cursed! Méheust does, however, end his book by drawing the reader's attention to an interesting French publication, Patrick Besson's novel, *La Titanic*,[825] which brings in, and blends together many of the facts and myths about *Titanic* in an intriguing, and amusing, way.

It seems, overall, that Méheust overreaches himself in his book. He touches on a number of issues that he devotes scarcely any space to examining, and he dwells in detail on some people and books that bear very little, if any, relation to the *Titanic* story. Moreover, his treatment of evidence is sometimes inadequate and inconsistent. In particular, he occasionally refers to particular categories of statements

824 Méheust, pp. 297-312.

825 Patrick Besson, *La Titanic* (1999). In French, the gender of *Titanic* is masculine. Making it feminine in his book-title is one aspect of Besson's playfulness.

as unreliable, yet accepts them elsewhere. When talking of Stead's posthumous appearances, he argues that the witness statements by his surviving fellow-travellers on *Titanic* 'must obviously be taken with the usual precautions, since one must take account of the work that memory invariably carries out following such traumatic circumstances'.[826] Indeed, later on he refers specifically to the way in which memory deforms and reconstructs memories.[827] But the implications of this point are extremely far-reaching, and at other stages of his inquiry he is, inevitably, very heavily dependent on others' memory. Equally, his claim that, because Helen Bell's 'premonition' did not appear in *Light* until August 1912, 'one can do nothing with it'[828] appears to rule out a very considerable proportion of his other cases. Similarly, when he implies (pointlessly, since he mistakenly believes the percipient died on *Titanic*) that evidence that we have only 'via the filter of a survivor' is insufficient,[829] he risks undermining the reliability of many instances in his corpus. Other inconsistencies include the fact that while on some occasions Méheust shows awareness of, and takes account of, the fact that the morning newspapers of 15 April did not record *Titanic*'s sinking, on other occasions he writes as if he believes, like some of his percipients, that they did. He also sometimes allows for a difference between the time in either London or New York and ship's time, sometimes not.

826 Méheust, pp. 65-66.

827 Méheust, p. 145.

828 Méheust, p. 175.

829 Méheust, P. 187.

More broadly, *Histoires paranormales du Titanic* has a general structure and balance, giving great prominence to literary examples, that is not calculated to throw maximum light on premonitions as such. What is more, because Méheust, like Brown, presents anecdotal premonitions of the *Titanic* disaster chronologically, as a kind of – somewhat dramatised – narrative, the general impression left is that the whole story of the ship was one of menace and fear, whereas other books paint a very different picture, emphasising the celebrations, the sense of excitement, anticipation and hope for the future that prevailed up to the time of the collision.

CHAPTER 7

RESULTS AND METHODS

SINCE THE LITERARY PREMONITIONS WE EXAMINED are chronologically prior to the non-literary, it is appropriate to review our authors' treatment of them first. And as Gardner, who is the only author to bring up the two poems, makes no substantive comment on them, we may simply reiterate our judgement that there is no justification for regarding either poem as even a possible premonition of the *Titanic* disaster, and pass on to the four main fictional examples.

The different evaluations of the main literary cases, as well as the distinct ways in which they are treated, are especially noteworthy. Brown and Stevenson devote very little space to the fictions of Stead and Robertson, as does Behe, who classifies all three works as no more than curious coincidences. On the other hand, Gardner rather surprisingly regards Robertson's novel as the 'single most impressive example of seeming precognition of the *Titanic* disaster, or any other disaster'.[830] And, sceptic though he is, he takes up the bulk of his book in presenting and reproducing Robertson's *Futility* and extracts from Stead's 'From the Old World to the New' (although he devotes only a single paragraph to 'How the Mail Steamer Went Down …', which he does not even name). Méheust goes even further than this in comment, focusing both the first and final parts of his book on these two writers and dwelling at some length on the broad matter of premonitions in literature.

It is very striking that none of our authors expresses a clear belief that 'How the Mail Steamer Went Down …' constitutes or even contains a premonition of the *Titanic* disaster. The emphasis falls broadly on Stead's warning regarding an insufficient number of lifeboats, and even Méheust is concerned above all to argue – without success – that the story foretells Stead's death. On the other hand, 'From the Old World to the New' does at least incorporate the sinking of a liner by collision with an iceberg, though Méheust presses the case for wider paranormal content in the tale rather than making much attempt to link it to the *Titanic*.

All of our authors, on the other hand, note the many points of similarity between Robertson's *Futility* and the *Titanic* story. Stevenson is not impressed, but Gardner is. Without quoting a source, or elaborating on the matter, Brown claims that Robertson had an 'astral partner' and was in a state of trance when he wrote the story,[831] yet Behe

830 Gardner (1), p. 27.

831 Brown, pp. 21-22. Occasionally, one reads more detailed accounts of Robertson's 'trances', but no creditable sources are ever given.

regards the apparently uncanny similarities as perfectly understandable. Although there is a general inclination to believe that most of these can be explained by Robertson's knowledge of the evolution of ships and his rational anticipation of further developments, Méheust dwells at length on the obvious parallels, even – rather implausibly – extending the list. But he both refers to the 'unintentional' prophecy with which Robertson's name is now associated and says Robertson is a writer-medium who could write only in a state of trance. He is rather vague, even confused about the whole pattern into which the writer allegedly fits.

While Stevenson and Brown appear not to know of Garnett's 'The White Ghost of Disaster', Gardner finds it a more surprising coincidence than Robertson's novella. But he believes this is because it came out at the same time as the *Titanic* sinking, and sees it as one of a large number of stories about liners colliding with icebergs. Behe regards it as one more curious coincidence, and Méheust seems to give it a very low rating as a premonition. He, too, is especially struck by the date of publication, but he makes a good deal less of Garnett than his emphasis on literature and seeing all literary examples as a group would lead us to expect, treating him almost as an afterthought.

All in all, the literary cases of alleged premonition are not particularly well treated by our authors. Understandably, uncertainty governs the significance of parallels between the stories and the *Titanic* catastrophe. And there is certainly no obligation to see these items, in the way that Méheust does, as a significant *group* of literary works. The fact that three authors, in the quarter century before the *Titanic* disaster, wrote about the sinking of Atlantic liners is not particularly remarkable.[832] Neither is the point that their fictional liners had some resemblances to *Titanic*. Indeed, it is a very great deal more extraordinary to consider that these writers all had some kind of supernatural power and that they all experienced premonitions of the *Titanic* tragedy. Méheust is the only one of our authors to come even close to believing the latter, and he duly follows this up in almost the only possible way, by mentioning a theory that links the paranormal features of the works of the three separate writers. However, his 'risky' idea of a telepathic network linking the works beneath the surface without the knowledge of the authors as the most likely explanation raises infinitely more questions than it answers. It is speculative in the extreme and so undeveloped that it does not merit serious consideration.

Méheust also touches on the possibility of one writer influencing a later one, but regards the hypothesis that Robertson drew on Stead's stories as 'unlikely on the psychological level', although he argues that we cannot absolutely exclude it as an unconscious phenomenon. Nonetheless, as we have already indicated, a thorough examination of literary premonitions would certainly

832 It is worth mentioning that any claim that the novel *Atlantis* by Gerhart Johann Robert Hauptmann, published in 1912 and said to have been written a month before the *Titanic* disaster, anticipates the disaster can be dismissed out of hand. The dissimilarities between *Titanic* and the fictional steamer *Roland* are far too numerous to mention, and the *Roland* sinks (probably after a collision with a derelict) half way through this long, romantic novel, the rest of the story taking place on land, in America.

involve both a more detailed consideration of Stead's possible influence on Robertson, and of Garnett's debt to both authors.

It does need to be remembered, however, that the 'literary premonitions' of Stead and Robertson were not seen as anything of the sort for up to more than twenty years, until the *Titanic* tragedy occurred. A detailed investigation might show exactly when their stories first came to be regarded as premonitions, who first publicly declared them to be such, and the precise nature and sequence of subsequent recognitions. Coates's book in 1913 certainly considered Stead in this light,[833] but it implies that the alleged paranormal elements were noted – and discussed – still earlier. It is not clear by whom and when Robertson was first considered to have foreseen the disaster. The extraordinary timing of the publication of Garnett's story (7 April, 1912) raises rather different issues, as so much was known about *Titanic* at that time, making this the only literary case that *could* have been seen as a premonition of disaster for the ship at the very moment the story came into the public domain. Interest in *Titanic* premonitions surely encompasses the need for a clearer detailed understanding of the circumstances in which the literary instances came to be considered as such.

None of our commentators, moreover, registers the point that, broadly speaking, the similarities with *Titanic* seem to increase in importance in the chronological order of publication of our four items. It would have been good to

833 James Coates, *Has W.T. Stead Returned? A Symposium* (1913). See especially Chapter XI, 'Do Coming Events Cast their Shadows before?'

see this recognised and examined, since it may increase the likelihood that it is inference from 'present' conditions rather than anything paranormal that has produced resemblances to *Titanic* in the works of literature concerned.

A further weighty fact is that even Méheust, for all his emphasis on premonitions in literature, gives almost no attention at all to the extremely important question of whether these authors are supposed to have had a number of premonitions, then later to have incorporated them into a story, or whether the suggestion is that the whole act of writing itself was carried out in some kind of paranormal state. This would appear to be a crucial question for the investigation of the paranormal, yet the detail of it is almost totally ignored by our commentators. In short, even where the simple correlation of actual and fictional facts in a literary work is agreed to be significant, careful examination of possible premonitions must necessarily involve more than this. Some scrutiny of the nature and circumstances of any alleged premonition proper, and its recognition as such, is surely an absolutely minimal requirement. It may be particularly complex and difficult in the case of old literary texts, but this is no reason for omitting or avoiding it.

Altogether, far more space is devoted in the texts to premonitions regarding Stead's death than to any other specific topic or type of premonition. They constitute more than 17% of our total number.[834] Our suggestion that

834 For various reasons, it is extremely difficult to be *absolutely* precise in counting cases, so that numbers in this chapter need to be treated with a degree of caution, although any 'errors' should not be significant enough to affect the argument.

they are a special instance of non-literary premonitions, since initially they clearly actually circulated within the circle of Stead's acquaintances, is borne out by the fact that 21 of the 32 cases for which sources are given quote books by either Stead's daughter, Estelle, or Edith Harper, Stead's secretary, or James Coates, who knew Stead well. Even so, only one instance is mentioned by all 5 of our authors, and 15 by just one author.

There is, furthermore, some common agreement with Coates's view that neither Stead himself nor, perhaps, any of those said to have foretold his death issued a specific warning about *Titanic*. None of the commentators is willing to argue that Stead's vision of death by violence in a 'mob' relates significantly to the ship.[835] And only Méheust appears to regard Stead's speech in which he imagines himself shipwrecked as having any relationship to *Titanic*.[836] All of the other cases allegedly illustrating Stead's predictions of his own death are characterised by great uncertainty and vagueness. At the same time, of the 24 cases where someone else is said to have had a premonition of Stead's death, 8 are examined by only one of our commentators, and another 11 are considered only by Behe and Méheust. But Méheust comes back to only 4 of these to give them a star grading, and amalgamates 3 of them with other cases to rate them in Part III.[837] Hence, it can be said that any measure of agreement on this topic

835 **(IS,9c)**.

836 **(IS,9d)**.

837 May de Witt Hopkins **(GB,wts,11)**; Kerlor **(IS,11a)**, **(IS,11b)**, **(GB,wts,14)**; Mme de Thèbes **(GB, wts,3)**.

between Behe and Méheust on these 11 instances really is minimal.

There are only 4 cases of someone predicting Stead's death that are examined by more than two of our authors, 2 of them relating to Kerlor. Gardner does not mention Cheiro, and Brown does no more than repeat the information of Stevenson, who considers Cheiro's predictions as rather impressive. Both Behe and Méheust, however, have serious doubts.[838] Four of our authors, moreover, are – in varying degrees – sceptical about the case of Mrs Tweedale.[839] As far as Kerlor himself is concerned, while Gardner does not mention him at all, neither Stevenson nor Brown makes any significant comment on the 'strongest' case of Kerlor's vision of Stead's trip to America and a 'huge black ship'.[840] And, since Behe looks at this in his chapter on Stead we do not know how he would have rated it in relation to his categories of curious coincidence, possible, and probable psychic phenomena. Moreover, while Behe draws our attention to a clear mistake in Kerlor's premonitions (that Stead will be trampled upon or kicked to death), Méheust, although rating the case highly, thinks that Kerlor may have heard of Turvey's prediction.

One can say, in general, that where there is some agreement concerning others' predictions of Stead's death, this is as much dismissive as positive, and does not help in the least in making a case for precognition. Moreover,

838 (IS,10).

839 (IS,12).

840 (IS,11a).

Goss and Behe suggest explicitly that the evidential value of these predictions is greatly reduced by the fact that they were mostly recorded long after the event. And, regardless of the timing issue, Méheust's observation that Kerlor may have heard of Turvey's experience – despite the fact that the latter case does not relate to Stead – raises the point that a much closer look ought to be taken at the interaction between members of Stead's circle and the possibility of the premonition of one influencing that of another. This is a clear reality in connection with Stead's 'appearances' after his death, but none of our authors seriously explores the phenomenon in relation to premonitions that allegedly took place before it. Yet the inter-relations of subjects within Stead's orbit, whilst by no means a factor in all of the predictions of his death, may well have played a significant part in many of them.

For a general review of alleged non-literary premonitions, it is useful to begin our assessment at the end, with Méheust's 8 favoured, three-star cases. We find that 3 of them had not been unearthed by Stevenson, and that an additional 4 are not mentioned by Behe, despite the fact that they are covered by Stevenson. In fact, the only one of Méheust's 8 actually examined by four authors – and the only case that he classifies as a premonition rather than as telepathy – is the Kerlor case concerning Stead's death already mentioned.[841] In short, looking at the writings of our five authors as a whole, there is little justification for seeing Méheust's selection as picking out particularly special cases of premonition.

841 **(IS,11a)**.

Again, if we look at Behe's 35 'probable' cases, we find that only 2 are awarded three stars by Méheust (Jessie and Marcelle Navratil), and another 2 two-star-plus (Butt and Esther Hart).[842] In fact, Méheust quite often classifies Behe's best instances as only one-star or one-star-plus. And even when we examine the 4 cases where there appears to be something like a common (positive) judgement, the results are disappointing. The complicated, 'long-lasting' and changing nature of Butt's anxieties makes it extremely difficult for either Behe or Méheust to see this as an entirely convincing case of premonition, and there are considerable differences of emphasis in the presentation of it by all five authors. Moreover, each of the other 3 items is somewhat undermined by problems concerning sources. In short, none of the 4 cases apparently rated highly by both Behe and Méheust, when scrutinised, stands out as compelling in the context of the writings of our five commentators.

Since none of the cases first introduced by Brown is considered by Gardner as well as by Behe and Méheust, the only other class of general premonitions that can be examined for potential agreement among more than three of our authors takes us back to those presented by Stevenson in his first article. This is a mixed bunch of cases. Three commentators have reservations of some kind about Connon Middleton's dreams, and while Stevenson is inclined to see the New York woman's dream about her mother as telepathy, and Méheust rates it highly as such, Gardner's criticism carries some weight. There is a certain

842 6 are rated as two stars by Méheust, 10 one star or one-star-plus; 13 are not rated.

agreement on the plausibility of Blanche Marshall's vision, but Méheust has some reservations. Both Stevenson and Gardner are rather critical of Mrs Potter's dream, but Méheust attaches credence to it as an example of remote viewing, not precognition. Neither Stevenson nor Brown is critical of the story concerning Reverend Morgan's choice of hymns: Gardner is, of course, and Méheust grants the experience only one star. Méheust also awards only one star to Charles Hays's predictions, and Behe regards them as just a curious coincidence; Gardner is particularly dismissive, and Stevenson himself makes no comment. Apart from Gardner, all our authors take the case of Vincent Turvey pretty seriously, but there is considerable confusion over the exact details. Both Stevenson and Brown rather weakly endorse the warning given to Edith Evans, but Gardner, Behe and Méheust are all doubtful. And only Brown shows any inclination to believe that John Coffey had a premonition.

It is somewhat easier to compare reactions to the 7 experiences that Stevenson brings to light in his second article, since neither Brown nor Behe refers to any of them! Gardner makes no substantive comment on two of the cases, but is strongly and specifically dismissive of the other five. Méheust has his reservations about the case of Mr M., and, for reasons that he does not make entirely clear, awards Mr Black's dream only one-star-plus. He also makes little of Colin Macdonald's feelings, once more rating them as one-star-plus. But he is intrigued by Norah Mathews's premonition, awarding it two stars. And he regards three of Stevenson's later cases highly. He rates

Mrs Henderson's case, as three stars and includes it in his favoured eight, although the timings confirm Stevenson's view that it was definitely not an instance of premonition. Furthermore, Méheust again classifies the dreams of Ida Lorenz, and Mrs Hughes as three stars, and includes them in his eight strongest cases. Although it is difficult to see any particular significance in the point, it is rather remarkable that 3 of Méheust's 8 strongest cases should come from the 7 in Stevenson's second article, despite the fact that two of our commentators fail to take the 7 cases into account at all.

All things considered, surprisingly little general agreement is to be found on the part of our five authors (or even – if we exclude Gardner, as a firm sceptic – on the part of four of them) regarding specific alleged premonitions. It is true that the actual body of cases considered by each varies quite considerably. Moreover, fewer than 20 of our 201 experiences in all are examined by four or five of them. This low number in particular is significant in itself, especially when 7 of the cases are either literary ones or concern Stead. In other words, there is no discernible consensus on which instances are the most convincing, and no single example which meets with the broad approval of, say, four – perhaps even three – of our commentators. Even if it is considered unsurprising that there are some rather remarkable discrepancies in the judgements of our authors on particular cases, it is well worth recording the simple fact that no kind of confirmation of the reality of premonitions is to be found in a concordance in their views.

More than this, it is also noticeable how little clear commitment there is to the reality of premonition as such on the part of all of our authors except Brown. Gardner's scepticism can, of course, be taken for granted, but Stevenson is generally much more cautious than many references to his work would suggest. And, above all, he concedes that many of his cases are instances of telepathy rather than premonition, suggesting in a later article that only ten of his 'nineteen' cases were precognitive.[843] Behe carefully and explicitly limits himself to, at best, 'probable' examples of psychic phenomena (and has claimed in an Internet forum that he is now more sceptical about the paranormal). Méheust is a believer in the paranormal, but goes even further than Stevenson in claiming that instances of premonition as such are rare, and vastly outnumbered by cases of telepathy.[844] Whilst we have acknowledged that the boundary between premonitions and telepathy can be a very indistinct one, it is clear that the 'standard' case of premonition involves just one individual, and it ought to be possible to arrive at a judgement on premonitions that excludes virtually all alleged telepathic experiences. It is clear, therefore, that the assessments offered by our authors fall considerably short of the unambiguous affirmation of the reality of premonition that one might have expected from four of them.

When we turn back to the premonitions themselves, we find that, because literature is out there, in the public eye, and the 'warnings' to Stead were originally confined to

843 Ian Stevenson, 'Precognition of disasters' (1970), p. 205.

844 Méheust, pp. 207-208.

his acquaintances, the question arises of where the other, general cases came from (apart from earlier authors in our sequence). Since Stevenson effectively started the process of investigation we have been pursuing, it is interesting that he notes in his first article that all materials he quotes have already been published elsewhere. Nevertheless, in a significant number of instances he mentions making personal contact with the percipient or someone close to the percipient – something more feasible when he was writing, around fifty years after the event – and little, if any, of this material was previously published. The process of making direct contact with individuals actually predominates in his second article, where no fewer than 6 of his 7 cases fall into this category. In other instances in his first article he uses correspondence already available in books or journals (mostly journals of psychic research). On 6 occasions he draws on books by Lord and Coates; almost all of the other books he cites are by percipients themselves or those who knew them. It is perhaps a mark of his academic training and environment that his sources do not include newspapers.

As mentioned in the Introduction, both Brown (who was herself a newspaper writer and columnist) and Behe rely heavily on newspapers as sources of the cases they cite. Brown names 28 newspapers in her bibliography, though she does not say, in the body of her text, where or how she has used them. Behe is more systematic, naming at least one source – newspaper or other – for each of his cases. Remarkably, he cites around 76 separate English-language newspapers (principally from America, Britain, and Canada – none, for instance, from France, although there were over thirty French passengers on *Titanic*), and uses nearly 30 of these more than once.[845] Interestingly, only 3 of the 28 newspapers listed by Rustie Brown are used as Behe's sources. Sometimes Behe quotes three or more papers as his sources for a particular case. From the present point of view, what is more significant is that around 100 of his references to newspapers are to editions dated April, 1912 (some 13 are to May, 1912, and only 9 to a later date). There is no mention of an edition pre-dating the *Titanic* disaster itself, but this demonstrates beyond any doubt that the first and original written source of most *Titanic* premonitions is newspapers.

Since many people attach particular weight to individual eyewitness testimonies in the case of the *Titanic* catastrophe as a whole, some will regard newspaper reports of the time as authenticating accounts of premonitions, especially as so many of them are based on interviews with passengers or crew from the ship itself. Yet there is no justification for automatically taking this step, for serious questions have to be raised about the accuracy and reliability of reporting in newspapers. While some may argue that, in principle, there is no more reason to doubt newspaper reports in themselves than accounts in journals or books, it is far from certain that, in general,

845 In 'Acknowledgements' Behe talks of the 'hundreds of newspaper microfilms which yielded many of the accounts discussed in this work'. It is perhaps surprising that the website 'Encyclopedia Titanica', which refers extensively to newspapers in its biographical entries and includes links to articles in innumerable cases, has not systematically included the newspaper articles specifically mentioned as sources in Behe's book.

this position can be sustained. Newspaper reports are produced more quickly, even hastily; they are not peer-reviewed in the way and to the extent that the texts of most journal articles or books are; newspapers vary more in quality, and their reporters – bearing in mind that we are referring here in many instances to local or regional papers – are, on the whole, less qualified than authors; there is a greater need, with newspapers, to present the type of material that is wanted, and will sell – a greater tendency, on the whole, to select and dramatize.

Despite Behe's heavy reliance on newspapers in his earlier book, these points are explicitly recognised in *Lost at Sea*, where Goss and Behe point out that accounts in national newspapers or commercially oriented magazines 'may (rightly or wrongly) be open to charges of bias; the argument is that such publications exaggerate, colour or otherwise "adapt" – or falsify – their material to suit the perceived tastes of a particular, often uncritical, unobjective and non-scientific readership'.[846] In his *A Death on the Titanic* (2011),[847] moreover, Behe refers to the 'questionable reliability of many 1912 newspaper interviews with *Titanic* survivors, since many reporters appear to have embellished or fabricated interviews that they later attributed to specific survivors'.[848] He lists the survivors whose newspaper interviews he has deliberately refrained from using, giving his reasons for doing so. In one case he speculates whether an unnamed *Titanic*

846 Goss and Behe, p. 245.

847 This is an abridgement of the third volume of Behe's *Archie* (2010).

848 *A Death on the Titanic*, p. 359.

survivor was 'merely inventing tall tales about things that occurred on board the *Titanic* while the great vessel was sinking'.[849] Although his further statement that 'Indeed, sometimes individual survivors granted second newspaper interviews which made it clear that their earlier statements … were fabrications created by imaginative reporters'[850] is somewhat paradoxical in its own reliance on newspapers, one might wish that Behe's generally critical attitude towards newspapers had been adopted in his earlier book on premonitions.[851]

These views on newspapers are generalities: there are, and always have been, newspaper reports that are more careful and considered than some books and articles. But to rely on newspapers in general, without distinguishing between them, or to rely on a particular newspaper article as a source without seeking to know more about the reporter or circumstances of the item, and without cross-checking its content in some way, is short-sighted. Referring to more than one newspaper for an individual case may temper the more outrageous of inventions, but does not avoid the general objections to reliance on newspapers.[852] Of course, equivalent distinguishing and checking needs to be carried out on articles and books,

---

849 *A Death on the Titanic*, p. 368.

850 *A Death on the Titanic*, p. 369.

851 It is interesting to note that, although for its detailed reconstruction of events between the collision and the sinking *On a Sea of Glass* (2012) relies extensively on statements in newspapers, it is scrupulous in cross-checking one account against another and frequently categorises a particular comment or report as inaccurate or embellished.

852 Some 40 of Behe's (70) curious coincidences alone rely in part or in whole on newspapers as their sources. Méheust refers to only one newspaper as a direct source.

too, and there are many cases where these procedures are difficult, tedious, even impossible. Yet confidence in results ultimately depends upon them and, in the broadest terms, it will be weaker when what we have to take for granted is found in a newspaper rather than a book or a journal article.

Somewhat tentatively, Goss and Behe pursue the general argument concerning the unreliability of newspapers a little further, suggesting that 'not far removed from this category, certain specialist publications may be accused of utilising unreliable material not for direct financial gain but to promote a defined view or belief system favoured by the editors and/or the readers'.[853] They claim, reasonably, that some sources are 'traditionally afforded higher respect than others' and that cases documented by the British or American Societies for Psychical Research or 'comparable bodies composed of accredited parapsychologists' tend to carry more weight. Yet they clearly have some reservations, despite the fact that they contrast the accounts of these organisations with those in 'a national newspaper or commercially oriented magazine'. It is true that those who are sceptical about the paranormal are likely automatically to question the authenticity of items that appear in spiritualist publications, but it is not clear that this is entirely reasonable: there really is no serious alternative to scrutinising such items themselves on their individual merits.

Our insistence on sources is by no means an arbitrary matter. It is entirely reasonable to criticise a commentator

853 Goss and Behe, p. 245. This echoes Behe's point in his earlier book (p. 61).

for not quoting a source for a particular premonition. Perhaps we have sufficient faith in the commentator to exclude the possibility of invention on his or her part, and indeed of any intention to deceive. We may even be confident that the commentator has done his or her very best to record the incident accurately. This still does not eliminate the possibility of error of memory or in transmission, and without a source we are unable to check for this ourselves. What is more, we certainly need to be absolutely sure of the dating and timing of the premonition, and an unsourced experience does not allow us to verify these, or to scrutinise the original account, to check for error, to look for further details, or perhaps to see the circumstances in a different perspective.

To carry out these tasks thoroughly in the face of such a large number of instances would be, as we indicated from the first, a massive task. It is far from clear that even Stevenson, with his twenty-six cases, carried it out fully, or that Gardner went quite that far for all of his limited range. As the number of potential premonitions increased dramatically with first Brown, then Behe, and – less substantially – Méheust, the very likelihood of truly comprehensive checking diminished accordingly. Behe's thoroughness in particular is admirable, and he is by far the most conscientious of our authors in giving sources. His work in this respect, however, raises two major points. We have seen that his heavy reliance on newspapers as sources is questionable in itself, but this in turn brings out the fact that all of the questions of reliability that we need to deal with in the case of a commentator also need to be dealt with in connection with any given source. In short, while quoting a source for an alleged premonition is indispensable, it solves nothing, since the source itself has to be evaluated in one way or another.

To complicate matters further, in many cases the source is not the product of the subject or percipient himself or herself, but of another party reporting on the subject's experience. The very same questions of reliability arise, of course, with regard to this third party. And even if the appropriate checks could be carried out at all of these levels, it would still be possible for an extreme sceptic to doubt, since one may question, and refuse to rely on, *anything*. Even if our commentators had assiduously followed their own best advice and cast the methodical, Cartesian doubt on all of their subjects, and even if there were corroboration of some kind on the part of other people in the cases they regarded as genuine, it would still be possible to refuse to accept the authenticity of what was left. There is simply no way of totally eradicating all possibility of doubt by someone who is determined to pursue it and continues to persist in questioning evidence. This needs to be borne in mind as much as gullibility in any attempt to establish, or undermine, the reality of premonitions.

In general, of course, all four authors following Stevenson draw on the work of their predecessors. But this is a surprisingly unsystematic and patchy process rather than a smooth, linear one. Brown indicates early in her book that she knows of both of Stevenson's articles, and that she visited him in 1977. Yet she fails to mention 4 of the 19 cases in his first article, and makes not a single reference to any of the 7 cases in his second article. It is true that in only one of these latter instances was the percipient actually on the *Titanic*, but distance from the scene does not prevent Brown from using such experiences in her book. In general, she adds substantially to the number of cases, but although at the beginning she acknowledges her debt to dozens of people by name ('Hundreds of people have played a part in making this book a reality'),[854] and has an extensive bibliography at the end, she is less conscientious than any of the other authors about quoting her sources in connection with particular cases. From certain details in the book, one is bound to wonder, as we have already mentioned, to what extent incidents reported to Edwina MacKenzie constituted a major source for Brown.

Gardner's sources, on the other hand, are quite clear. In addition to his literary items, the only cases that he discusses are Stevenson's cases from both articles, which he takes up one by one.[855] His book has no footnotes or endnotes, no Index or Bibliography, but where he refers to specific articles or books in his commentaries he gives basic details in the body of his text. However, he makes no reference at any point to Brown's book, which he may have been unaware of.

Behe was aware of at least the first of Stevenson's articles, which he mentions by name in 'Further Reading'.[856] He

854 Brown, p. iv.

855 Gardner promises to look at Stevenson's ten cases 9-12 (Gardner (1), p.19), but, in introducing his Stead extracts, omits to mention the Cheiro and Kerlor items.

856 Behe, p. 173).

claims that he discusses 'only a few' of the cases Stevenson takes up. The reasons for this are unclear, since, in general, Behe is attempting to be more comprehensive than earlier contributors. In any event, all of Stevenson's cases are more worthy of space than many of Behe's 'curious coincidences'. In fact, while Behe treats 15 of the 19 instances mentioned in Stevenson's first article, like Brown he refers to none at all of the 7 mentioned in his second. He cites an edition of Robertson's novel as his source for Stevenson's first article,[857] but although Stevenson has 19 *numbered* cases over both of his articles, Behe's reference to Stevenson's 19 cases is not absolutely conclusive evidence that he is taking both articles into account, since, counting the separate items relating to Stead and the 'extra' cases, Stevenson's first article itself actually includes 19 cases! In any case, Behe's failure to mention specifically Stevenson's second article or anything in it remains a puzzle.

Behe does, however, cite in 'Further Reading' the books of both Rustie Brown – 'a lively, entertaining and informative work…' – and Martin Gardner. Yet, perhaps because he considers them of poor quality, he neglects 14 of Brown's cases. He also argues that Gardner makes each of Stevenson's cases 'childishly simple to explain away', but claims that 'the book should be read because of its excellent discussion of coincidences, and how they can sometimes appear to be of a psychic nature'.[858] More generally, one has to note that, although the fact that 29 of Behe's 35 'probable' cases are ones that he himself brings

857 *The Wreck of the Titan* (1974).

858 Behe, p. 173.

to light, this means that only 6 of the 47 non-literary cases not concerning Stead introduced by earlier authors make it into Behe's list of his best cases. The chapter in Goss and Behe's book uses 2 cases from Behe's earlier work, and 3 from our other authors; 3 of its 8 new cases come from psychic journals and 4 from newspapers.

Méheust frequently refers to Stevenson and examines every individual case covered by both of his articles, except for one.[859] And we need to remember that, although his book examines fewer than half of the same cases as Behe (who is often cited in footnotes),[860] it is twice as long, takes up a number of instances of possible paranormal activity that Behe does not, and is more detailed on theoretical matters and questions of methodology. Yet Méheust gives no indication of having read either of the books by Brown (who first introduced 9 of the cases that he considers)[861] or Gardner. And, although he treats one of 'their' cases, there is no concrete evidence that he is aware of the book by Goss and Behe. Furthermore, it is unfortunate that, in addition to omitting to produce an Index to his book, Méheust is much less systematic than he ought to be about providing sources for all of his cases, although some instances where he quotes no source are clearly derived from Behe.

In general, therefore, in the texts we have studied it is very far from the case that the matter of examining premonitions is a steadily accumulating one, with each author systematically taking up all of his or her

859 Coffey (**IS,12b**).

860 He mentions 16 of Behe's curious coincidences, 10 of his possibles, 25 of his probables.

861 9 of which are treated in Behe's book.

predecessor's alleged instances and adding to them. Gardner has more restricted aims, but since he ignores Brown one might even talk, in general, of a certain degree of neglect of previous authors on the part of four of our commentators.

On the other hand, all five authors display, in varying degrees, a measure of self-consciousness about the methods of investigating precognitive phenomena once these have been identified. At the highest level of generality, it might be said that they all five tackle anecdotal premonitions in much the same way. Having located a source (specified or not), they begin by recounting the experience, amalgamating the items of information where it has more than one provenance. Then, usually, they make some comment on, or offer an evaluation or assessment of, the story. Stevenson and Behe sometimes have a sub-heading, 'Comment', in connection with particular cases (although in his first article Stevenson groups most of his comments under 'DISCUSSION' later in the piece). Méheust runs through his anecdotes more or less without comment in Part II, but makes a major feature of evaluating those he returns to in Part III. Gardner usually criticises as he goes along: his negative assessment is clearly implicit where he does not comment. Brown's common failure to make any explicit judgement strongly implies and encourages belief.

We said in the Introduction that there is no well-established protocol for investigating paranormal anecdotes, but Stevenson rightly pointed out in a lecture that certain procedures that rather resemble the methods used by lawyers in reconstructing a crime and historians in understanding the past, are, in fact, followed. However, he says only that they involve considering alternative explanations and eliminating them until only the single most probable one remains. Then, by further observations, we may seek to 'confirm or reject the initially preferred explanation'.[862] This is no more than a very broad guide to aspects of how our authors proceed, or at least *should* proceed. If we examine or analyse their detailed procedures, and where they do so themselves, additional details of method and further issues invariably arise, although these vary a great deal in importance.

If we look, for example, at the matter of how to treat the *motives* of those who claim to have paranormal experiences, we find that Goss and Behe are particularly concerned to comment. They believe that such people are not self-publicists but have a 'natural desire to share' and often to canvass explanations for the unusual. They say that the editors of the journals involved agree that the stories merit retelling to larger audiences, but answer '"Yes" and … "No"' to the question of whether the editors publish in the hope of promoting a particular set of beliefs, and even of whether the percipients, too, have that in mind. They are anxious to stress that their cases cannot be dismissed because some of them have a 'taint' of spiritualism. Evidence is always required, they say, to back up peculiar claims, and all of their percipients could have done better had they wanted to work on the susceptible reader's conviction. However, Goss and Behe's general claims that

862 Ian Stevenson, 'Some of My Journeys in Medicine – A Lecture about Science and Reincarnation' (1989).

paranormal precognition does not function in an obvious fashion, and that any paranormal experience relating to *Titanic* will have a 'personal, ambiguous quality', are, as we noted, rather vague and unhelpful ones, which fail to advance the argument.

Their points, moreover, are just one aspect of a broader issue concerning what or whom we may trust or rely on with regard to paranormal claims. Gardner's critical mind-set and Behe's Part II, 'Mistaken accounts and deliberate hoaxes', may seem to show a greater awareness of the possibility of error and deceit than is present in the other three authors, but Méheust and Stevenson also both make judgements on the quality of evidence. Yet none of our authors quite faces up to the matter of exactly what makes a particular statement believable, trustworthy or reliable, and what undermines our faith in it. Indeed, the question may in itself be too general to be answered except in philosophical terms, but a considerably stronger sense of the ways in which an individual may be 'sincere' but wrong and, perhaps above all, susceptible to the highly complex process of self-deception is required in the texts we have examined.

Brown is the only one of our five authors who does not take serious account of the possibility of fraudulent claims with regard to the paranormal and premonitions. Stevenson says he has excluded instances where fraud may have been involved; Gardner and Behe go into some detail concerning the nature and mechanisms of some such claims; and while Méheust rarely mentions fraud as such, in his detailed examination of cases he is fairly rigorous in certain respects in seeking out ways in which accounts of premonitions may have been doctored after the event. In general, therefore, there is likely to be little, if any, deliberate, significant and serious fraud in our two hundred cases that has been overlooked by our authors.

Error and self-deception, however, are quite different matters. It is quite remarkable – and this is the stage at which to emphasise a point that might otherwise be neglected – that in examining and comparing the accounts of premonitions by different authors one comes across so many discrepancies in the details of particular cases. Inevitably, varying levels of detail are noticeable, but the incompatibilities and contradictions are, in many instances, very striking indeed. Whether or not these arise from the use of different sources or in some other way, there is often no logical option but to classify *some* of the assertions made as erroneous. One might, loosely, have assumed that this would scarcely occur when dealing with responsible commentators, but we have seen that the phenomenon is widespread. So much so that simply recording the discrepancies in different accounts of an experience may, in some instances, be sufficient to raise severe doubts about its validity as a premonition. Whether or not this weakens the case for premonitions in general, with reference to *Titanic* it certainly does not strengthen it in any respect.

It is true, of course, that the fact that we are talking of 'seeing' something in the future makes for additional complications. Where there may be question of error in the perception of the subject, the opportunity of checking a perception, or of suggesting that a subject has misdescribed his or her perception is limited in the extreme. Indeed, later 'corrections' – or, in fact, modifications of any kind – of an original 'premonition' almost automatically weaken its apparent authenticity significantly. And not only do subjects sometimes misremember the *timing* of their experience, error can – and does – occur in the transmission and re-transmission of accounts of premonitions. Yet where it is a matter of possible error in a third party's account of the subject's original perception – and this must apply in a very great many instances – there is rarely any independent means of verifying this.

In any case, there are simple and straightforward mistakes in the alleged premonitions themselves. Foreseeing *Titanic* upside down or capsized should count as an 'error', as do significantly mistaken numbers or more complex clashes between an account and known facts (for instance, in those many cases where it is erroneously implied that the high number of casualties on *Titanic* was known early on 15 April 1912). Nevertheless, in instances where a preponderance of perceptions accompanying the error appear to be accurate, the premonition is not wholly undermined by specific mistakes. It is not that our authors are unaware of this. Merely by examining premonitions in the way that they do, they show that they are alive to the possibility of error. It is more that they are not always as scrupulous or vigilant as one would have hoped in detecting it.

There is also obvious truth in Stevenson's contention that the unexpectedness of the sinking of *Titanic* may have generated an emotional shock not present in less surprising disasters. The surprising, disorienting, and traumatic nature of the *Titanic* disaster produced circumstances that probably increased limitations and confusions in the perceptions and judgement of many participants. Moreover, as both Gardner and Behe point out, quite apart from those who lie, even honest people tend to exaggerate without realising it.

Perhaps an even more important point is that, insofar as a reason or motive is required, the desire to receive attention or feel important after the event would be more than enough to generate self-deception in some people. In any event, one must always be conscious of the *possibility* of self-deception in the spoken or written statements of both witnesses and those reporting their words. In principle, this has to be regarded as potentially a major feature of premonition accounts. Yet none of our authors treat self-deception, as they probably ought to have done, as on a par with chance/coincidence and inference when it comes to considering alternative explanations for apparently paranormal experiences.

Self-deception may operate on at least two different levels. Granted that virtually all accounts postdate the *Titanic* disaster itself, the percipient may simply have deceived himself or herself regarding the degree of similarity between his or her alleged premonition and the actual events of the catastrophe (this could happen in accounts of dreams just as easily as of experiences in the waking state). Or perhaps a third party relating the percipient's account could be a victim of the same phenomenon. Again, either the subject or a third party might be self-deluded, not concerning the content of a 'premonition', but about exactly when the experience took place. Of course, where we can be absolutely certain that the subject was not aware of the relevant facts when offering the account, possible self-deception cannot be seen as undermining the suggestion of precognition. But our scrutiny of individual cases has shown just how difficult this is to establish, and, in any case, this situation could pertain in only a certain proportion of instances.

Where the possibility of self-deception is applicable, not to recognise this explicitly is an obvious and crucial mistake on the part of those examining alleged premonitions. While Brown seems frequently guilty of this kind of negligence, Stevenson, Behe and Méheust all slip into it from time to time. It may be because self-deception is such a complex and elusive phenomenon that it is not raised or engaged with seriously or often enough by our authors. Behe, for example, acknowledges that many people wished to somehow become involved in the *Titanic* saga, yet his 'probables' category is said to include ordinary people who 'had nothing to gain by lying', which sits rather uneasily with his earlier claim and makes no apparent allowance for the possibility or likelihood of self-deception.

Having mentioned the importance of the exact timing and dating of the premonitions themselves, one has to add that, in general, much less *careful* attention than is required is paid by our authors to this. Especially as so many instances involve the reporting of someone's alleged premonition by a third party, much more rigorous scrutiny and, above all, double-checking of dates and times is needed. There may be reasons for suggesting that circumstances in which someone would have a 'premonitory' experience and feel obliged to record it in writing before the event itself are bound to be rare (although, equally, emphasis on the remarkable intensity and vividness of premonitory feelings might begin to militate against this view). In any case, the plain uncertainties with regard to timing are very considerable – surely sufficient to undermine many cases. All five authors say or imply that the ideal case would be that of a *Titanic* premonition documented before the disaster. For this, we clearly require something in print earlier than 14 April, 1912, or possibly – with all checks regarding time-differences properly made – on 14 April itself. But, as we have repeatedly pointed out, this condition is *extremely* rarely met in our two hundred cases.

Of course, cancellation of tickets on *Titanic* by prospective passengers – of which more than fifty are said to have been authenticated[863] – was necessarily carried out before the voyage, and there are doubtless written records of some of these that ante-date the sinking. But no obvious record exists of a cancellation made because of a specific premonition that *Titanic* would sink, much less that the ship would hit an iceberg and sink. Behe cites 9 specific cases of cancellation as curious coincidences, significantly

863 See www.encyclopedia-titanica.org/canceled-titanic-passages.html John Eaton, in this article, says vaguely that 'Some cancellations (most not noted here), were apparently based on various psychic forebodings', but only his reference to Mrs Bill gives any details (see **(GB,cc,14e)**).

ascribing them to 'maiden voyage phobia', which is a 'general, all-inclusive type of superstition … not directed specifically at *Titanic*'.[864]

Rather weakly, Méheust concedes that, although the paranormal experience must have left a definite trace fixed before the event in question, if there is no written record indirect testimony affirming that a certain person said something may be taken into account, on condition that *this* is properly registered in writing, although even then it will have inferior and only complementary value in evaluation. And when the condition of an earlier written account is fulfilled, it is still necessary, he says, to eliminate chance and inference, including unconscious inference, which Méheust believes has been neglected by existing analyses. Behe does talk of cryptamnesia – the emergence into the conscious mind of information once buried in the subconscious[865] – but this phenomenon needs looking into more systematically and thoroughly, since 'unconscious inference' seriously risks being a term that purports to explain premonitions in 'normal' terms without actually doing so. Establishing 'unconscious' processes is at least as tricky a matter as detecting self-deception.

A number of other theoretical matters and issues of methodology remain, one might say, unresolved, or insufficiently pursued, in our commentators' writings. Some are broad in nature, others are fairly particular and pertain more specifically to the *Titanic* disaster.

864 Behe, pp. 23-25.

865 Behe, pp. 56-57.

Rather more than a quarter of our cases centre on predicted risk or danger to a particular person, but without reference to *Titanic* (more than half of these concern Stead), which raises the general matter of personal links with *Titanic*. As we saw, there is serious confusion and inadequacy in Stevenson's claim that the ratio of 'stranger' cases to 'personal relationship' cases is higher with *Titanic*. Goss and Behe suggest that what little is known of psychic events suggests that an 'emotional bond between percipient and subject' increases the likelihood of some kind of premonition. Méheust argues that in the majority of cases, the percipients had a link with the ship, direct or indirect, but his claim that the lack of such a link is 'very rare' is something of an exaggeration. There is clearly no such link in the vast majority of Stead cases, and none at all in the literary ones. And in around 35 of the general (non-Stead) cases no relationship exists between the subject and any *Titanic* passenger. Moreover, it is unclear whether Méheust has a number of different categories in mind, since, in explaining why he has *not* rated certain cases highly, in addition to the general 'people having a link with *Titanic*', he also refers to 'people due to travel on *Titanic*, or knowing others were on the ship', and to 'people having a link with *Titanic* (for instance, a direct, visual link)'. This is more than a trivial matter, as from a particular point in his book onwards he seems to believe that anyone with some such link can be suspected of auto-suggestion or unconscious inference.

It may be that potentially the most impressive 'premonitions' are experienced by those neither on *Titanic* nor knowing anyone on the ship, but this would include cases like that of Blanche Marshall, who definitely had a direct, visual link.[866] In theory, there is no reason at all for downgrading all cases where the percipient is due to board *Titanic* or knows someone who has done so, although a personal emotional involvement in the disaster may increase the chances of distortion in recounting an experience.

A further unresolved issue is whether other paranormal experiences by the percipient count as reasons for authenticating alleged premonitions. Sometimes the fact that the percipient has *not* had previous premonitions seems to be taken to count in favour of the hypothesis of precognition,[867] but Méheust, for one, occasionally assumes that other visionary experiences strengthen the case for premonition. Goss and Behe stress that something depends upon the accuracy of the other premonitory experiences, but do not come to any conclusion. This is a slightly more complex matter than it might appear, since it assumes that other premonitions have already been authenticated. In principle, even if this is so, it does not in the least weaken the need for the closest examination of alleged *Titanic* premonitions, although it may in some way impinge upon our judgement of any individual case.

Behe himself claims that caution seems advisable in dealing with 'individuals who claim the ability to routinely utilise psychic phenomena', in the light of the fact that genuine psychic phenomena 'seem to have a rather

866 **(IS,4)**.

867 **(IS,2)**, **(IS,3)**. See also, Méheust, p. 240.

sporadic, spontaneous nature' (something which, in itself, deserves much closer scrutiny by our authors, and is not obviously compatible with Méheust's frequent reference to 'long-lasting' premonitions). Behe admits that some such individuals made extremely accurate predictions, but believes that all of their reports should be grouped together as only *possible* psychic events. Goss and Behe go even further than this, conceding that 'some spiritualistic accounts suggest that a believer is less prone to criticise a subjective experience than other folk, overemphasising its "evidential" aspects'. Once more, the implications of this view are extremely far-reaching. Yet it should not be thought to justify the dismissing out of hand of all of the cases discussed in a book like that of Coates. Our clear obligation is to look in great detail at each experience on its merits: it is precisely this that makes the abundance of material concerning *Titanic* a problem in its own right.

This is also bound up with the whole matter of exactly what counts as a *Titanic* premonition as such, an issue that remains unclear (and one that comes into play especially acutely in connection with Behe's treatment of curious coincidences). There obviously has to be a clear indication that we are dealing with a premonition, rather than just a warning, or a fear, or a stated possibility. Apart from the point made by a number of our authors that a general warning to 'beware of water' is commonly given by fortune-tellers, we must certainly discount the rational warnings issued concerning liners going too quickly across the Atlantic despite the dangers of fog, ice, and derelicts. A number were published before 1912, some from sea captains and some of which portray vessels very similar to *Titanic* encountering ice. For instance, in a long article published in *The Atlantic* in May 1910 Charles Terry Delaney writes of a liner with 3,300 aboard, saying that it is only by good luck that such a vessel has not yet been 'sent to the bottom' through collision with an iceberg.[868] He imagines a ship 'somewhere in the vicinity of the fog regions, the Banks of Newfoundland', and asks whether it is right for ships' masters 'sixty years of age or thereabout' to command in case of emergency. He also recounts an experience when a ship he was on was suddenly almost alongside an iceberg three hundred feet high: 'The ship passed within twenty feet of it, going at the rate of twenty-one knots; had there been a submerged trailer attached to the berg the ship's bottom would have been ripped open'. There is no suggestion of premonition or the paranormal here, just the rational fears and warnings of an experienced mariner.

However, even discounting such warnings, we find that the boundaries limiting which experiences may legitimately be considered to fall within our range are, in principle, difficult to define. A number of the cases examined appear to be general worries about a person or future events, bearing no specific reference to *Titanic*. A premonition does not necessarily have to mention *Titanic* by name. (Méheust often takes the absence of a reference to *Titanic* itself as a mark of *authenticity* in a premonition,

868 'The Man on the Bridge', *The Atlantic* (1910). Others wrote that the builders of ocean steamers were losing sight of safety, and that watertight bulkheads had recently failed to save ships from sinking.

whereas Stevenson, at least, sees it as a weakness.) Slightly more than a half of our cases are definitely specific to *Titanic*, while around one eighth refer to an unspecified liner in some kind of danger. A 'premonition' has to be detailed enough in some way to enable us either to identify the ship, or to pin down the dating or timing, or the nature of the disaster. Hence, a prediction that a liner would strike ice and sink at some unknown date would not count, but one that this would happen in April, 1912 is somewhat more impressive. And a forecast dated before 14 April, predicting that a transatlantic liner would strike ice and sink, or perhaps simply would sink on 15 April certainly rates as a possible (*Titanic*) premonition.

Méheust often stresses the importance of finding some particular, special detail to confirm the authenticity of the experience, going so far as to argue that the precision of the special details given by the percipient is the 'major criterion' for distinguishing whether an experience is a genuine act of clairvoyance or not. But the justification for this is anything but clear, and the consistent application of the principle difficult to envisage.

Raising the matter of what counts as a *Titanic* premonition, as we have just seen, presupposes that the question of what a premonition as such is has already been answered. Yet different aspects of this more general issue sometimes arise in our authors' texts. They occasionally touch, for instance, on the question of whether a premonition has to involve its recognition or acknowledgement as such by the percipient. Stevenson raised the matter of 'recognising' unconscious premonitions at the beginning of his first article, but failed to cast any further light on it. And Brown quoted an author who talks of percipients having 'some conscious recognition', even when they pretend it is not there.[869] We saw that, in introducing his curious coincidences, Behe implicitly broaches the question, but he fails to convince us that a third party could not interpret an experience as a premonition, despite the percipient's denial.[870] This also impinges on Behe's treatment of possible psychic phenomena, since he suggests that the percipient's failure to comment on his/her experience may constitute a major reason for not considering a case as a 'probable', genuine one.[871] Again, the situation of a percipient not being conscious of having a premonition, but feeling that the experience was an especially unusual one in some way is entirely feasible and relevant. It is here that hindsight might also legitimately come into the picture. In short, on the matter of awareness that one has had a premonition, a certain flexibility in interpretation is probably appropriate, although special circumstances seem to apply in the case of literary premonitions, where parallels between the literary piece and subsequent real events appear to be virtually the only criterion. As with some of the earlier problems, there are refinements here that are impossible to set out in advance, so that establishing tight or precise conditions seems hardly feasible. Yet in spite of this, it is tempting

869 Brown, p. 63.

870 Behe, p. 15. Goss and Behe talk of Sophia Laitinen's friends wondering whether one of her dreams might have constituted a premonition (Goss and Behe, p. 227).

871 Behe, pp. 88-89.

to believe that some initial attempt to establish limiting principles might help considerably with an examination of *Titanic* premonitions. At least if we could eliminate certain cases on the grounds of irrelevance to begin with, the process of investigating those that remained might be somewhat tighter and more focused.

It is, equally, the case that, since all of our authors set out the cases they present in broad chronological order, it would have been good to see the first four of them carry out, as a complement to this approach, a more systematic examination of the *processes* of premonition as such. This might well have made the business of structuring and assimilating the abundant material somewhat easier. Méheust undertakes a brief review of this kind in the last chapter of Part III of his book ('Analysis of the Processes'): 'Freed from the need to find proofs, I will now examine in themselves the processes involved in the experiences.'[872] The alleged premonitions we have examined are, of course, of many different kinds and an extended attempt to categorise them would be very welcome. Unfortunately, Méheust's efforts are insubstantial and obviously incomplete. On the basis of the two hundred cases dealt with here, he appears to be right statistically in claiming that although dreams are a major channel for the paranormal, they are not the predominant mode of premonitions, although the precognitive dream may, in fact, be the most

872 Méheust, p. 211. In describing the procedures followed in investigating paranormal phenomena, Stevenson suggested that we 'search through series of apparently similar phenomena for recurrent features that may provide clues to causative conditions and processes of occurrence', but he achieved little success in this respect in his own two articles.

common type of premonition, as Gardner claims. (But Gardner's specific point that the details of a dream need to be written down and dated is a very strong one, and this, together with other points that he makes about dreams, is sufficient to undermine many of the dream cases in our corpus.) Méheust's own attempt to delineate the major characteristics of premonitory dreams (they use a variety of materials, have an exceptional emotional charge, and are often repetitive) fails to distinguish them from other dreams and suffers from his desire to both relate his analysis to, and differentiate it from, Freudian psycho-analysis.

The division between dreams and what one 'sees' in the waking state is fairly straightforward, but neither Méheust nor any of our other authors has anything significant to say about daytime 'visions' or 'dreamlike' events that would enable us to distinguish these clearly from other types of premonition. And in contrasting visions with premonitions that were just ideas, or anxieties without cause, Méheust generalises to little effect and fails to substantiate on these other categories. His comments on the very important matter of the role of language in paranormal processes, moreover, are sketchy in the extreme, as are his references to long-lasting premonitions, which are said to be distinct from the sudden, spontaneous ones more commonly considered.

What is more, Méheust's very brief argument that psycho-analysis is no more than a branch of the broader discipline of parapsychology is especially unconvincing, and his own postulation that the commonest channel for premonitory processes is emotional impact does not suggest a category at all, but merely offers one of their prominent features. Once again, much more analysis of the strength and intensity of emotions in premonitions is required. While claiming that the emotional shock generated by the sinking of *Titanic* is part of the reason for the sheer number of *Titanic* premonitions, Stevenson suggests that strong emotions are not necessary to extrasensory perception, but that they facilitate its occurrence, and in general our authors recognise their importance, associating them with a certain intensity. Behe, for example, asserts that 'One characteristic of a true precognitive dream is its *vividness*, coupled with the powerful influence it has on the dreamer after he awakens.'[873] Yet in *Lost Ships* he and Goss acknowledge that there is no way of distinguishing between a genuine premonition and a strong feeling, even when the latter seems borne out by subsequent events. Furthermore, they acknowledge that some people may have experienced their worry that the 'arrogance' associated with talk of *Titanic*'s unsinkability would exact some kind of divine retribution as a strong feeling verging on a premonition.[874]

When one tries to arrive at an overall assessment of the results of our five authors' work and the methods they use, a number of major features come to light: considerable omissions; discrepancies in the outcome of their inquiries; the relative timidity of their commitment to belief in

873 Behe, p. 159.

874 Goss and Behe, pp. 242-243.

precognition; unresolved issues of methodology; their failure to make significant inroads into the classification of premonitions. None of these factors encourage belief in a paranormal element in 'premonitions', but neither do they – individually or collectively – in themselves invalidate such a belief. What they certainly do is to indicate that the examination of alleged *Titanic* premonitions is an incomplete, ongoing process. It is best to see the results of comparing the work of our five commentators as a spur to understanding better all of the issues they raise.

CONCLUSION

HERBERT ASQUITH DESCRIBED THE *TITANIC* DISASTER as 'one of those terrible events in the order of Providence which baffle foresight'. Yet there may be reason to believe that the number and range of alleged precognitive experiences in connection with the *Titanic* disaster is exceptional, possibly even unique. Behe, for instance, argues that there is no 'normal' explanation for the overwhelming volume of supposed premonitions concerning *Titanic*'s fate, which are 'more numerous and better documented than those of any other event'.[875] But he himself adds to the cases some 45 'curious coincidences', many of which hardly merit consideration as premonitions. Moreover, certain comments by Gardner – his apposite statistical cautions and his reference to problems that are not 'well formed' – may cause us to hesitate before fully accepting Behe's contention: it is simply impossible to calculate what proportion of people, given the precise circumstances

875 Behe, pp. 160-162.

of the *Titanic* disaster, might be expected to focus on paranormal aspects of the tragedy, and documentation on the topic is on many occasions inadequate. Nevertheless, the very number of apparent premonitory experiences cannot fail to impress, even though, leaving aside the literary instances and Stead, there is very little indeed by way of significant records that actually pre-date the catastrophe.

All of the cases of alleged premonitions of the *Titanic* disaster treated in this book are contained in the writings of our five authors. There are still other cases, scattered in writings and websites of various kinds, and it is, of course, possible that some of these are as significant as any of those examined.[876] But, apart from anything else, sources are rarely given for such instances.[877] Still more cases may come to light, but it is obvious that none made public before 2006 forced their way into texts by authors scrutinising the subject between 1960 and 2006, and it seems unlikely in the extreme that any more hard information will surface on those they treated. The task

876 Behe's claim, in 'Acknowledgements' (p. 172), that 'it is almost certain that new cases will come to light as time goes on' has proved accurate.

877 Here are just a few examples, recorded in various places. One Jim Mullholland, taken on as a crewman in Belfast, is said to have left *Titanic* in Southampton, having seen the ship's cat Mouser leave down the gangplank with her four kittens: 'The cat knew something.' It is sometimes claimed that Annie Sage, whose husband and nine children died with her on *Titanic*, predicted the disaster (though the strength of her premonition might be doubted, granted that she nevertheless boarded the ship with her whole family). John Clarke, the orchestra's bass violinist, may have suggested that it might be his bad luck to go down with the ship. Of over one hundred cases registered on the French website 'Le Site du Titanic' (titanic.pagesperso-orange.fr), quite a number are 'extra' cases, although no sources are given for any of them.

of listing and assessing 'extra' cases must be left to others.

In any case, if we are bound to wonder why this particular drama generated so many paranormal experiences or claims, it has to be said that our five authors make almost no progress at all with this question. One or two points concerning the very *shock* of the sinking of an 'unsinkable' ship are worth bearing in mind, but perhaps certain other matters need to be weighed in the balance. While the eruption of Krakatoa in 1883 and the San Francisco earthquake of 1906 were both entirely natural catastrophes, human agency as well as natural forces played a part in the *Titanic* tragedy. Its immediate human consequences were more limited,[878] but many of the people who died were especially prominent in the western world, as were some of the many survivors. This factor means that the human interest of the story is greater. What is more, although it was not the first large-scale catastrophe to become known world-wide quite quickly, the *Titanic* sinking did take place at a time when telegraphs, the telephone and the press were newly geared-up to spread news immediately. The disaster – which incorporated not only the two hours and forty minutes of the actual sinking (of which there is, of course, no photographic record at all), but equally the rescue and its lengthy aftermath of suffering, inquiries, and legal proceedings – directly touched a great number of people and has long indirectly engaged countless others.

We should remember, too, that the early twentieth

878 In addition to vast destruction of property, the Krakatoa eruption is said to have been directly responsible for some 36,000 deaths; the San Francisco earthquake caused some 3,000 deaths.

century was a period when interest in matters paranormal was especially intense, perhaps at some kind of peak. H.G. Wells was scathing about 'these absurd days … when we are all trying to be as psychic and silly and superstitious as possible'; and George Bernard Shaw saw the decades before the Great War, when people were 'addicted' to spiritualism, as a 'drift to the abyss'. The Society for Psychical Research was founded in 1882, and Stead, in his *Review of Reviews*, regularly surveyed the pages of a number of spiritualist journals.[879] None of this fully explains the unusual number of claims of paranormal activity in relation to *Titanic*, but it may make it somewhat easier to understand. Certainly, once such claims were publicly recorded in some way or other, the topic was bound to continue to be explored.

The fact is that the very abundance of anecdotal material in connection with the *Titanic* is almost excessive. Two hundred and one cases in all, of various kinds, are dealt with here (though this includes more instances of alleged premonitions, since a number of cases involve more than one premonition).[880] These are extremely difficult to encompass and evaluate together,

879 For the specific quotes and these points, see John Wilson Foster, 'The Titanic Disaster: Stead, Ships and the Supernatural' (2004). Foster adds to Shaw's list of 'table-rapping, materialisation séances, clairvoyance, palmistry, crystal-gazing', 'telepathy or thought-reading, clairaudience and "phone-voyance" (seeing through a telephone wire) … mesmerism, hypnotism and levitation, automatic writing, astrology and astral voyaging … magic and ritual, theosophy'.

880 Incidentally, it is difficult to see any significance in the gender-balance of the cases examined, with nearly a quarter more male percipients being involved overall (and a very much stronger preponderance of men among Behe's 'curious coincidences'). But this does rather run counter to any suggestion that women are particularly likely to have paranormal sensitivities.

especially as their quality varies enormously. The worst are utterly trivial and/or bear absolutely minimal relation to *Titanic*, yet the task of locating the strongest experiences remains an extremely tricky one. What the work of our authors as a whole brings out particularly clearly is the very great difficulty of getting to the bottom of cases that are more than one hundred years old, and the sheer complexity of the issues that they raise. We emphasised in the Introduction the distinction between anecdotes and parapsychological experiments, and we are now in a somewhat better position to understand some of the problems of dealing with the former, especially when they are in considerable numbers and of variable quality.

In any case, it is worth reflecting on what the considerable number of alleged paranormal experiences does *not* mean. If, for instance, there is any useful sense in which *Titanic* premonitions constitute some kind of 'collective' experience, this has yet to be established. Stevenson makes no headway with the term, and simply referring to C.D. Broad's 'disseminated co-referential hallucinations' takes us no further at all. Again, it certainly does not follow from the volume of experiences that any are genuinely psychic; nor does it make it more likely that they are, much less that the paranormal is a reality. Moreover, the argument that, although the individual cases may all be attributed to coincidence or other normal factors, collectively they add up to some kind of evidence for the paranormal is obviously entirely invalid.

When we look at all of the anecdotal *Titanic* cases we have listed, it is already surprising that fewer than half are covered by more than one of our authors, and a great deal more puzzling that only 8 cases (of the total of 26 examined by Stevenson) are treated by all five. Yet in itself this is of less significance than the fact that very little indeed by way of harmony and agreement on the substantive issues of premonitions emerges from the writings of these writers. It is true that some will regard Gardner's resolute scepticism about the small number of cases he considers as unjustified, even doubt the proposition that evidence for the paranormal needs to be quite *exceptionally* strong. Nevertheless, a more critical approach to the topic than that of Rustie Brown is certainly required. Her introductory case for premonitions is an extremely thin, unsystematic, and feeble one, and her 'narrative' of the different cases itself appears to indicate a lack of reflection or scrutiny. As for Stevenson, Behe and Méheust, it is unsurprising that their focus sometimes slips. Their judgement is occasionally faulty, and some inconsistency and vagueness can be found in their work. It is true that the general stance they adopt may be recognised as the appropriate one: all three have a degree of objectivity and take their material very seriously, sifting and assessing it with considerable care. Unfortunately – though significantly – this by no means brings them to the same conclusions. In fact, the differences in their opinions on premonitions are one of the most striking things to emerge from scrutiny of their works.

Of course, all of our authors may be assumed to have ventured into print because they had something new to say, and this may go some way towards explaining disparities in their judgements. It could even be argued that the diversity of opinions – both concerning individual cases and some matters of general principle – shows the independence of the commentators, which is a good, healthy sign. Yet, quite apart from the fact that there are serious oddities in the number of instances from their predecessors taken up, or neglected, by the four individual authors following Stevenson, the evaluations of the ninety or so cases commented on by more than one of the five authors vary much more considerably than might have been anticipated. One might have expected at the very least a certain consensus on the most convincing or plausible cases on the part of all or nearly all of our authors, even one or two remarkable instances that commanded common approval. That this is far from what we find may not be sufficient to undermine belief in the reality of *Titanic* premonitions, but it has to be regarded as a major factor in an overall view of the phenomena concerned.

We have seen that Stevenson set the scrutiny of premonitions in motion, and that, while both Brown and Behe extended the range of the inquiry considerably, and Gardner's more limited investigation acted as a useful kind of brake on the process, Méheust's book revived interest in the topic, approaching it from different angles. Yet both individually and collectively the five commentators failed to clarify certain major theoretical questions concerning premonitions, and none of them managed to maintain throughout the persistence and rigorous consistency required in the examination of particular cases. In short, it is not at all clear that – even if the range of alleged cases is by now more extensive – we understand either the individual experiences or the fundamentals of premonitions much better than in Stevenson's time. Yet to stop trying to gain a clearer view would be a kind of betrayal of the efforts of our five commentators.

Abstract inquiry into premonitions *as such* should perhaps be dealt with by philosophers, while psychologists and historians may look into more empirical aspects of the topic. Exactly how anecdotal evidence and experimentation will fit into the picture that results remains uncertain, but there is no doubt at all that more systematic and penetrating work on *Titanic* premonitions is required. We have indicated many directions in which such work should be pursued. It could possibly be carried out by the sort of team of researchers who have applied themselves to more general features of the *Titanic* story. They might take into account the cases not touched upon by our five authors, and examine or re-examine *all* of the relevant documentary evidence available, including the numerous relevant newspaper reports and interviews. Some kind of searchable computerised database could be established as an invaluable tool. While this would not teach us more about the ship itself or the factual and technical aspects of its fate, it might help to clarify some of the outstanding theoretical matters raised by the writings of our authors, as well as casting further light on particular 'premonitions'. More than this, it could hardly fail to contribute something more to the cultural history of the disaster, in which tales of the paranormal figure quite prominently. As with discussion of feminism, racism, religion, and the class question – all broad issues that are still very much open, and subject to regular or constant review – scrutiny of the question of premonitions specifically in connection with *Titanic* indisputably provides especially poignant examples, as well as much general material for exploring the issues at stake. The case of *Titanic* will not *solve* any of these general issues. Yet further refinement of our understanding of relevant premonitions can only bring greater awareness of the extent to which, and different ways in which, the sinking of *Titanic* made an impact on so many people. This in turn will help to explain why the ship left such an enduring legacy and add to our grasp of a major twentieth-century catastrophe.

APPENDIX 1

FULL LIST OF CASES

Cases are listed in the order in which they are introduced in this book. Their identification number (see 'Foreword') is given, as is the main name associated with the case. In most cases, where a person is named, it is that person who had the premonition, but this is not so in every single instance. Also included are identification numbers to show which later authors have taken up particular cases, and Méheust's star-gradings of cases, where these are offered (bracketed where different cases are amalgamated).

Chapter 1. Poems, Stead, Robertson, Garnett

MG,25 – Thaxter's 'A Tryst'.
MG,26 – Melville's 'The Berg (A Dream)'.
IS,9a – Stead ('How the Mail Steamer Went Down …' – **(RB,32)**, **(MG,20)**, **(GB,cc,1)**, **(BM,wts,1)**.

IS,9b – Stead ('From the Old World to the New') – **(RB,33)**, **(MG,21)**, **(GB,cc,3)**, **(BM,wts,2)**.
IS,1 – Morgan Robertson – **(RB,12)**, **(MG,1)**, **(GB,cc,4)**, **(BM,mr,1)**.
MG,24 – 'Mayn Clew Garnett' – **(GB,cc,55)**, **(BM,72)** *+.

Chapter 2. Premonitions of the Death of Stead

IS,9c – Stead (vision of a mob) – **(MG,22)**, **(GB,wts,2)**, **(BM,wts,3)**.
IS,9d – Stead (shipwrecked) – **(RB,34)**, **(MG,19)**, **(GB,wts,6)**, **(BM,wts,8)**.
RB,20 – Stead (Egyptian mummy story) – **(GB,cc,36)**, **(BM,26a)**.
RB,29 – Stead (his own premonitions).
RB,35 – Stead (predicts he will be killed).
GB,wts,5 – Stead (discusses his death, in Toronto) – **(BM,wts,7)**.
GB,wts,12 – Stead (predicts his violent death) – **(BM,wts,14)**.
GB,wts,17 – Stead (no anxieties about *Titanic*).
BM,wts,21 – Stead (says goodbye emotionally).
BM,wts,22 – Stead (writes to Harper).
BM,wts,23 – Stead (letters from Queenstown).

IS,10 – 'Cheiro' – **(RB,30)**, **(GB,wts,8)**, **(BM,wts,10)** *.
IS,11a – Kerlor (huge black vessel)– **(RB,31)**, **(GB,wts,9)**, **(BM,wts,11)** (***).
IS,11b – Kerlor (Stead drowning) – **(RB,31)**, **(GB,wts,9)**, **(BM,wts,12)** (***).

IS,12 – Mrs Tweedale – **(MG,23)**, **(GB,po,21)**, **(BM,73)** *+.
GB,cc,61 – Cross/crucifix.
GB,wts,1 – 'Teresina' – **(BM,wts,4)**.
GB,wts,3 – Mme de Thèbes – **(BM,wts,5)** *.
GB,wts,4 – Unnamed clairvoyant – **(BM,wts,6)**.
GB,wts,7 – Etta Wriedt – **(BM,wts,9)**.
GB,wts,11 – May de Witt Hopkins – **(BM,wts,13)** *+.
GB,wts,13 – Archdeacon Colley – **(BM,wts,15)**.
GB,wts,14 – Kerlor (Stead encircled in stone) – **(BM,wts,16)** (***).
GB,wts,15 – R. Penny – **(BM,wts,20)**.
GB,wts,16 – Stead (advice not to sail).
GB,wts,18 – May de Witt Hopkins – **(BM,wts,27)**, **(BM,63)**.
GB,wts,19 – Miss Scatcherd (Stead warns a friend).
GB,wts,20 – Adela Harper.
GB,wts,21 – Lady Campbell – **(BM,wts,28)**.
G&B,6 – Shaw Desmond – **(BM,wts,17)** **.
G&B,10 – Mrs Chase.
BM,wts,18 – Unnamed medium.
BM,wts,19 – Miss Scatcherd (Stead has a short time left).
BM,wts,24 – Mrs Wesley Adams – **(BM,39)** *+.
BM,wts,26 – Pardoe Woodman – **(BM,49)** **+.

Chapter 3. Stevenson

IS,2 – Connon Middleton – **(RB,3)**, **(MG,2)**, **(BM,19)** *.
IS,3 – New York woman – **(RB,46)**, **(MG,3)**, **(BM,65)** ***.
IS,4 – Blanche Marshall – **(RB,5)**, **(MG,4)**, **(GB,pr,21)**, **(BM,38)****.

IS,5 – Mrs Potter – **(MG,5)**, **(BM,61)** **.

IS,6 – Rev. Morgan – **(RB,21)**, **(MG,6)**, **(BM,50)** *.

IS,7 – Charles Hays – **(MG,7)**, **(GB,cc,45)**, **(BM,51)** *.

IS,8 – Vincent Turvey – **(RB,7)**, **(MG,8)**, **(GB,po,20)**, **(BM,wts,25, BM,46)** **.

IS12a – Edith Evans – **(RB,26)**, **(MG,9)**, **(GB,cc,49)**, **(BM,59)** *.

IS,12b – John Coffey – **(RB,13)**, **(MG,10)**, **(GB,cc,34)**.

IS,12c – Archibald Butt – **(RB,28)**, **(MG,11)**, **(GB,pr,3)**, **(G&B,7)**, **(BM,16)** **+.

IS,13 – Mr E.M. – **(MG,12)**, **(BM,62)** **.

IS,14 – Mrs Henderson – **(MG,13)**, **(BM,69)** ***.

IS,15 – Mr Black – **(MG,14)**, **(BM,48)** *+.

IS,16 – Ida Lorenz – **(MG,15)**, **(BM,68)** ***.

IS,17 – Mrs Hughes – **(MG,16)**, **(BM,47)** ***.

IS,18 – Norah Mathews – **(MG,17)**, **(BM,21)** **.

IS,19 – Colin Macdonald – **(MG,18)**, **(BM,10)** *+.

Chapter 4. Brown and Gardner

RB,1 – Mr Finlay.

RB,2 – Nora Keane – **(GB,cc,33)**, **(BM,44)** *+.

RB,4 – Mary Tripp.

RB,6 – Mrs Milling.

RB,8 – Male stranger to Mrs Henry Harris – **(GB,cc,29)**.

RB,9 – Mrs Pettet's father.

RB,10 – Alfred Vanderbilt – **(GB,cc,14f)**.

RB,11 – Edith Rosenbaum/Russell – **(GB,po,17)**, **(BM,12)** **.

RB,14 – A stoker – **(GB,cc,32)**, **(BM,41)**.

RB,15 – Anna Ward – **(GB,po,6)**, **(G&B,3)**.
RB,16 – Lady Duff Gordon.
RB,17 – Hutchinson – **(GB,cc,35)**.
RB,18 – A steward – **(GB,cc,42)**.
RB,19 – Mrs William Bucknell – **(GB,pr,13)**, **(BM,40)** *+.
RB,22 – Mrs Hocking (cock crowing)– **(GB,cc,44)**, **(BM,30)** (*).
RB,23 – Esther Hart – **(GB,pr,14)**, **(BM,24)** **+.
RB,24 – A crewman – **(GB,cc,37)**.
RB,25 – Mr Chandler – **(G&B,1)**.
RB,27 – Col. Gracie's wife – **(GB,pr,30)**, **(BM,60)** **.
RB,36 – Miss Griffin.
RB,37 – Falling oil lamp, Miss Eliza Wellsted.
RB,38 – Death of Straus's horse – **(GB,cc,51)**.
RB,39 – Wallace Hartley's mother.
RB,40 – Jessie – **(GB,pr,25)**, **(BM,55)** ***.
RB,41 – Harry Widener – **(GB,cc,22)**.
RB,42 – *Titanic* unchristened.
RB,43 – *Titanic* harmed because of name.
RB,44 – Mrs Bishop.
RB,45 – Graham Greene – **(BM,64)** *.
RB,47 – Edwina MacKenzie.

Chapter 5. George Behe

GB,cc,2 – Time-capsule.
GB,cc,5 – Emil Taussig.
GB,cc,6 – Arthur Newell.
GB,cc,7 – Alexander Robins.
GB,cc,8 – John Phillips.

GB,cc,9 – A.J. Pierce.
GB,cc,10 – Capt. Smith – **(BM,8)**.
GB,cc,11 – Rev. Bateman.
GB,cc,12 – Table collapses.
GB,cc,13 – Postponement of sea trial.
GB,cc,14a – Unnamed man.
GB,cc,14b – M. Forster.
GB,cc,14c – Unnamed man.
GB,cc,14d – Unnamed man.
GB,cc,14e – Mrs Bill – **(BM,31)** *.
GB,cc,14g – Mrs Vanderbilt – **(BM,32)***.
GB,cc,14h – Lady Duff Gordon.
GB,cc,14i – Mrs Ryan.
GB,cc,14j – Mrs Anderson.
GB,cc,15 – Ernest Farenden.
GB,cc,16 – Mrs Leeford.
GB,cc,17 – George Clifford.
GB,cc,18 – Mary Mack.
GB,cc,19 – The Fitzpatricks.
GB,cc,20 – A crewman.
GB,cc,21 – Fred Clark.
GB,cc,23 – Arthur Lewis.
GB,cc,24 – Sidney Collett.
GB,cc,25 – George Wick.
GB,cc,26 – The boat train.
GB,cc,27 – Mrs Hocking (ship's too big) **(BM,30)** (*).
GB,cc,28 – Member of kitchen staff.
GB,cc,30 – Charles Clarke.
GB,cc,31 – Mr Duane.
GB,cc,38 – Mrs Daughtrey.

GB,cc,39 – Rev. Brown.
GB,cc,40 – Rev. Chew.
GB,cc,41 – Rev. Byles and Rev. Peruschitz.
GB,cc,43 – A Frenchman.
GB,cc,46 – Rev. Carter.
GB,cc,47 – A rat.
GB,cc,48 – Constance Willard.
GB,cc,50 – Fred Barrett.
GB,cc,52 – Suva, Fijis – **(BM,70)** **+.
GB,cc,53 – Capt. Smith – **(BM,14)**.

GB,po,1 – Dr Minahan – **(BM,3)** *+.
GB,po,2 – *George Washington* officer – **(BM,5)** *.
GB,po,3 – John Hume's mother – **(BM,13)** *.
GB,po,4 – Edwina Mackenzie.
GB,po,5 – Rumoured prophecy of sinking.
GB,po,7 – Mme de Thèbes – **(BM,7)**.
GB,po,8 – Caroline Endres.
GB,po,9 – Alice Fortune – **(BM,9)** **.
GB,po,10 – George Wick.
GB,po,11 – Jacques Futrelle.
GB,po,12 – Mrs Holden.
GB,po,13 – Unnamed woman.
GB,po,14 – Unnamed woman warns Andrews.
GB,po,15 – Mother from Athenry – **(BM,18)** *.
GB,po,16 – Unnamed businessman.
GB,po,18 – A steward.
GB,po,19 – A greaser.
GB,po,22 – Mrs von Walden.
GB,po,23 – Houston newspaperman – **(BM,66)** ***.

GB,po,24 – Alfred Stead.
GB,po,25 – Wife of Arthur Lewis.

GB,pr,1 – Jennie Hanson – **(BM,15)** *+.
GB,pr,2 – Mrs Shepherd.
GB,pr,4 – Helen Bell – **(BM,20)** *.
GB,pr,5 – Mr Battle.
GB,pr,6 – Charity Rouse – **(BM,23)** *.
GB,pr,7 – Fred Smith.
GB,pr,8 – Margaret Devaney – **(BM,22)**.
GB,pr,9 – Mrs Adelman.
GB,pr,10 – Mr Steer.
GB,pr,11 – William Klein.
GB,pr,12 – Jackie Ward.
GB,pr,15 – Isaac Frauenthal – **(BM,53)** *+.
GB,pr,16 – Stephen Jenkin – **(BM,29)** *.
GB,pr,17 – Col. John Weir – **(BM,28)** *+.
GB,pr,18 – Slade brother – **(BM,27)** *+.
GB,pr,19 – Harry Burrows – **(BM,34)**.
GB,pr,20 – Mr T. Brown – **(BM,37)** **.
GB,pr,22 – Patrick O'Keefe – **(BM,42)**.
GB,pr,23 – Eugene Daly – **(BM,54)** **.
GB,pr,24 – William Rodgers – **(BM,45)** *+.
GB,pr,26 – Benita Guggenheim– **(BM,52)** *+.
GB,pr,27 – Laura Cribb– **(BM,58)** *.
GB,pr,28 – Edward Kent.
GB,pr,29 – Margaret Hays.
GB,pr,31 – Mrs Gatti– **(BM,11)** **.
GB,pr,32 – Henry Forbes Julian– **(BM,17)** **.
GB,pr,33 – Marcelle Navratil– **(BM,57)** ***.

GB,pr,34 – Louise Logsdon.
GB,pr,35 – Babysitter for Prangnell– **(BM,71)** *.

G&B,2 – Sophie Laitinen.
G&B,4 – Elizabeth Sims.
G&B,5 – Angus McCormack.
G&B,8 – Estelle Barnes.
G&B,9 – M. Abrahams.
G&B,11 – Bert John.
G&B,12 – Alfred Adler– **(BM,67)** *.
G&B,13 – Edward Dorking.

Chapter 6. Bertrand Méheust

BM,1 – Draughtsman.
BM,2 – Cabin boy.
BM,4 – Mary MacCormick.
BM,25 **+ – Mrs A.
BM,26 * – Col. Long.
BM,33 * – George Beedem.
BM,35 ** – Rosalind Hodge.
BM,36 – Mrs Hakesworth.
BM,43 *+ – Henry Wilde.
BM,56 *+ – Mme Maréchal.

APPENDIX 2

TABLE OF CONTENTS OF MÉHEUST'S HISTOIRES PARANORMALES DU TITANIC [PARANORMAL STORIES OF THE TITANIC]

BIBLIOGRAPHY

THIS IS NOT A *TITANIC* BIBLIOGRAPHY, BUT ONE listing only the various texts, books and articles used or mentioned in this work.

TEXTS EXAMINED

Ian Stevenson (1), 'A Review and Analysis of Paranormal Experiences Connected with the Sinking of the *Titanic*', *Journal of the American Society for Psychical Research*, vol. 54, October 1960, pp. 153-171.

Ian Stevenson (2), 'Seven More Paranormal Experiences Associated with the Sinking of the *Titanic*', *Journal of the American Society for Psychical Research*, vol. 59, July 1965, pp. 211-225.

Rustie Brown, *The Titanic, the Psychic and the Sea*, Blue Harbor Press, Lomita, California, 1981.

Martin Gardner (1), *The Wreck of the Titanic Foretold?*, Prometheus Books, New York, 1986.

Martin Gardner (2), *When you were a tadpole and I was a fish. And other speculations about this and that*, Hill and Wang, New York, 2009; paperback edition, 2010.
George Behe, *Titanic. Psychic Forewarnings of a Tragedy*, Patrick Stephens, Wellingborough, 1988.
Michael Goss & George Behe, *Lost at Sea. Ghost Ships and Other Mysteries*, Prometheus Books, New York, 1994 (first Galahad Books (Edison) edition, 2005).
Bertrand Méheust, *Histoires paranormales du Titanic*, J'ai lu, Paris, 2006.

TEXTS FOR CHAPTER 1

Celia Thaxter, 'A Tryst', 1874, in *The Poems of Celia Thaxter*, Houghton, Mifflin and Company, Boston, 1896. Included in Gardner (1).
Herman Melville, 'The Berg (A Dream)', 1888, in *John Marr and Other Poems*, Princeton University Press, Princeton, 1922. Included in Gardner (1).
W.T. Stead, 'How the Mail Steamer went down in Mid-Atlantic, by a Survivor', *Pall Mall Gazette*, 22 March, 1886. Subsequently published in the *Review of Reviews* (1912) and other journals.
W.T. Stead, 'From the Old World to the New', *Review of Reviews*, Christmas edition, December, 1892. Extracts included in Gardner (1).
Morgan Andrew Robertson, *Futility*, M.F. Mansfield, New York, 1898. Variously reprinted as *Futility, Or the Wreck of the Titan* or with a similar title. Included in Gardner (1). See in particular: Morgan Robertson, Ian

Stevenson, *The Wreck of the Titan: Or, Futility; Paranormal Experiences Connected with the Sinking of the Titanic*, 7 C's Press, Riverside, Connecticut, 1974; and *Le Naufrage du 'Titan'*, Corsaire Editions, Orléans, 2000.

'Mayn Clew Garnett' (Thornton Jenkins Hains), 'The White Ghost of Disaster', *The Popular Magazine*, Vol. 24, No.2; May 1, 1912, pp. 165-180. The story is also printed in *The Chief Mate's Yarns. Twelve Tales of the Sea*, G.W. Gillingham Company of New York, 1912, and is included in Gardner (1).

OTHER ITEMS REFERRED TO

James E. Alcock, 'Give the Null Hypothesis a Chance. Reasons to Remain Doubtful about the Existence of Psi', *Journal of Consciousness Studies*, 10, nos. 6-7, 2003; pp. 29-50. (Also in *Psi Wars. Getting to Grips with the Paranormal*, ed. James. E. Alcock, Jean E. Burns, Anthony Freeman, Imprint Academic, Charlottesville, 2003.)

Pierre Bayard, *Demain est écrit* [*Tomorrow is Written Down*], Éditions de Minuit, Paris, 2005.

Lawrence Beesley, *The Loss of the Titanic. Its Story and its Lessons,* W.H. Allen, London, 1979. First published by Heinemann, London, 1912.

George Behe, *Archie*, Lulu.com, North Carolina, 2010 (3 volumes).

George Behe, *A Death on the Titanic*, Lulu.com, North Carolina, 2011.

Patrick Besson, *La Titanic*, Éditions du Rocher, Paris, 1999.

Bruce Beveridge, Scott Andrews, Steve Hall & Daniel Klistorner; Art Braunschweiger (ed.), *Titanic. The Ship Magnificent. Volume One: Design & Construction*, The History Press, Stroud, 2009.

Bruce Beveridge, Scott Andrews, Steve Hall & Daniel Klistorner; Art Braunschweiger (ed.), *Titanic. The Ship Magnificent. Volume Two: Interior Design and Fitting* Out, The History Press, Stroud, 2009.

Steven Biel, *Titanica, the Disaster of the Century in Poetry, Song, and Prose*, W.W. Norton, New York, 1998.

Matthias McDonnell Bodkin, 'The Ship's Run', in his *The Quests of Paul Beck*, T.F.Unwin, London, 1908; reprinted in Rosemary Herbert, *Murder on Deck*, Oxford, Clarendon Press, 1998.

C.D. Broad, *Lectures on Psychical Research*, The Humanities Press, New York, 1962.

Rustie Brown, *The Mariner's Trivia Book*, Blue Harbor Press, Lomita, California, 1986.

Archibald Butt, *Taft and Roosevelt: The Intimate Letters of Archie Butt*, Doubleday, Doran & Co., Washington D.C. (two volumes), 1930.

Cheiro, *Cheiro's Memoirs: the Reminiscences of a Society Palmist*, William Rider and Son, London, 1912

James Coates, *Has W.T. Stead Returned? A Symposium*, L.N. Fowler & Co., London, 1913.

W.E. Cox, 'Precognition: An Analysis, II', *Journal of the American Society for Psychic Research*, 50, No. 3, 1956, pp. 99-109.

Charles Terry Delaney, 'The Man on the Bridge', *The Atlantic*, May 1910.

Shaw Desmond, *My Adventures in the Occult*, Rider and Co., London, 1946.

Lucy Duff Gordon (Lady), *Discretions and Indiscretions*, Jarrolds, New York, 1932.

John P. Eaton and Charles A. Hass, *Titanic. Destination Disaster. The legends and the reality*, Haynes Publishing, New York, 3rd edition, 2011.

Jule Eisenbud, *Parapsychology and the Unconscious*, North Atlantic Books, Berkeley, 1983.

C. Ferruli, *"Titanic": l'aventure, le mystère, la trag*édie, Hachette, Paris, 2004.

Tad Fitch, J. Kent Layton, & Bill Wormstedt, *On a Sea of Glass. The Life and Loss of the RMS Titanic*, Amberley Publishing, Stroud, 2012.

John Wilson Foster, 'The Titanic Disaster: Stead, Ships and the Supernatural', in Tim Bergfelder and Sarah Street, *The Titanic in Myth and Memory: Representations in Visual and Literary Culture,* I.B. Tauris, London, 2004, pp.37-51.

Robin Gardiner and Dan Van Der Vat, *The Riddle of the Titanic*, Weidenfeld & Nicolson, London, 1995. See: Robin Gardiner, *L'Énigme du 'Titanic', myst*è*res et dissimulations*, Michel Lafon, Paris, 1998.

Archibald Gracie, *Titanic. A Survivor's Story.* The History Press, Stroud, 2008. First published as *The Truth About the Titanic*, J.J. Little & Ives, New York, 1913.

J. Grant, *Far Memory*, Harper & Bros., New York, 1956.

Graham Greene, *A Sort of Life*, The Bodley Head, London, 1971.

Herbert Greenhouse, *Premonitions: A Leap into the*

Future, Bernard Geis Associates, New York, 1971.
David Haisman, *'I'll See You in New York'. Titanic. The Courage of a Survivor*, Boolarong Press, Brisbane, 1999.
Samuel Halpern *et al*, *Report into the Loss of the SS Titanic. A Centennial Reappraisal*, The History Press, Stroud, 2011.
Jack W. Hannah, *The Futility god: Spiritist Power, Occultism and Futility*, Didactic Pub. Associates, Mansfield, Ohio, 1975.
Jack W. Hannah, *The Titanic: its prophecy, philosophy, & psychology*, Didactic Pub. Associates, Mansfield, Ohio, 1980
Edith Harper, *Stead, the Man: Personal Reminiscences*, William Rider and Son, London, 1918.
Gerhart Johann Robert Hauptman, *Atlantis*, B.W. Huebsch, New York, 1892.
Bernhardt J. Hurwood, *Strange Talents*, Ace Books, New York, 1967.
'J.B.K' (ed.), *Morgan Robertson the Man*, published by *McClure's Magazine* and *Metropolitan Magazine*, New York, 1915.
Carol King & Richard Havers, *Titanic. The Unfolding Story*, Haynes Publishing, Yeovil, 2011.
Yves Lignon, 'Le Titan-ic ?', *La Gazette fortéenne*, vol. 4, October 2005, pp. 243-247.
W. Lord, *A Night to Remember*, (Illustrated Edition), Penguin Books, London, 1978 (first published by Henry Holt & Co., New York, 1955).
Maurice Maeterlinck, *La Sagesse et la Destinée*, Bibliothèque Charpentier, Paris, 1899.
Bertrand Méheust, *Un voyant prodigieux, Alexis Didier*,

Les Empêcheurs de penser en rond, Paris, 2003.
Connon Middleton, Correspondence, *Proceedings of the Society for Psychical Research*, vol. 15, (June) 1912, p.264.
R. de W. Miller, *You Do Take It with You*, The Citadel Press, New York, 1955.
Elizabeth Navratil, *Les Enfants du 'Titanic'*, Hachette jeunesse, Paris, 1998.
Charles Panati, *Supersenses – Our Potential for Parasensory Experience*, Quadrangle/The New York Times Book Co., New York, 1974.
C.F. Potter, *Beyond the Senses*, Doubleday, Doran & Co., New York, 1939.
W.F. Prince, 'Some Coincidental Dreams (Continued)', *Journal of the American Society for Psychical Research*, vol. 13, no.3 (March, 1919), pp. 172-182.
Jane Roberts, *The Nature of Personal Reality*, Prentice-Hall, New York, 1974.
Morgan Robertson, 'Gathering No Moss. An Autobiography', *Saturday Evening Post*, 28 March, 1914. Also in *Morgan Robertson the Man*, *McClure's*, 1915; and in Hannah (1980).
Nicholas Royle, *Telepathy and Literature, Essays on the Reading Mind*, Blackwell, Oxford, 1991.
Stephen Rudley, *Psychic Detective*, Franklin Watts, New York, 1979.
H.F. Saltmarsh, *Foreknowledge*, G. Bell & Sons, London, 1938.
David Seabury, *Pull Yourself Together*, Science of Mind Publications, Los Angeles, 1967.
Mrs Henry Sidgwick, 'An Examination and Analysis of

Cases of Telepathy between Living Persons', *Proceedings of the Society for Psychical Research*, vol. 33 (1923), pp. 23-30.
W.T. Sloper, *The Life and Times of Andrew Jackson Sloper, 1849-1933*, self-published, Kensington, Conn., 1949.
Estelle Stead, *My Father*, George H. Doran Co., New York, 1913.
W.T. Stead, *Borderland. A Casebook of True Supernatural Stories*, University Books, New Hyde Park, New York, 1970.
Isabelle de Steiger, 'Mr Turvey's Prevision of the 'Titanic' Disaster, *Light*, XXXII, 29 June 1912, pp. 310-311.
W.O. Stevens, *Unbidden Guests*, Dodd, Mead & Co., New York, 1945.
W.O. Stevens, *The Mystery of Dreams*, Dodd, Mead & Co., New York, 1949.
Ian Stevenson, 'Precognition of disasters', *Journal of the American Society for Psychical Research*, 64, April 1970, pp. 187-210.
Ian Stevenson, 'Some of My Journeys in Medicine – A Lecture about Science and Reincarnation', The Flora Levy Lecture in the Humanities, University of Southwestern Louisiana, Lafayette, Louisiana, 1989.
Sidney Tyler, *A Rainbow of Time and Space: orphans of the Titanic*, Aztec Corp., Tucson, 1981.
G.N.M. Tyrrell, *Apparitions*, Pantheon Books, New York, 1953.
Vincent N. Turvey, *The Beginnings of Seership : Astral Projection, Clairvoyance and Prophecy*, 1909 (reprinted by Kessinger Publishing, Whitefish, MT, 2004). Some sources name the book *The Beginnings of Seership, or Super-Normal*

Mental Activity and date it to 1911 (reprinted 1954).

C.L. Tweedale, 'Mr Stead and the "Titanic" disaster', *Light*, XXXII, 4 May 1912, pp. 212-213.

C.L. Tweedale, *Man's Survival After Death*, E.P. Dutton & Co., New York, 1921.

G.N.M. Tyrrell, *Apparitions*, Pantheon Books, New York, 1953.

Alan Vaughan, *Patterns of Prophecy*, Hawthorn Books, New York, 1973.

William Young Winthrop, *A 20th Century Cinderella or $20,000 Reward*, Abbey Press, New York, 1902.

Pardoe Woodman and Estelle Stead (eds.), *Blue Island, Experiences of a New Arrival beyond the Veil, communicated by W.T. Stead*, Hutchinson & Co., London, 3rd edition, 1922.

Marie Young, 'Lest We Forget', *National Magazine*, October 1912.

... 'E.T. Cook and the death of W.T. Stead', *The Contemporary Review*, June, 1912. Reprinted in Frederick Whyte, *The Life of W.T. Stead*, Jonathan Cape, London, 1925; vol. II, pp. 353-356.

INDEX OF NAMES

ABOUT THE AUTHOR

Terry Keefe taught and researched in French literature and philosophy at Leicester University (becoming Head of French and Dean of Arts), then as Professor of French at Lancaster University. He published six academic books, and numerous articles, then, following early retirement, wrote two local books, edited a conservation journal, and began lecturing extensively on mysteries, especially *Titanic*. Having made a few contributions to specialist internet forums on the disaster, he became aware of the need for a serious book on *Titanic* premonitions. Married for almost sixty years, he now lives with his wife near his grandchildren and his son and daughter, both of whom are professors at Sheffield University.